BEYOND THE WEST

New Global Architecture

gestalten

Table of Contents

Intro
Local Architecture in a
Globalized World
_____ 4

*The Search for
South African Architecture*
by Graham Wood
_____ 8

Local Studio
Hillbrow Counselling
Centre
ZAF _____ 14

Porky Hefer—Vernacular
Architecture and Design
The Nest @Sossus
NAM _____ 16

Malan Vorster Architecture
Interior Design
Tree House Constantia
ZAF _____ 22

SAOTA
Kloof 119A
ZAF _____ 28

*Beit Beirut: Architecture
Shaped by War, Collective
Memory, and Democracy*
by Doreen Toutikian
_____ 34

CAAT Studio
Mahallat Residential
Building No. 3
IRN _____ 38

Dar Arafa Architecture
Al Abu Stait Mosque
EGY _____ 42

OUALALOU + CHOI
Fez Medina
Renovation
MAR _____ 50

Driss Kettani Architecte
Laâyoune Technology
School
MAR _____ 54

*West African Architecture:
Yesterday, Today,
and Tomorrow*
by Mathias Agbo Jr
_____ 64

Atelier Masōmī
NER _____ 66

Kunlé Adeyemi / NLÉ
Floating School
NGA _____ 74

Ramos Castellano
Arquitectos
Terra Lodge
CPV _____ 78

Orkidstudio
Swawou Girls' School
SLE _____ 86

Kéré Architecture
BFA _____ 92

Localworks
Multipurpose Hall
UGA _____ 102

*The Architecture
of Mexico's Evolving
Identity*
by Natalia Torija Nieto
_____ 110

PRODUCTORA
Centro Cultural Comunitario
Teotitlán del Valle
MEX _____ 112

Taller Héctor Barroso
Entre Pinos
MEX _____ 118

Fernanda Canales
Casa Bruma
MEX _____ 126

TACO (Taller de
Arquitectura Contextual)
Pórtico Palmeto
MEX _____ 132

Roth Architecture
SFER IK Museion
Tulum
MEX _____ 138

Comunal
Social Housing
Production
MEX _____ 144

TAX
(Taller de Arquitectura X)
Torre 41
MEX _____ 148

Frida Escobedo
MEX _____ 154

Brazil: Uncertainties and Stabilities
by Marina Pedreira de Lacerda and Pedro Vada
_____ 162

Arquitetos Associados
Claudia Andujar Gallery
BRA _____ 168

Campana Brothers:
Fernando + Humberto Campana
Zunino House
BRA _____ 174

Nicolás Campodonico
Capilla San Bernardo
ARG _____ 178

Ortúzar + Gebauer Arquitectos
Pollo House
CHL _____ 184

MAPA
Sacromonte Landscape Hotel
URY _____ 190

Freddy Mamani
Neo-Andina
BOL _____ 196

A Grid of Columns and a Roof: A Brief Overview of Architecture in Southeast Asia by Calvin Chua
_____ 202

WHBC Architects
Chempenai House
MYS _____ 206

SHAU
Microlibrary
IDN _____ 212

Formzero
Planter Box House
MYS _____ 216

Palinda Kannangara Architects
Frame / Holiday Structure
LKA _____ 220

Farming Architects
VAC-Library
VNM _____ 224

Narein Perera
Estate Bungalow
LKA _____ 228

Tropical Space
VNM _____ 230

Manoj Patel Design Studio
Residential Dwelling
IND _____ 236

Chaukor Studio
Minaret House
IND _____ 238

unTAG
Vrindavan
IND _____ 240

Bangkok Project Studio
THA _____ 244

Locating Chinese Architecture
by Mimi Cheng
_____ 252

MONOARCHI Architects
Treewow Villa O
CHN _____ 256

WEI Architects
Springstream Guesthouse
CHN _____ 262

People's Architecture Office
Shangwei Village Plugin House
CHN _____ 270

RSAA
Tongling Recluse
CHN _____ 276

Neri&Hu
CHN _____ 282

OPEN Architecture
UCCA Dune Art Museum
CHN _____ 292

Index _____ 300

Local Architecture in a Globalized World

Today, architects around the world face an unprecedented series of challenges. Issues such as the rapid growth of populations, societal and political instability, and climate change present those working on the built environment with new levels of complexity. This impacts the myriad decisions that go into any architectural assignment: selecting materials and organizing labor, the use of space, and the interaction between a building and its surroundings.

Globalization brings faster and more streamlined knowledge-sharing and integrative solutions, but also the risk of standardization and homogenization. This is particularly true in our ever-expanding cities, where skyscrapers and high-tech construction systems define our image of what cities "should" be, dominating not only the skyline but the headlines and prevailing academic discourse. In this context, the progression of architecture continues to be shaped by an overtly

Introduction

Western perspective. Size, technological advancement, territorial dominance, material innovation, and engineering prowess are often privileged in the professional conversation, according to a Western idea of what constitutes progress. Even beyond these borders, in regions where colonization has marked the architectural landscape, systemization and mass production—the pillars of our integrated international culture—threaten to neuter local knowledge and tradition.

Architectural practitioners are, then, presented with a unique opportunity. Beyond satisfying the basic human need for shelter, the profession now has the potential to profoundly reshape the way we live in the twenty-first century. The tools of the global economy—the powers of communication and production—equip designers and builders to make decisions that will affect our future livelihood and that of the planet. *Beyond the West* explores the diversity of global architectural cultures and, in doing so, proves that this approach is possible, and indeed will flourish.

This book investigates architecture that challenges our current grasp of the discipline, looking beyond the Western world to discover alternative solutions to globally relevant issues such as sustainability, transport and migration, material innovation, and even wellness. It aims to uncover the architecture of regional cultures and unpack what localization can mean in a global context by investigating how regional social, cultural, and economic conditions can produce intuitive and original architectural strategies. *Beyond the West* looks to thriving practices and projects in parts of the world that are seldom recognized in this arena. We highlight what progress looks like in Asia, Africa, and the Americas, with a focus on vernacular applications. We discover how everyday needs are better met when approached from a place of authenticity—one that serves the requirements of a specific place at a particular time.

Architecture must respond closely to its environment to resonate with the landscape around it and the people who use it. It benefits humans when attention is paid to local surroundings—to weather patterns, economic restrictions, and cultural traditions. That is not to say that Western ideas have no place outside of their borders. Our featured projects and architects do not work in blind isolation; they understand the benefits of a globally integrated world and utilize knowledge gleaned in other parts of the globe. We also recognize and applaud the many projects in the West that adhere to principles of regionality, sustainability, and respect for context and environment. We have chosen, however, to place our focus outside the West, uncovering projects with a sensitivity to local strictures in countries such as Brazil, Burkina Faso, Vietnam, and elsewhere.

A deep consideration for the local climate, resources, and cultures can initiate tremendous advances in the built environment. The projects featured here—from a low-impact mountainside bungalow modeled on Sri Lankan watch huts to an isolated Namibian desert retreat inspired by the nest of a local bird—are examples of a careful, research-driven, and localized approach. In many cases, tradition and intuition are the driving forces behind the overall concept. Working with available materials and in harmony with the surrounding terrain, architects find inspiration in traditional knowledge and skills. Bricks, stones, or bamboo from the surrounding landscapes are made or cut by local hands, creating local employment, and instilling local pride. These are appropriate responses when challenges include transport logistics,

Introduction

restricted budgets, technological limitations, and the availability of materials.

Many of the practices producing these trailblazing projects model new ways of thinking and working by their very make up. They often have younger and more gender-balanced workforces, and they employ open-ended, democratic decision-making processes with a distinctly contemporary and thoughtful working culture. This facilitates innovative and original problem-solving, and may, in time, contribute to a shift in mindset within the discipline as a whole.

Diversity and attentiveness to new voices are crucial for the development of contemporary architectural practices, just as localism and consideration for the environment are for individual projects. This book does not present a comprehensive list of localized architecture; instead, it offers an intriguing glimpse into this design category beyond Western borders, and we hope that it becomes a starting point for further exploration of these regions and the individual architects affecting change. Our goal is for the book to spark curiosity and encourage readers to explore the immense opportunities that arise when we cast our vision beyond the architectural cultures of Europe and North America.

The featured projects offer solutions to some of the challenges faced by the inhabitants of our planet, and together they represent the possibility of a better future. The architects showcased here, often working in response to rapid urban growth, climate change, and political and economic instability, have doggedly drawn on their training, the knowledge of their peers, and their own intuition to develop unique local solutions. This grounded, curious approach should inspire other members of the profession. It is a local call to arms for an international industry.

The Search for South African Architecture

The history of South African architecture, like that of many former colonies, is fragmented and contradictory, perhaps understood as much through its local interpretations of imported styles as through its search for an authentic regional identity.

01

The architecture of South Africa involves a disjointed relationship between precolonial vernacular influences and imported colonial styles. The need to find or create a national character has proved influential at various points in the history of the country's architecture, reflecting the preoccupations of the time. The tendency to follow international trends and import stylistic references from around the globe characterizes South African architecture as much as it does in any other modern industrial country. South African cities are unique, however, in their inheritance of the scars of apartheid urban planning and racial segregation, which continue to define the broader context in which all its architecture exists.

Precolonial Architecture

A broad overview of the history of South African architecture, therefore, needs to start in a few places at once. Some of the oldest and most significant historical structures in the region are the medieval stone cities of Mapungubwe in Limpopo and nearby, just across the border, the ruins of Great Zimbabwe. These prosperous and sophisticated iron-age cities supported complex social structures and advanced trade, and they are the largest antique built forms in Africa after the pyramids in Egypt. Great Zimbabwe dates to 1200 AD, and Mapungubwe is even older, dating back to 900 AD. Their distinctive stone and adobe structures, however, are archaeological influences rather than examples of vernacular architecture.

Precolonial architecture commonly found around South Africa ranges from the adobe and thatched homesteads and villages of various Nguni peoples to the intricately woven grass "beehive" huts of the Zulu people.

01 Stone buildings in Great Zimbabwe.
02 Entrance to a traditional Zulu house near the Drakensberg, South Africa.
03 Typical Cape Dutch facades in the South African Karoo.

Ndebele villages often receive special mention because of the distinctive brightly colored geometric patterns painted on their whitewashed walls. Ndebele architecture represents a relatively modern encounter between the vernacular architecture of Limpopo and Mpumalanga with Cape Dutch architecture and later industrial forms.

Early European Influences

Colonialism brought with it another starting point, as first Dutch and then later British settlers arrived on the southern tip of Africa, which became an important stopover on the trade routes to the East. Early European military engineers built the very first structures, predominantly fortifications, which included the fort and the distinctive pentagonal castle in Cape Town, which dates back to 1666.

As the Cape of Good Hope became more than a way station and the population grew, the Dutch, German, and French settlers developed what has become known as the Cape Dutch style, which is still widely considered to be the only authentic South African style of colonial architecture.

Although the whitewashed walls, distinctive gables, and thatched roofs have undeniable European influences, the style evolved in response to the landscape, climate, and locally available materials, and eventually came to be seen as belonging in the landscape as much as indigenous architecture. It also bears the influence of some of the traditions associated with enslaved people brought to South Africa from Africa's coastal regions and the Eastern Dutch territories, particularly wood carving and plaster molding, which influenced the local evolution of Cape Dutch gable design.

As Cape Town grew, neoclassical influences took hold. In the 1800s, British settlers brought prefabricated industrial materials like corrugated iron, influencing the direction of local architecture, which is evident in the distinctive Victorian veranda houses with their sloping "cat slide" roofs and decorative cast-iron "*broekie* lace" details.

The Cape was ruled by the British in the early 1800s. Although they had no real interest in further colonization, tensions between the Afrikaan and British populations precipitated an exodus of Afrikaners from the Cape around 1840. They ventured into the interior and began establishing farms and homesteads in the vast grasslands. A new simple, unadorned style, partly adapted from the Cape Dutch tradition, developed into a humble agricultural vernacular.

Industrialization

The discovery of gold and diamonds in the second half of the nineteenth and the rush of fortune seekers that followed, led to more ad hoc quickly assembled wood-framed, corrugated-iron-clad structures. This was the advent of the industrial architecture that some architects now call South Africa's "second vernacular."

On a grander scale, however, the architecture of empire was taking hold. Probably the single most influential architect of the late nineteenth and early twentieth century was Herbert Baker, whose close association with the rapacious British empire builder Cecil John Rhodes gave his work a platform both in the Cape and on the Highveld. Baker was essentially a proponent of the British Arts and Crafts movement, and brought many of its principles to South Africa, applying them across several styles ranging from neoclassical to Cape Dutch revivalism. He laid the template for much of the civil architecture of the time, which developed in response to the need for political unification and reconciliation after the Boer War fought between the British and Afrikaans populations around the turn of the nineteenth century. His distinctive mansions on the ridges of Johannesburg, which were particularly popular with the city's newly rich Randlords who profited from the discovery of gold, also pioneered distinctive new directions for local architecture in their use of local materials and skills.

Modernism and the Twentieth Century

As the twentieth century drew on, Baker's influence petered out into a rather stagnant conservatism, and very little came to replace it. Meanwhile, the architectural movement that would become perhaps the single greatest architectural influence in South Africa for the best part of the rest of the century was brewing in Europe. The modernist movement, pioneered by the likes of Swiss architect Le Corbusier and the German Bauhaus school, steered the direction of South African architecture more than any of the other early-twentieth-century styles, including art deco, that were enthusiastically adopted in Johannesburg, Pretoria, and particularly the subtropical port city of Durban on the east coast.

South Africa can be considered one of the earliest international centers of European modernism or the International Style, as it was also known. This development occurred largely through the influential character of a young architect and academic at Wits University's architecture school named Rex Martienssen, who

04

made pilgrimages to visit Le Corbusier and corresponded with him, bringing the purest local interpretation of the machine aesthetic to Johannesburg.

Modernism developed slightly differently in South Africa's major cities. It remained pure in Johannesburg under Martienssen's influence, but in Cape Town and the capital city of Pretoria, regional expressions developed.

The recently revived legacy of Pretoria architect Norman Eaton, for example, reveals a distinctly regional brand of modernism influenced more by the likes of US architect Frank Lloyd Wright and Brazilian architect Oscar Niemeyer than their European counterparts. Clean-lined modern aesthetics were interpreted with a more climate appropriate approach—deeper overhangs, window shades, cooling volumes, and so on—with local materials, and, in the case of Eaton specifically, an interest in local craft and decorative detailing.

In the Cape, architects such as Gawie and Gwen Fagan and Revel Fox reenvisioned Cape Dutch architecture through the lens of modernism. They reinterpreted and abstracted the distinctive proportions of Cape Dutch architecture—its restraint, and sculptural quality, as well as its distinctive gables, chimneys, and pergolas.

It should be added that the regionalism at the time was somewhat tainted by a romantic search for expressions of national identity influenced by the white nationalist government's desire to find new ways of legitimating its place in South Africa. Still, the best examples of regional modernism touched on a uniquely local quality in their designs.

The materials shortages and economic restrictions in the wake of the Second World War resulted in more organic regionalism, driven by the need to be creative with limited means, and by the pioneering work of architects such as Bauhaus graduate Steffen Ahrends, with his almost Arts and Crafts-inspired mid-century houses and his protégés Michael Sutton and Donald Turgel, who realized their own versions of modernism using local skills and humble materials.

04 The Union Buildings, seat of the South Africa Government in Pretoria, designed by Herbert Baker.
05 A township on the borders of Cape Town.

The political ideologies of the time are inscribed not only into the urban infrastructure but in the township developments close to metropolitan areas.

05

Neo-Brutalism and Apartheid

The prosperity of the 1960s and 1970s, however, brought a more slavish imitation of international styles, evident in the proliferation of steel-and-glass modernist architecture in the 1960s and the neo-brutalism of the 1970s.

The apartheid government developed massive projects in the 1970s to project a self-justifying image of South Africa as modern, progressive, and prosperous. Vast educational precincts, hospitals, broadcast centers, sports stadia, airports, and other civic structures were constructed in the heavy raw concrete that was in vogue internationally at the time. Together with the ambitious skyscrapers thrown up by big business in the economic boom that fueled the era's rapid development, these buildings still define Johannesburg's iconic skyline.

It must be noted, however, that these buildings were being developed in the broader context of the racist political policies of the apartheid government, which came to power in 1948 and ruled until 1994, and created an urban landscape

06

characterized by radical racial segregation. The political ideologies of the time are inscribed not only into the urban infrastructure but in the township developments close to metropolitan areas where the black population was housed as a source of cheap labor. Informal settlements proliferated around these "townships" as rapid urbanization took place. This racist urban landscape continues to define the character of South African cities. It is the starting point of much of the significant architecture of the democratic era since 1994, and its ongoing attempts to undo the legacy of apartheid urban planning.

Architecture in a New Democratic South Africa

The late twentieth and early twenty-first centuries saw the architectural landscape, particularly suburbia, swamped with faux Tuscan, Georgian, Provençal, Balinese, and Classical styles, along with a bland contemporary style with origins in twentieth-century modernism. This cluttered pastiche of styles reflected the inability of swathes of the population to imagine South Africa on its own terms and betrayed its persistent fantasies of belonging elsewhere.

The era of democracy after 1994, however, brought with it a reengagement with local concerns, injecting new vitality into local architecture and design. The imperative of transforming the fractured architectural landscape with symbolic and catalytic interventions, and a return to regionalism both in the pursuit of identity and environmental sustainability have pioneered exciting new directions in local architecture.

Perhaps the most significant post-apartheid civic project is Constitution Hill, which was formerly a military fort and prison where many well-known political figures including, Nelson Mandela, were incarcerated. The transformation of this site of pain and injustice into the Constitutional Court and the symbolic heart of South Africa's new democracy was made through subtle interventions that integrate art, craft, and architecture to embody a subtle, multivalent language. It remains the benchmark for the reframing of the South African architectural landscape. The way it harnesses an acknowledgment of a shared painful and shameful past and turns it into a

07

06/08 The Zeitz Museum of Contemporary Art Africa, at the V&A Waterfront, Cape Town, which opened in 2017.
07 The Nest @Sossus, designed by South African architect Porky Hefer, and drawing on the skills of local Nabibian artisans.

symbol of hope and reconciliation is a feat of architectural meaning-making unparalleled in South Africa.

When South Africa hosted the FIFA World Cup in 2010, large-scale construction presented another opportunity to create national symbols and portray a positive, progressive image of the country to the outside world. Football stadia such as FNB Stadium (known affectionately as the Calabash) on the outskirts of Soweto, South African's largest township, were as much symbols of national pride (if somewhat exoticized for a global audience) as attempts to realign the city's heritage of racial segregation and activate the social and economic life of the township.

A battle has ensued between blandly internationalist architectural styles and a more critical regionalist direction, still preoccupied with the search for identity, but suspicious of nostalgic nationalist narratives. Residential architecture continues to be driven significantly by modernism's as yet unexhausted potential to reconnect architecture with its context.

A number of grand inspirational architectural statements such as Cape Town's Zeitz MOCAA designed by British maestro Thomas Heatherwick have sprung up. This museum of contemporary African art was pursued mainly as a commercial partnership and sponsored by German billionaire Jochen Zeitz to house his personal art collection. Heatherwick's design transformed an industrial grain silo in the harbor district into an inspiring and inviting space by carving out the heart of its cellular interior, creating beautiful curves and arcs. It echoes Constitution Hill's narrative of transformation and hope in a more commercial context.

Attempts to improve the urban fabric in the country's suburbs and Central Business Districts (CBDs) range from the sensitive interventions that converted industrial buildings into a mixed-use precinct in Maboneng in Johannesburg's eastern CBD, to the city's new Council Chamber in Braamfontein, which reframes the neo-brutalist apartheid-era Metro Centre. Various attempts to transform the public space around them and the creation of new pedestrian thoroughfares are gradually helping to create safe public spaces that counter the high walls of private residences and the commercial disdain for connecting meaningfully with the urban fabric around buildings.

The era of democracy after 1994 brought with it a reengagement with local concerns, injecting new vitality into local architecture and design.

08

As the tensions persist, there is no single new direction in South African architecture. While critical regionalism, sustainability, and dialogue with the past are important influences, South African architecture cannot be distilled to one thing. It remains a hodgepodge of styles, a jumble of references, and an idiosyncratic combination of influences, but in amongst them, many buildings have a local flavor that perhaps best defines what South African architecture is: not an approach so much as an influence itself.

Graham Wood is a South African journalist who focuses mostly on architecture, art, design, and lifestyle more generally. He lives in Johannesburg with his wife and two daughters, a bulldog, and four chickens.

Architect   Local Studio
Project   Hillbrow Counselling Centre
Location   Johannesburg/South Africa

Transparency Supports Confidentiality

The inner-city Johannesburg neighborhood of Hillbrow is known for its vibrant migrant community. South African architecture firm Local Studio partnered with four local Argentinean contractors (an electrician, steelworker, mason, and cabinetmaker) to construct the Hillbrow Counselling Centre, which was conceived as a safe space in a notoriously crime-ridden area.

Local Studio founder Thomas Chapman describes the current climate in Johannesburg as "an unsure time," and therefore he designed the center to be "ephemeral and anti-monumental." The steel structural frame, covered in multiwall polycarbonate on two sides, looks almost temporary alongside a landmark historical church and the social infrastructure in this busy precinct.

Although silhouettes can be identified inside the center, and vast levels of natural light enter the building via the polycarbonate, its fluted form provides privacy, maintaining the confidentiality of the people undergoing counseling.

The two levels contain four individual counseling rooms and a space for group sessions. A converted shipping container links the top story with a sewing outreach project housed in the neighboring building, encouraging a natural flow from one area of support to another. "It's an interesting hybrid building," says Chapman of the result, explaining how the bridge acts as a study area.

Steel-box windows ensure comfortable climatic conditions. They support natural ventilation and act as rain covers and sunshades. "We always look for pragmatic ways to make interesting shapes," says Chapman. The asymmetric semi-pitched roof and diagonal recess of the side wall follow the incline of the indoor staircase, highlighting this notion. "This makes the building read like a floating object," says the architect.

Prior to this development, various counseling facilities were scattered around the site. Bringing them together in a single cocoon-like space has increased the impact of the services for those who need them most.

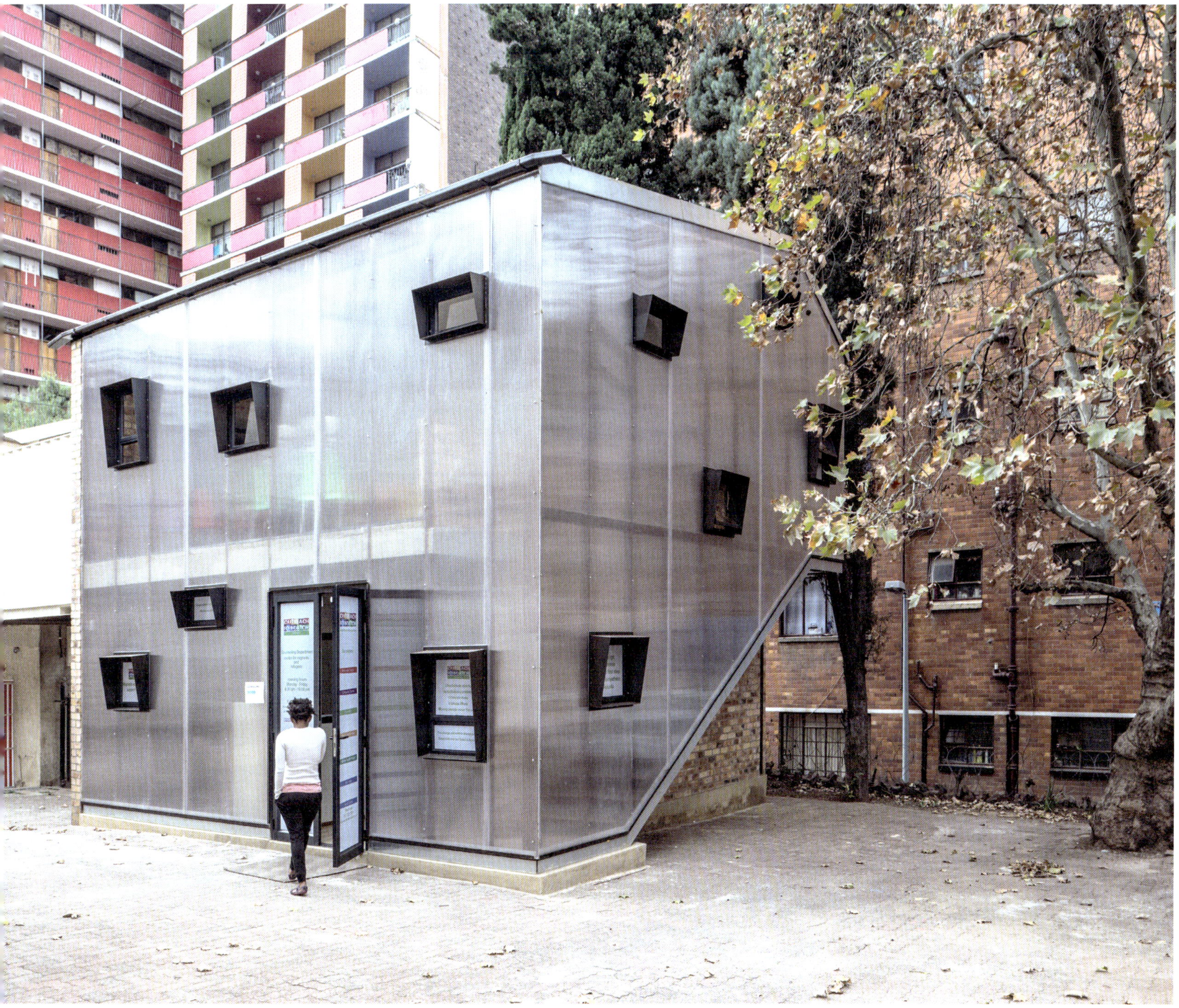

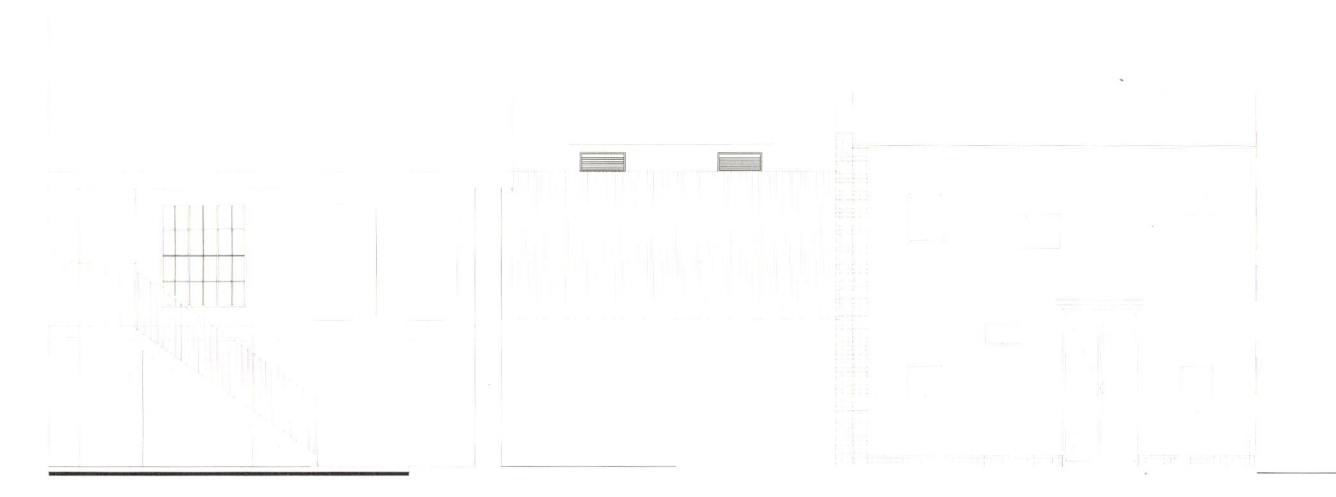

Architect Porky Hefer—Vernacular Architecture and Design
Project The Nest @Sossus
Location Namib Tsaris Conservancy / Namibia

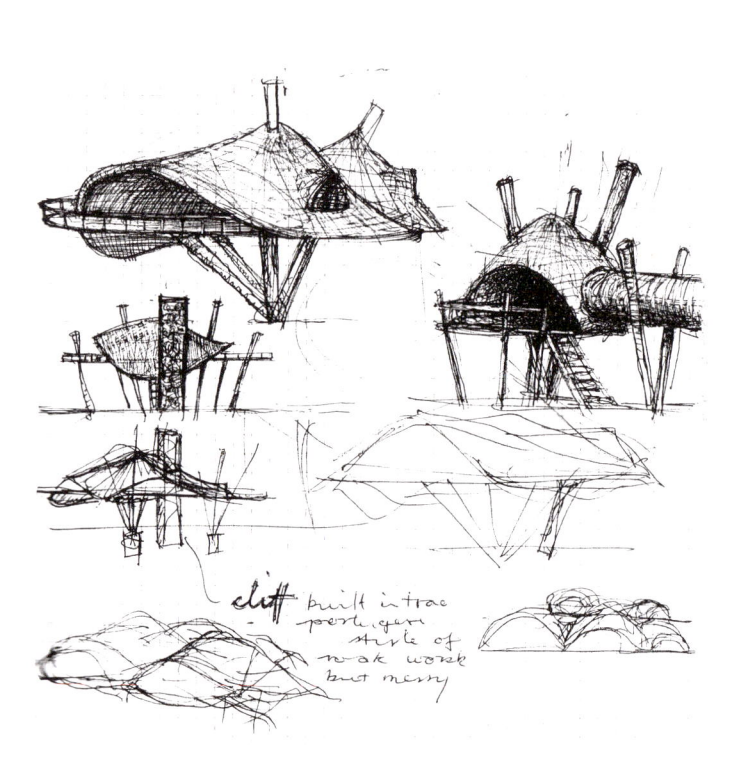

Weaver's Nest Inspires a Social Habitat

Former creative director Porky Hefer has been challenging perceptions of everyday objects ever since he left the advertising world to focus on product design. The South African's first foray into architecture continues the visual language he's become synonymous with—nesting environments in human scale—and is a progression of his handcrafted seating pods.

Porky Hefer—Vernacular Architecture and Design is named to highlight the designer's commitment to utilizing indigenous knowledge and local materials. The Nest, a residential and hospitality property in the Namib Tsaris Conservancy of Namibia, adheres to this ethos and reflects its desert location.

"It is tucked away in a lush valley against the great escarpment in the Namib Desert, in a true desert oasis boasting natural pools and waterfalls," says Hefer of the site that lies 155 miles (250 kilometers) from any notable town, and is only accessible by dirt road. "Materials and labor were very difficult to source," he admits, as was finding a builder prepared to work under such peculiar conditions. But Hefer insisted on "employing local people with local skills" to create this dwelling based on the form of the sociable weaver's nest—a bird abundant in the region. "It was all built by local artisans, with steel, stone, sustainable wood, thatch that was sustainably harvested in Namibia by Namibians, and bricks handmade on-site," he says.

The domed villa was sketched entirely by hand. It features four en suite bedrooms, living spaces with indoor and outdoor lounges, dining areas, an open-plan kitchen, and a study.

"The building carries the lowest possible environmental footprint," explains Hefer of the self-reliant system used to harvest solar energy. Water is drawn from a natural underground well, securing its off-grid existence.

From the earliest sketches to the realization of the final structure (page 21), all drawings for the dwelling were created by hand as they were concept developed from one stage to the next.

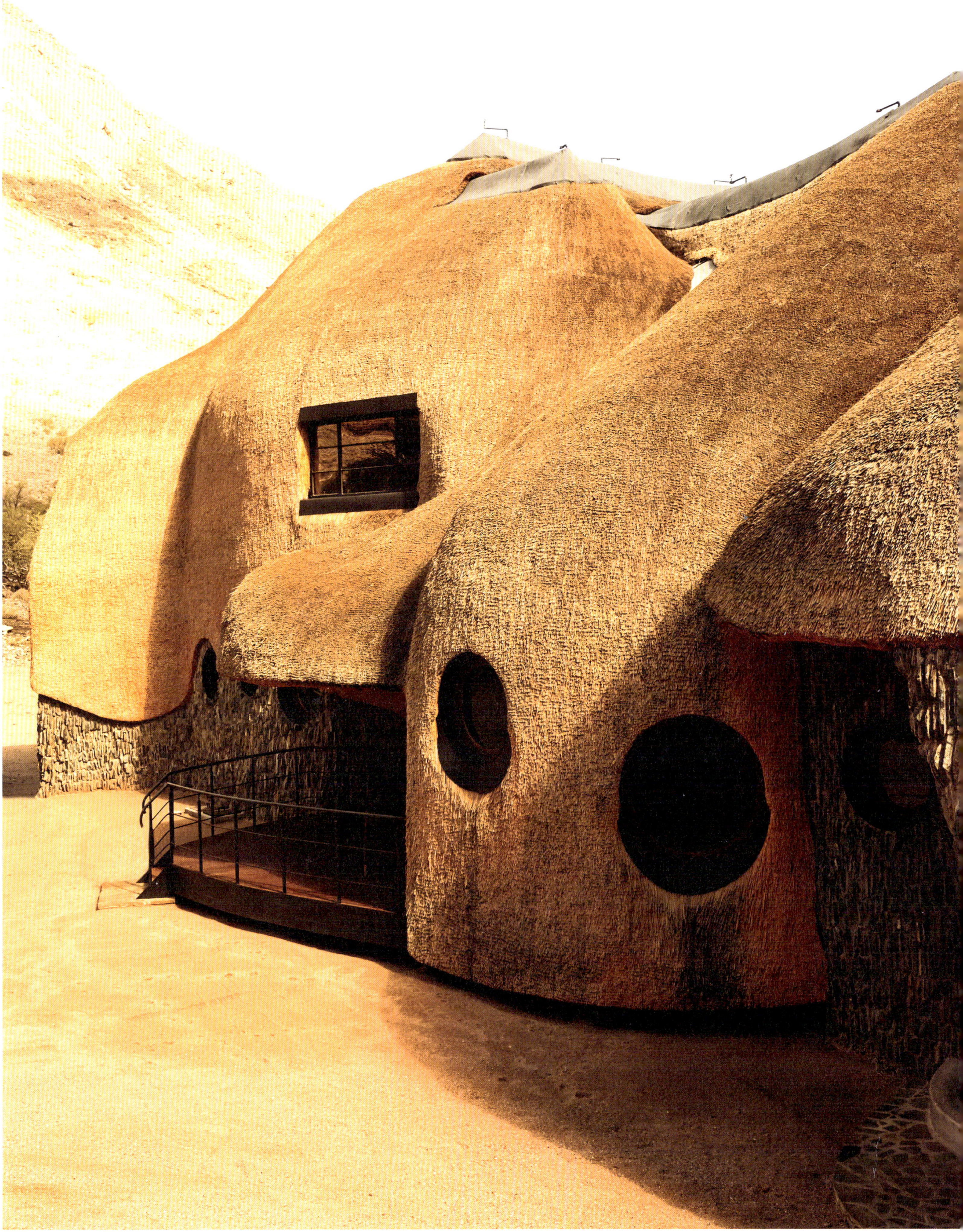

The Nest @Sossus

"It was all built by local artisans, with steel, stone, sustainable wood, thatch that was sustainably harvested in Namibia by Namibians, and bricks handmade on-site."

Most of the furniture within the dwelling was custom made—for example, the sunken lounge seating. Here and there, a few select pieces contribute to the somewhat modernist vibe of the place. Constructed from local stone, bricks, and sustainable wood, the dwelling blends in with the surrounding Namib Desert, mirroring its rich, earthy tones.

The Nest @Sossus

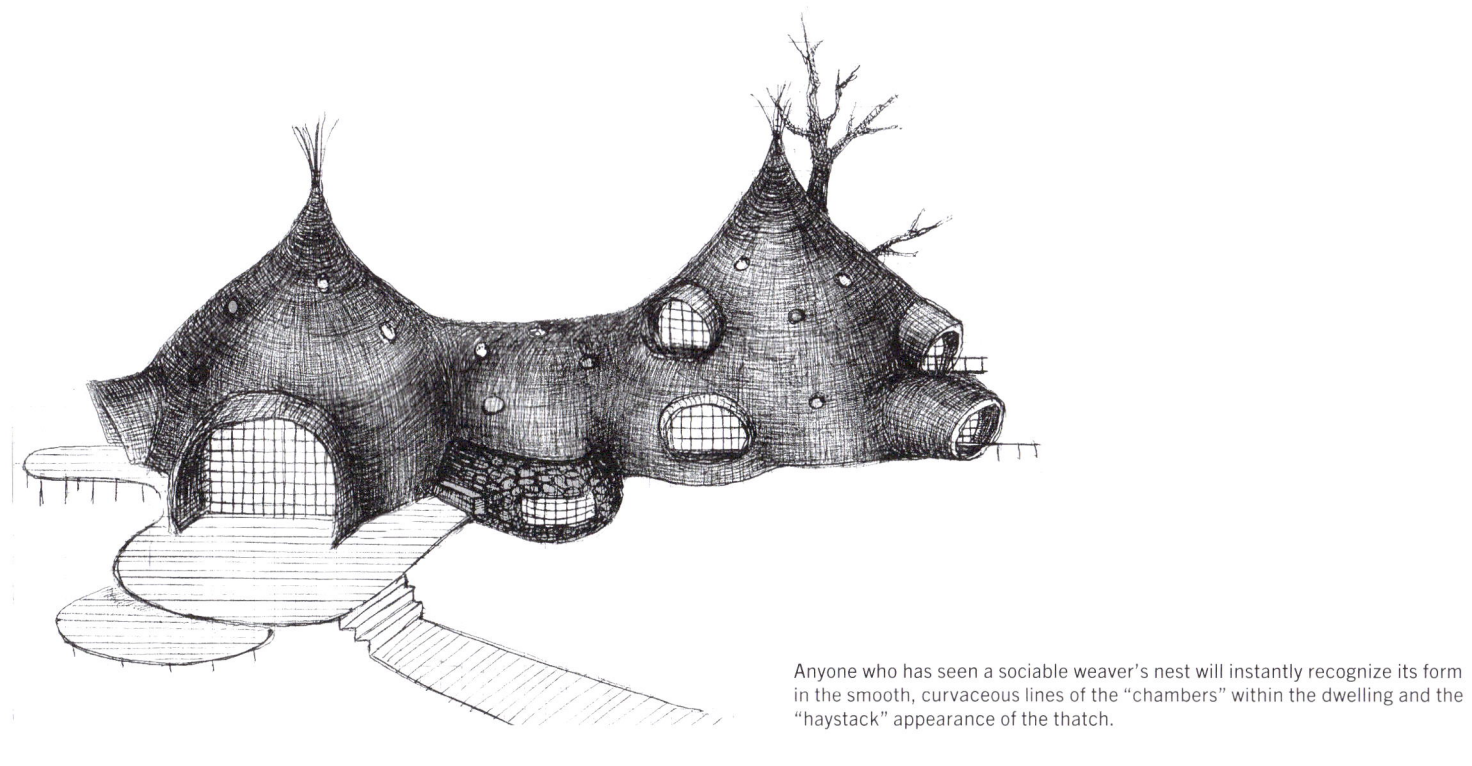

Anyone who has seen a sociable weaver's nest will instantly recognize its form in the smooth, curvaceous lines of the "chambers" within the dwelling and the "haystack" appearance of the thatch.

21

Geometry Informs a Tree-Like Sanctuary

Architect   Malan Vorster Architecture Interior Design
Project   Tree House Constantia
Location   Cape Town / South Africa

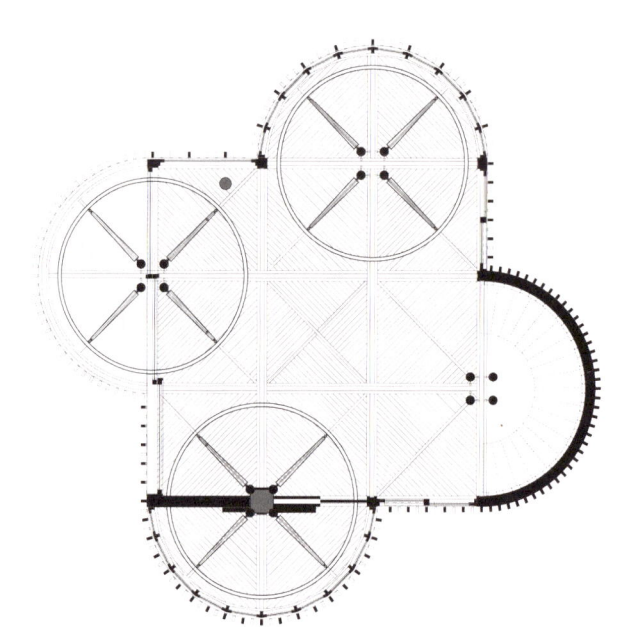

This one-bedroom hideaway resembling a contemporary tree house revitalizes a Cape Town property teeming with trees. Designed by local studio Malan Vorster Architecture Interior Design, the structure complements the layout of the property, which is a modern interpretation of a typical South African farmyard with several separate buildings.

The cabin, located in a small clearing in the forest-like garden, is elevated on stilts to take advantage of spectacular views of the verdant landscape, and the design reflects the verticality of the trees towering around it. The timber slats on the facade are untreated and have been left to weather naturally, creating a rustic aesthetic.

The layout is based on four cylinders with a square in the center. The cylinders create curved spaces on each of the three levels, reflecting the organic, natural surroundings. The square aligns with the north-south axis of the site. In the middle of each cylinder stands a Corten steel-plate column that supports the ceiling beams and connects with four branch-like arms, held by a circular ring. Each column is divided into four "trunks" to maintain transparency and light in the rooms. Attractive hand-turned brass components connect the steel and timber, adding interest to the focal points.

The ground level contains the main living space, and the semi-circular bay includes a patio and dining alcove. The bedroom lies on the level above with an en suite bathroom in the curved area. On the top is a roof deck with a built-in curved seat, and below the building lie a plant room and a timber and Corten steel ramp providing access.

Even at nightfall, the cabin blends in with its natural surroundings, its mirrored facade reflecting the colors of the sky.

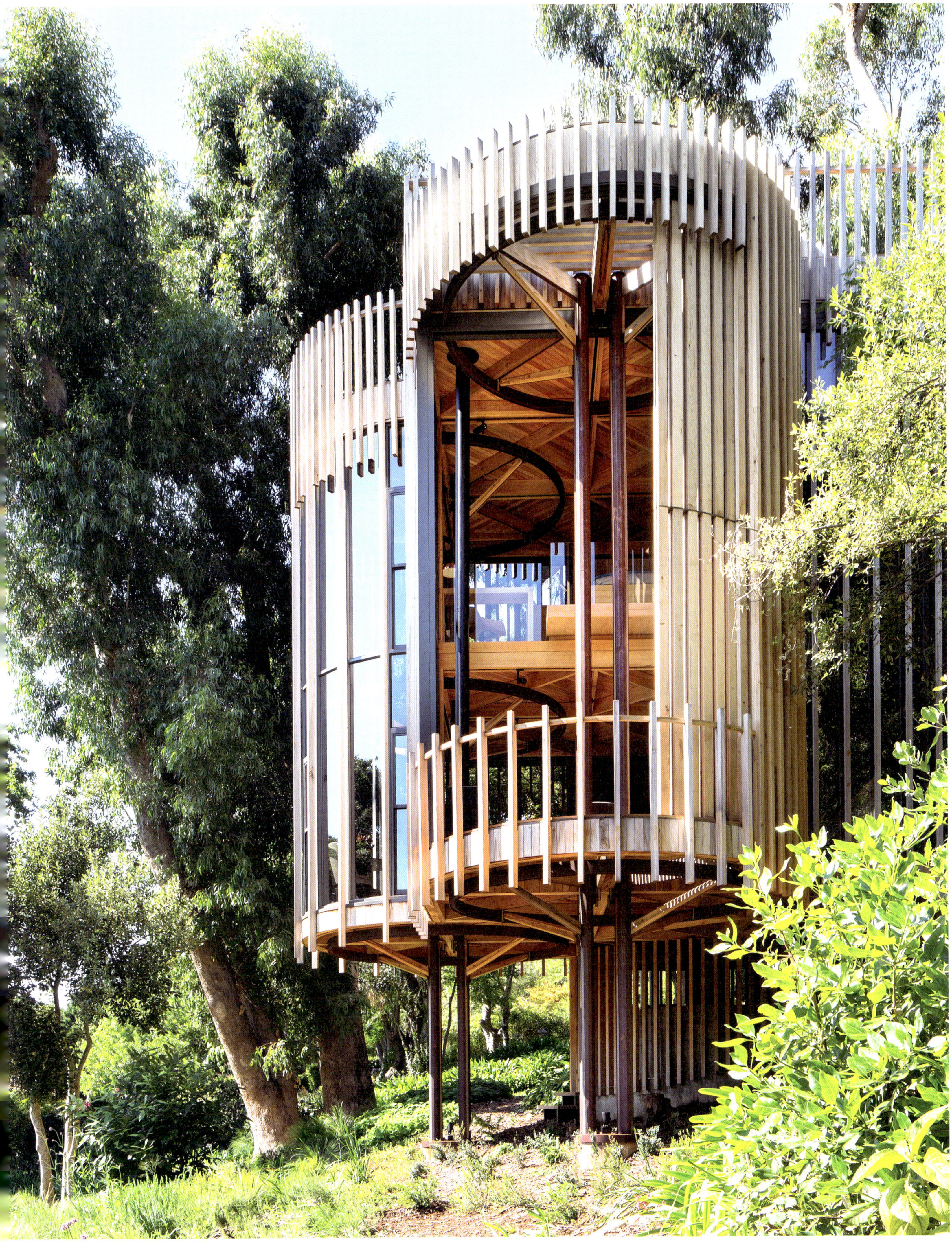

The timber slats on the facade are untreated and have been left to weather naturally, creating a rustic aesthetic.

Each cabin is divided in two along its length. To the front are zones for relaxation—bedroom, living room, and dining room. To the rear, behind a wooden partition, are the more functional areas, including the kitchen and bathroom.

Tree House Constantia

25

Tree House Constantia

With an entire "wall" made of glass, the cabin's occupants can enjoy the most spectacular, uninterrupted views of the open countryside.

At Home between Mountains and Sky

This family home in Cape Town makes the most of the city's cinematic views by opening up to panoramic mountains, ocean vistas, and the city sprawling below. Conceived by South African architectural firm SAOTA, the three-story house is designed to connect with the surrounding environment. This approach is exemplified by the clerestory window, which reveals Table Mountain and the Lion's Head peak.

Celestial views can be appreciated with a skylight through which the movement of the Sun and Moon can be tracked. The natural scenography continues with a courtyard flanking the entrance lobby, and verdant gardens screen every level of the house from neighboring properties and create an immersive experience. Acting as dividing "walls," the flora eliminates the need for imposing periphery walls and allows natural light to penetrate the home throughout the day, keeping the interior attuned to its surroundings.

The architects have not neglected the view of the city lying beneath the residence. The top-floor open-plan kitchen, dining room, and lounge open onto the swimming-pool deck, where the urban landscape is the primary view before the eye is drawn toward the Atlantic Ocean and Boland mountains in the far distance. The view from the master bedroom, one level below, is the same.

Built on a busy street, the tranquil setting of the home is surprising. The stone wall in front gives little indication of the contemporary architecture behind it. Created using a method of construction that is traditional in South Africa's Cape region, it acts as a visual shield and separator, and the natural material suits the mountain setting.

From the street, the only hint of the building's modernity is the clerestory that rises above the stone barrier, forming a giant light box that hovers in the sky at night.

Architect SAOTA
Project Kloof 119A
Location Cape Town / South Africa

The swimming pool is on the uppermost level of the site, where residents can swim almost among the treetops.

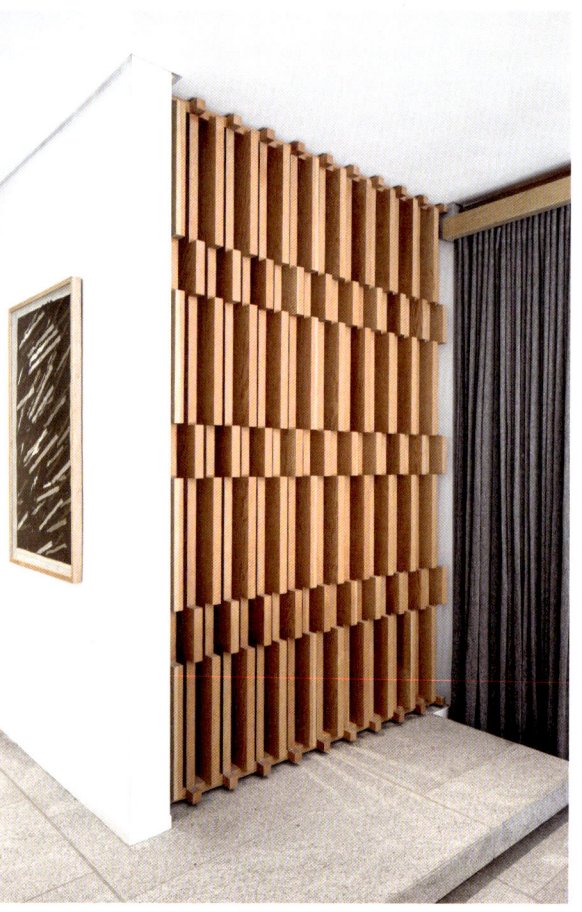

Rooms are furnished throughout with contemporary pieces, much of them from OKHA in Cape Town. Colors are predominantly muted and the prolific use of washed oak gives the spaces warmth.

Kloof 119A

31

Verdant gardens screen every level of the house from neighboring properties and create an immersive experience.

Elements of the design, in particular its linear structure, are reminiscent of mid-century houses in California, whose spectacular views were similarly captured through vast plate-glass windows.

Beit Beirut: Architecture Shaped by War, Collective Memory, and Democracy

How an Arab city on the Mediterranean reconciled fierce divisions and civil war to become a thriving cosmopolitan destination. But despite its progress, Beirut's new architecture remains cognizant of its past.

01

There are Arab cities from Morocco on the western border of North Africa to Iraq in West Asia. They share a common language, and their architecture reflects their interconnected political histories. The architecture in the cities of Egypt, Iraq, and Iran reflects their ancient origins. Cities in Algeria, Tunisia, and Morocco exhibit strong colonial influences. Metropolises on the Arabian Peninsula, such as Dubai, Doha, and Kuwait City, are renowned for skyscrapers, which represent their exponential economic growth since the late 1960s, when oil was discovered in the region.

Cities in Syria, Palestine, and Lebanon, however, are infamous for war-damaged architecture because they have been hot spots for political instability and conflict in recent decades.

Beit Beirut and the Civil War

Beirut is one of the most iconic Arab capitals. It encompasses all of the characteristics of Arab cities: the ancient, the colonial, the contemporary, and the war-damaged. Today, it is a vibrant Mediterranean cosmopolitan city that boasts world-renowned cuisine, a contagious creative energy, a liberal society, and nightlife that attracts tourists from all corners of the globe. Yet, it endured a harrowing civil war that lasted 15 years (1975–1990) and devastated the city. During that time, the city was divided into a Christian area in the east and a Muslim area in the west. Crossing the long demarcation zone separating these areas meant instant death by snipers or abduction by militias at checkpoints. Over the years, this no-go zone became a wilderness known as the Green Line.

Before the war, the Green Line was known as Damascus Road (as it is today), and it was the

01 Beirut's coastline from the air.
02 The Mohammed al-Amin Mosque in Beirut, Lebanon, also known as "The Blue Mosque". It was inaugurated in 2008.
03 A road running through the sand dunes of Liwa in Abu Dhabi, UAE.

main artery of the city leading toward the Syrian capital. In 1924, Victoria and Nicholas Barakat, who owned a piece of land at one of its intersections, commissioned the Lebanese architect Youssef Afandi Aftimos to build them a yellow sandstone mansion. In 1932, when concrete-casting technology was developed, two floors with integrated precast concrete columns were added to the original stone construction by architect Fouad Kozah. The two wings were separated by a narrow atrium, connected by a thin balustrade, giving the building a distinctive aesthetic with hints of the art deco style. In all its magnificence, it was an emblem of the middle-class bourgeoisie.

02

03

When the civil war started, the Barakat family fled to the north of the country, and right-wing Christian militias turned their home into a sniper's den. By reappropriating Kozah's architectural design, they set the building's beauty against itself, forming a perfect redoubt with ideal sight lines for targeted assassinations. Soon, the junction where the building stood became known as "the intersection of death." Over the years, the militias also made adjustments to the structure. They destroyed the staircase, built walls from sandbags and concrete with openings for their artillery, and devised assassination contraptions. It is a perfect example of war architecture.

In the mid-nineties, when the war ended, the building was abandoned. Reconstruction began, and all evidence of the 15 years of destruction was eliminated. The warlords of the civil war returned to power to rule the country, and it was in their interest to help the people forget the crimes they committed. Simultaneously, Rafiq al-Hariri, an entrepreneur, began to rebuild downtown Beirut. He was from the Lebanese port town of Saida and accumulated his wealth in Saudi Arabia, where he formed alliances with the Saudi royal family. In 1992, he became the first postwar prime minister. He bought all of the real estate in Beirut's city center and turned it into a privately owned mini-empire. People started calling the heart of Beirut city "Solidere," the name of his company, and many citizens became increasingly worried about how the city was being developed. When the Barakat building was due for demolition in 1997, civil activists, spearheaded by a young architect, stepped in to save it and convince the state to turn it into a museum.

A Museum to Fight Amnesia

In 1994, while wandering the ravaged streets of Beirut, Mona Hallak (now a professor of architecture at the American University of Beirut) entered the abandoned yellow building formerly belonging to the Barakats. There she discovered hundreds of artifacts that had been there since war had erupted. Furniture, photos, diaries, and personal items that had belonged to the residents before the war and the militias who squatted the

04

building were scattered everywhere. From that moment on, she was convinced that the building must be preserved in memory of the war. She spent 20 years protesting along with colleagues to stop the government from destroying the only piece of architectural heritage remaining on what had been the Green Line. They eventually succeeded. The municipality of Beirut bought the building and partnered with the city of Paris, which offered a technical support team. Partnerships between Lebanon and France are common because of their colonial history. Together, they took on the project to turn the Barakat building into Beit Beirut, a museum commemorating the Lebanese Civil War. It was the first time in the modern history of the city that there had been a democratic process in preserving architecture. Hallak received the French medal of honor for her effort to save this heritage building.

Architect Youssef Haidar was commissioned to perform the restoration. He decided to preserve the building in its bullet-ridden state, exhibiting the militias' constructions, and making only minor adjustments to ensure the building's stability and functionality. This approach provoked a great deal of controversy from the municipality (who were initially appalled by the idea), the Lebanese public, and architects both locally and internationally. Most controversially, Haidar integrated new bullet holes on the facade, which were carefully detailed reconstructions of real ones; but to the general public, they looked fake, and some felt that this mocked the building's dark past.

Haidar admits that this was the most challenging project he ever undertook. The process involved renovating over 64,500 square feet (6,000 square meters), which took 10 years and cost $18 million. "This building has a huge emotional load; the complexity of dealing with these emotions and the attachment that people and activists have with it, alongside the demands of the state, was the main challenge," says Haidar.

"We have a duty as architects. People have a short and selective memory, and this building is linked directly to the collective memory of the city. We wanted to create a democratic and open space for public debate. The permanent collection of the museum is the preservation of the space itself and the traces of war and time. My frustration is that it is not fulfilling its job as it is still not open to the public as it should be."

War is not something that any of its victims want to remember, but in Lebanon, there is collective amnesia and misinformation that harbors hatred and aggression. While the people who took part in the war are alive, it is difficult to discuss or make peace with it. The war is not taught in schools, and there are no official history books about it. There is no official death toll, and thousands of families still do not know the fate of relatives who disappeared during the war. Beit Beirut reminds us of that.

Collective memory of a tragic war, democracy, and controversy make Beit Beirut an iconic piece of architecture. It is a building that cannot go unnoticed, and it makes a profound impression

04 Visitors walk through the interior of Beit Beirut. Bullet holes are visible in the structure's stone walls.
05 The building's restored facade.

> "We have a duty as architects. People have a short and selective memory, and this building is linked directly to the collective memory of the city. We wanted to create a democratic and open space for public debate."

on everyone who experiences it. People who did not live through the war, especially tourists and journalists, are mesmerized by the building's aura and the power of its destruction. Architects are outraged by the way it was restored, emphasizing the complete lack of adherence to restoration laws and undignified aesthetics. People who lived through the war are disturbed by the fact that its war identity has been preserved and shocked by the audacity of the "fake" bullet holes. It is a sensitive matter for many people in Lebanon, and today, in the absence of a museum program, the heated debate surrounding the renovation and use of the building is ongoing.

05

Democracy and Architecture

For most of the world, it is hard to imagine an Arabic city where democracy might influence architecture. Beit Beirut is unique. There are no other buildings that embody the destruction of a civil war, confronting the warlords who caused it and who are still in power. As dictatorships are on the rise, and radical politics come into play, democracy is in great danger. The majority of countries around Lebanon are governed by authoritarian dictators who are very unlikely to listen to the voice of a young female architect—or civil society—who wants them to face their past and make a statement with a public building. In this story, the true heroine is Mona Hallak. She did this out of an awareness of the value of collective memory in a city's architecture, at a time when the new postwar government was destroying everything in the name of neoliberal capitalism based on empty promises. Her years of activism are an example of exercising the right to democracy. If Gaza, Syria, and Yemen are rebuilt, will their governments listen to their people? Or will everything be designed according to the agendas of their leaders?

For now, Beit Beirut is used as an events venue. It still does not have a museum director nor strategic programming. Considering how long it took for the building to reach its current position, it may take many more years for it to fulfill its true destiny. But when the government is ready, and public funds are available, what will take place inside Beit Beirut will be a great achievement for the city. It would be a space that is filled with humanity, much like the Holocaust Memorial in Berlin or the Apartheid Museum in Johannesburg. A building of that nature in the region would be the first example of reconciliation.

Doreen Toutikian is a cultural producer with a background in human-centered design. She is founder of Beirut Design Week and MENA Design Research Center. She lectures on design research, history, and theory at Academie Libanaise des Beaux Arts, where she is also a member of the pedagogical committee.

Architect CAAT Studio
Project Mahallat Residential Building No. 3
Location Mahallat / Iran

A Home from Locally Mined Stone

CAAT Studio's architects Mahdi Kamboozia and Helena Ghanbari believe that "future architecture is not just about the advancement of design and construction technology, it is also about proposing ideas tailored to new conditions in social relations."

For a residential building on the outskirts of the hot, dry city of Mahallat, Iran, the architects combined two ideas and designed a house that allows living to flow easily between the three levels while demonstrating the capabilities of a stone found abundantly in the area.

Two mines located nearby—Haji Abad and Abbas Abad—are rich sources of travertine. The property owner is an independent travertine retailer and consultant, and is an expert in this material. He commissioned CAAT Studio to build his home using this local rock, cut and treated in Mahallat, to demonstrate its beauty and versatility.

The foundations and floor plates were already in place within the 59 × 33-foot (18 × 10-meter) site when Kamboozia and Ghanbari started work. The building sits close to neighbors on the left and right, and the southern elevation looks toward the mines and mountains, while the northern side offers views over Sarcheshmeh Park, where trees tower over a small spring.

The architects maximized these views by dotting windows along the facade, which echoes the organic curves of the mountains and treetops. The travertine walls are clad along these contours in different patterns, illustrating the decorative potential of the material. Inside, the curves lead fluidly from one area to the next while also creating spatial divisions. The result shows what can be achieved at a low cost with readily available materials, and it is a strong example for the region.

Travertine is a form of limestone and has a pitted texture by way of pores and pockets that develop during its formation. This gives the facades of this house a beautiful decorative quality, with subtle shifts in appearance as the sun passes overhead in the sky.

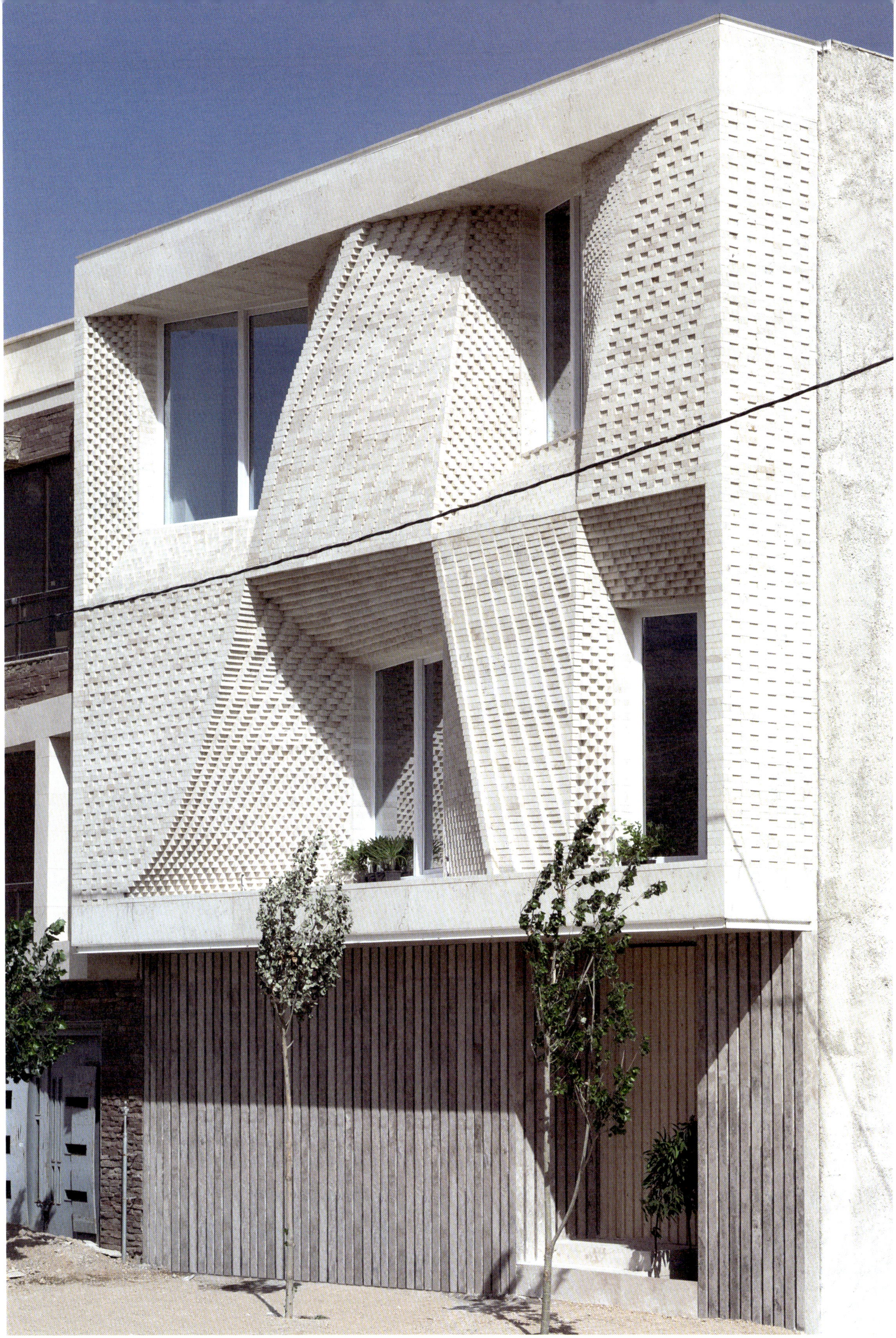

Inside, the curves lead fluidly from one area to the next while also creating spatial divisions.

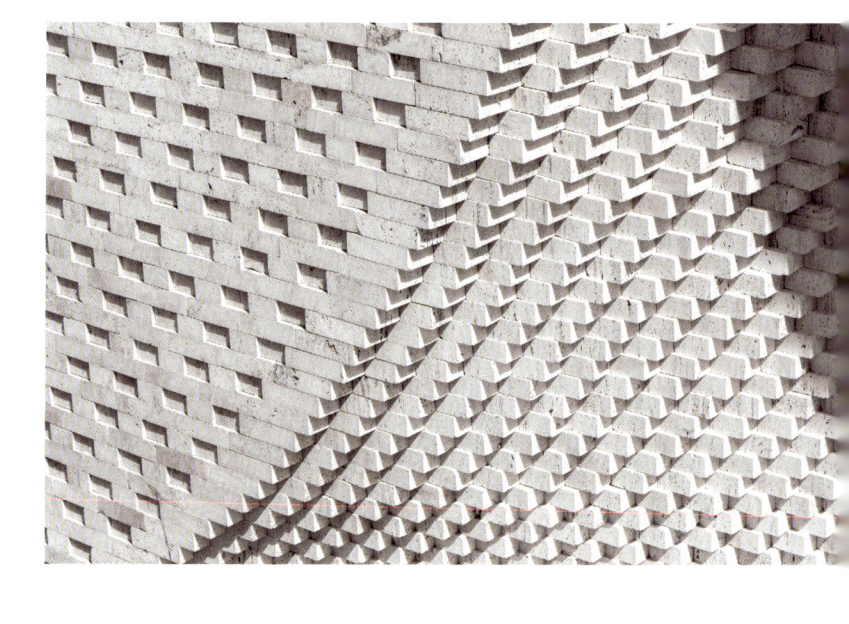

While the house's exterior is all about geometry, with the travertine bricks forming intricate curvaceous patterns, the corresponding curves inside the house are polished smooth and are devoid of decoration.

40   Mahallat Residential Building No. 3

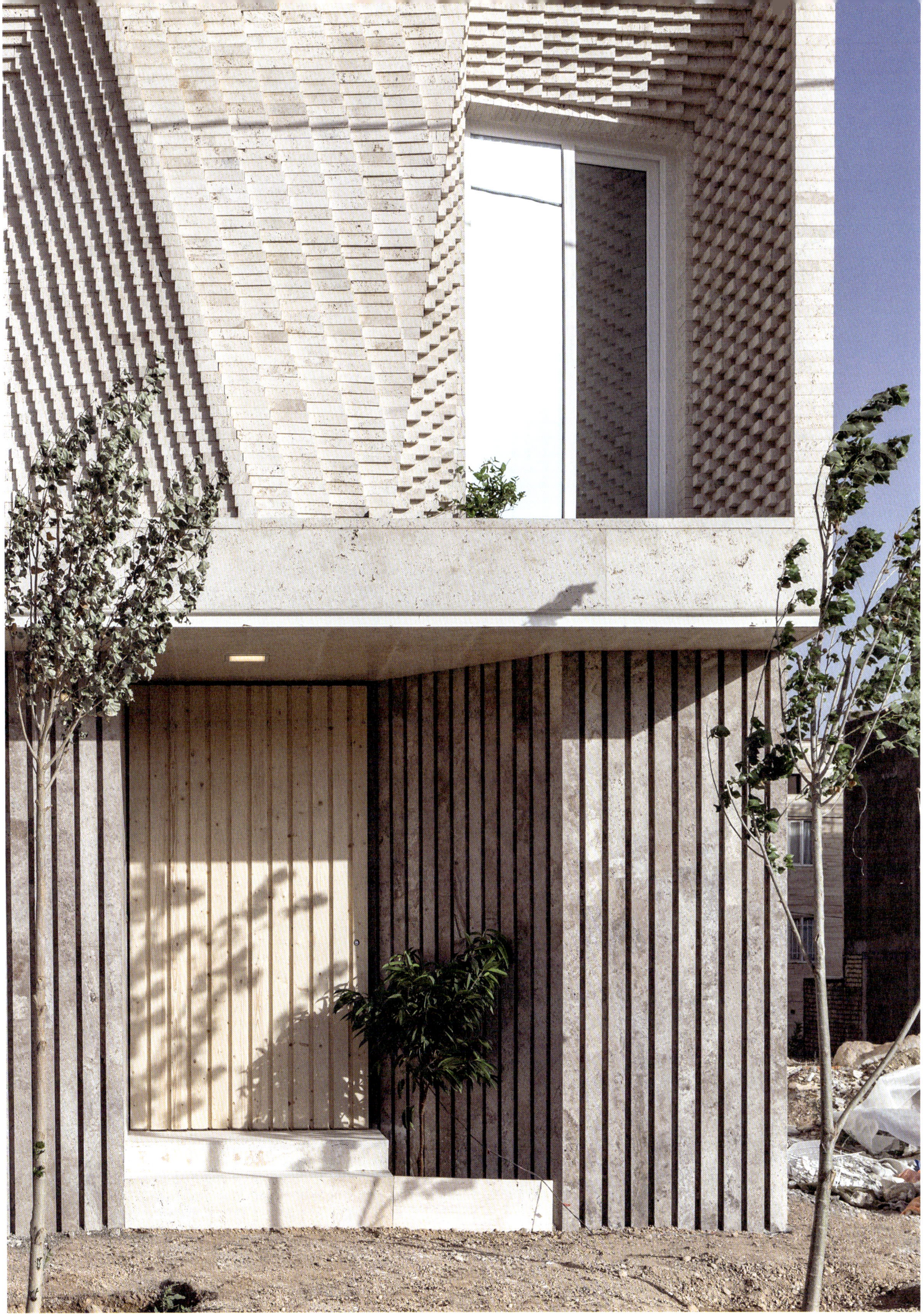

A Mosque Symbolizes Spiritual Growth

Dar Arafa Architecture, led by principal architect Waleed Arafa, is a Cairo-based studio focused on producing contemporary Egyptian architecture that recognizes the country's rich heritage. In the village of Basuna, Arafa and his team reimagined the 300-year-old Al Abu Stait Mosque after a flash flood rendered it unsafe for worship.

Its location in a densely built-up residential area adjacent to a cemetery and in front of a weekly market meant that noise, dust, and the odor of passing cattle needed to be taken into consideration while making provisions for climate control. "We decided to limit openings at, or close to, street level, to just the main entrance, while tackling these challenges on the roof," Arafa explains.

The roof features a dome constructed with blocks made of local sand and lime that insulates the interior from external noise. The staggered pattern of the blocks informed the design aesthetic for the whole building. "The stacked dome references the historic dome of the Great Mosque of Córdoba," says Arafa, "and serves as a reminder of the rich potential of historic architecture in both architectural discourse and construction innovations."

The roof also incorporates 108 small square skylights, which are partially covered by pendentive domes with operable glass panels, allowing natural light and ventilation to enter the building. These small domes represent abiding by God's will, respecting the movement of the wind and the Sun. "They allow the God-given breeze and light to flood the interior of the mosque while protecting it from glare and heat," Arafa explains.

Due to budget constraints and limited accessibility to machinery, Arafa depended primarily on manual labor and simple tools with assistance from specialized masons, resulting in a project that he says "seeks to learn from the past to create relevant innovations for the future."

Architect   Dar Arafa Architecture
Project   Al Abu Stait Mosque
Location   Basuna / Egypt

The northwestern facade and women's entrance (above), and the main entrance (top left) to the mosque. There are four entrances in all, two of them with wheelchair access.

Al Abu Stait Mosque

The mosque is striking in its contemporary features, from the interlocking volumes of the exterior to the grid of glass square skylights above the main hall. Pillars inside the main hall mimic the mosque's twisted minaret. Plans for the south face reveal how the slender minaret rises from the ground, nestling between the mosque's main hall and rear entranceway.

The roof features a dome constructed with blocks made of local sand and lime that insulates the interior from external noise.

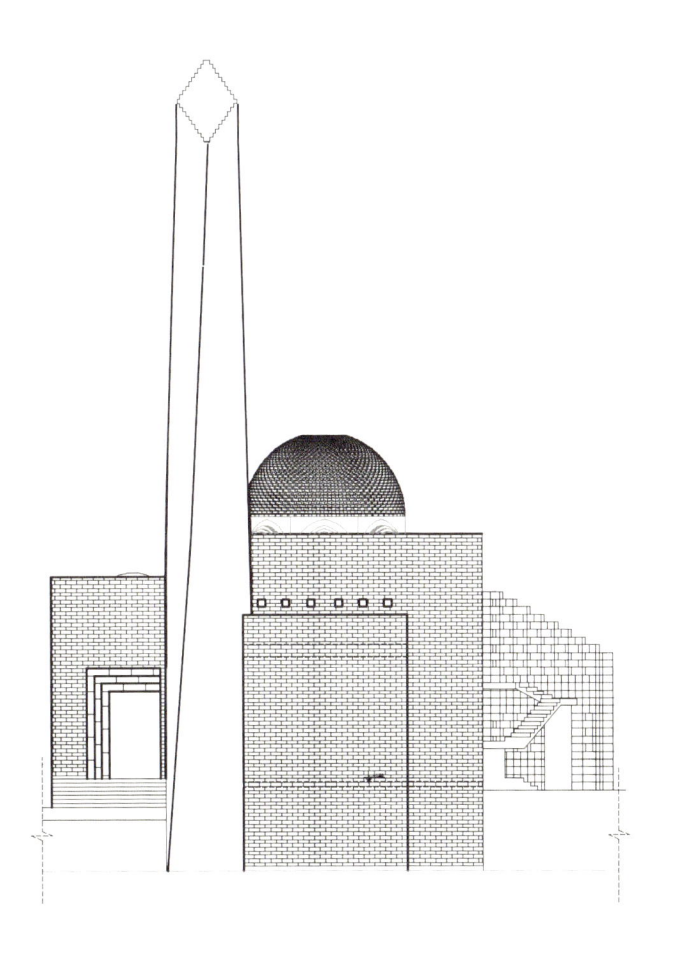

Al Abu Stait Mosque

There is the most fantastic play of light and shade throughout the development—from the shadows cast by the angular turns of the staircase to the geometric shafts of light on the brilliant white walls within.

47

Al Abu Stait Mosque

The shape of the mosque finds echoes in the rooftops of the maze of streets below.

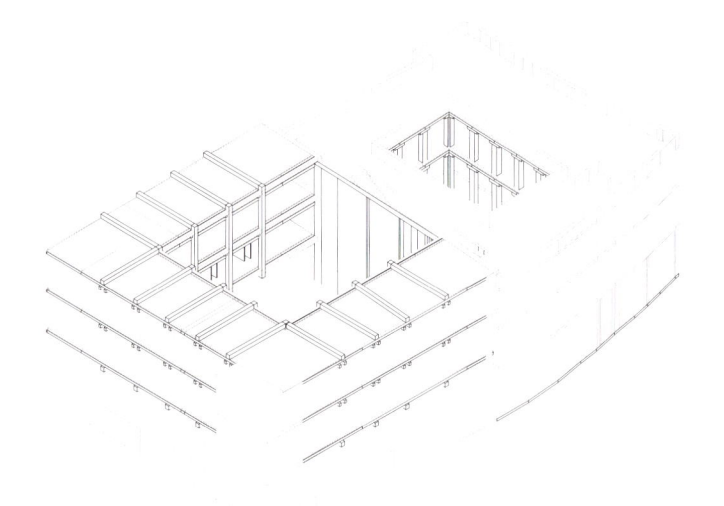

Heritage Calls for Sensitive Restoration

In 1981 the Medina of Fez (the oldest, walled part of the city) in Morocco was declared a UNESCO World Heritage Site to preserve its visual integrity. When architects Linna Choi and Tarik Oualalou of Morocco- and France-based architecture and urban design practice OUALALOU + CHOI were commissioned to renovate the four caravanserais in the Medina, they embarked on the task with utmost sensitivity.

The multidisciplinary project involved urban design, architectural restoration, and landscaping, with a particular focus on the city's ancient copper industry. The architects explain that they sought to investigate the "morphology, physical displacement, and environmental impact associated with this artisanal activity."

OUALALOU + CHOI reimagined the contemporary practice of copper work in Fez by rejuvenating structures dating from the fourteenth to seventeenth centuries and constructing a new building. They also piloted a restructuring of the main entrance to the Fez medina, Place Lalla Ydouna, a 275,000-square-foot (25,000-square-meter) plaza housing artisan and industrial functions.

Over the years, Fez has maintained its status as Morocco's cultural center. The medina once formed one of the largest Islamic metropolises, and in its heyday, it embraced a vast multicultural population.

Characterized by construction techniques, decoration, and town planning developed over more than 10 centuries, the wide variety of architectural forms and urban landscapes in the city reflect the Andalusian, Oriental, and African influences that have converged with local skills and knowledge. By maintaining this legacy, OUALALOU + CHOI has played a part in conserving the caravanserais so that future generations can appreciate the traditional lifestyle and culture inherent in this historical center.

Architect   OUALALOU + CHOI
Project   Fez Medina Renovation
Location   Fez / Morocco

The architects drew on the expertise of local craftspeople to ensure that all materials and building techniques—from the terra-cotta masonry to the woodwork, joists, and seals—followed strictly traditional methods.

Fez Medina Renovation

The architects sought to investigate the morphology, physical displacement, and environmental impact associated with this artisanal activity.

In renovating the existing buildings, the architects were careful to maintain their original structure, which essentially sees four tall units arranged around a central patio. Typically, the courtyard of each caravansary functions as a double-height space and would historically have been used by craftspeople and for trade.

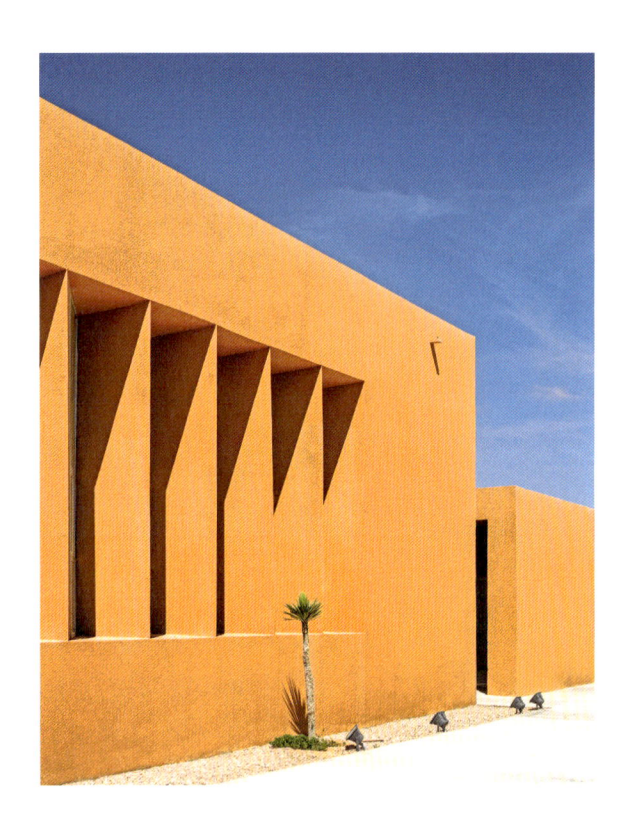

Building Blocks in an Earthy Palette

The Laâyoune Technology School in Morocco mimics the country's characteristic architectural style, which emphasizes the bond with the earth. By reinterpreting the traditional mud-brick buildings of Morocco with ochre concrete structures that reflect the colors in this region of the Sahara, the school maintains a dialogue with the land on which it stands.

For Driss Kettani of Casablanca-based Driss Kettani Architecte, who designed the school as part of the decentralized Ibn Zohr University, "place, culture, and the inhabitants" informed the initial reflections of the practice. In this collaboration with architects Saad el Kabbaj and Mohamed Amine Siana, Kettani designed a range of buildings—classrooms, workshops, and an amphitheater, as well as a library, offices, maintenance areas, and staff accommodation—with a unified aesthetic.

Away from the city center, the site called for a sense of community for staff and students. The architects achieved this by organizing the buildings on either side of a dividing axis that allows easy navigation and provides outdoor social spaces, plazas, and pathways interspersed with trees and gardens.

Inspired by the casbah (North African citadel), these walkways interrupt and connect the geometric blocks that constitute the school's structured composition. The sober, flat walls reduce cost and waste, and ensure maintenance is easy, while the limited material palette ensures the school buildings are coherent.

Vertical openings in these walls shelter the interiors from the harsh sunlight and heat while allowing sufficient light to penetrate classrooms and providing natural ventilation. Other sun-protection mechanisms include *brise-soleil,* double-skin walls, and covered walkways.

Architect Driss Kettani Architecte
Project Laâyoune Technology School
Location Laâyoune / Morocco

Echoes of the architectural style can be found in the layout of the communal spaces, with their block benches and geometric concrete paving.

The sober, flat walls reduce cost and waste, and ensure maintenance is easy, while the limited material palette ensures the school buildings are coherent.

The low rise of the university buildings, and their street-like configuration around the communal spaces, conjures a more urban feel to the development—almost like a mini village.

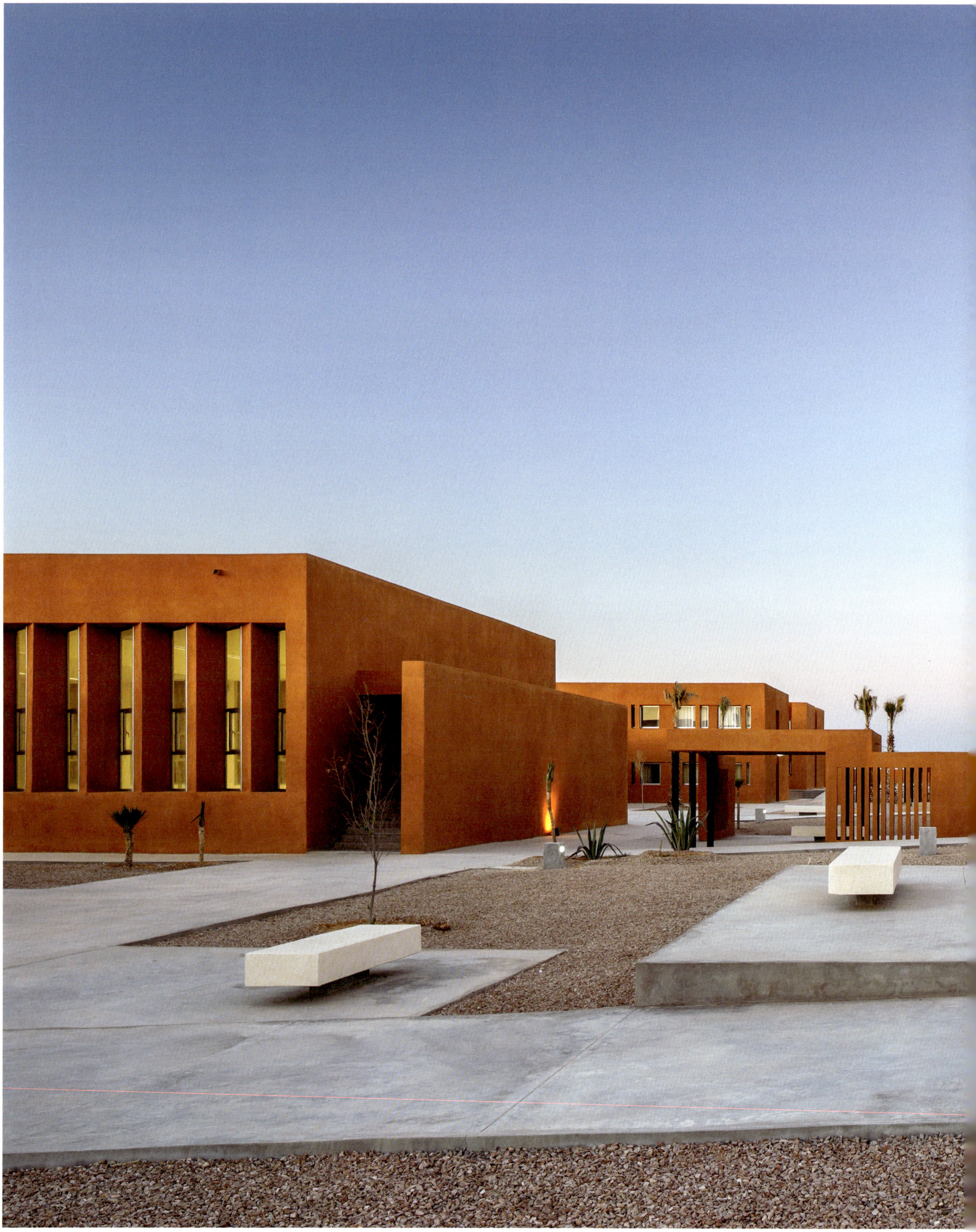

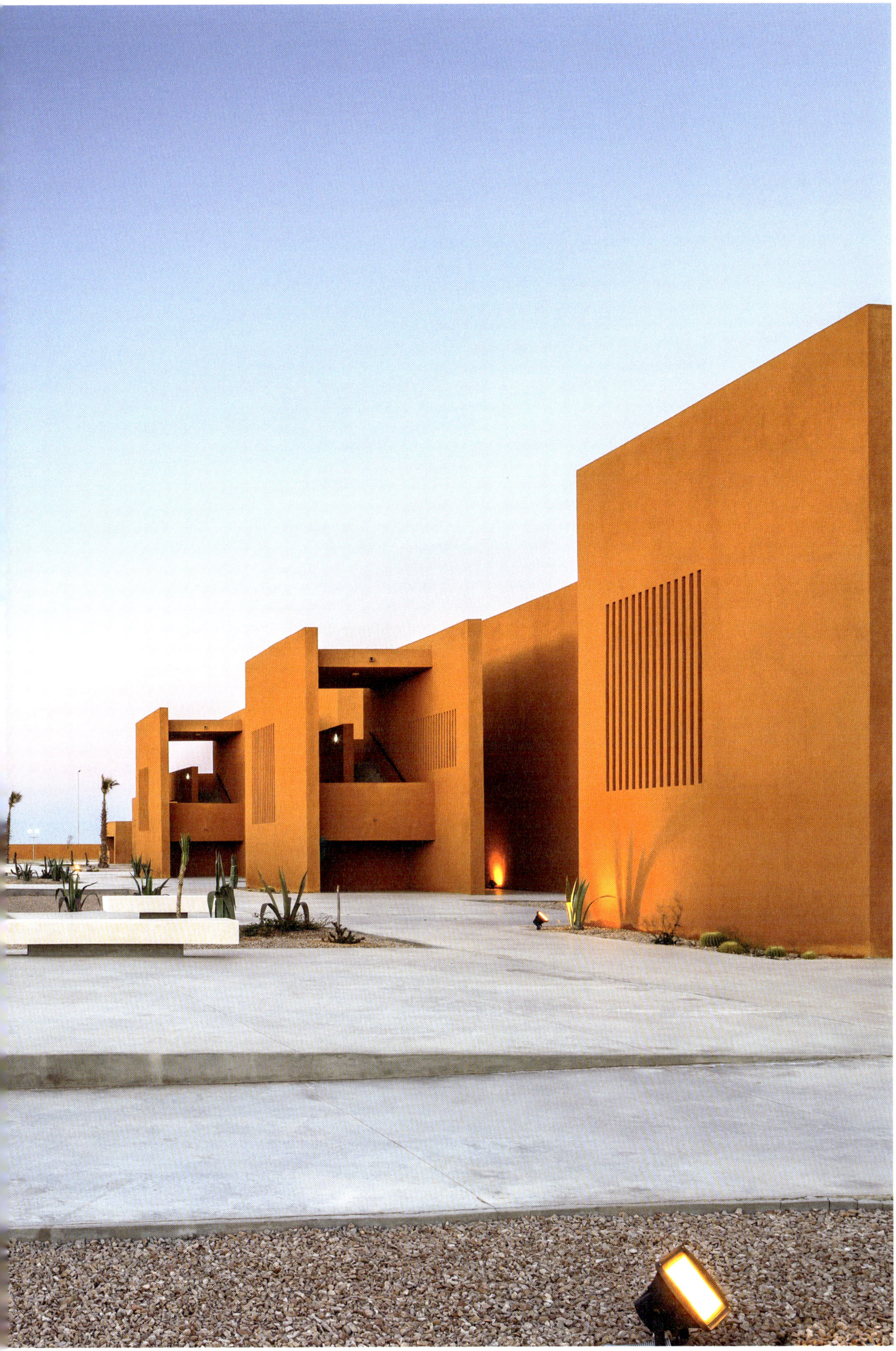

West African Architecture: Yesterday, Today, and Tomorrow

With new economic prosperity, this vast and varied region is giving way to rapid urban development at a megacity scale. Still, a cluster of contemporary architects are approaching vernacular heritage from a modern lens—and turning heads internationally.

01

The West African region lies between latitudes 4° N and 28° N of the equator and between 15° E and 16° W of the Greenwich Meridian. It has an estimated population of 362,201,579 people, inhabiting an area of about 2,000,000 square miles (5,119,976 square kilometers). The region consists of 16 mainland countries: Benin, Burkina Faso, Cape Verde, Côte d'Ivoire, Gambia, Ghana, Guinea, Guinea-Bissau, Liberia, Mali, Mauritania, Niger, Nigeria, Senegal, Sierra Leone, and Togo; and the offshore islands of St. Helena, Ascension, and Tristan da Cunha. Geographically, the region consists mainly of the Sahel region in the north, along the Sahara Desert, and its tropical south, along the Gulf of Guinea, which is bordered by the Atlantic Ocean.

West Africa is one of the continent's most vibrant regions, with diverse cultures, climate, geology, and vegetation. The area is home to several ethnic groups, who live across national boundaries. For instance, populations of Fulani, one of the largest ethnic groups, live in nearly every mainland country in West Africa, while the Yoruba live in southern Nigeria, Ghana, Benin, Togo, Ghana, Cote d'Ivoire, and Sierra Leone. There are hundreds of smaller ethnic groups living across the region, some of whom existed as independent tribal states in the precolonial era.

A Brief History of West African Architecture

The various ethnic groups living across West Africa have never had a homogenous indigenous architecture; instead, their architectural styles are as varied as the influences that inspired them. Each traditional tribal state in precolonial West Africa had a unique architecture morphology, iconography, and construction methodology influenced

01 The Larabanga Mosque in Ghana, built in the Sudanese Style, is one of the oldest in West Africa.
02 Depiction of a Portuguese man on one of the "Benin Bronzes" that would have originally decorated the Royal Palace in Benin City, present day Nigeria.
03 Traditional thatch buildings in Taneka Beri village in the Atakora region of Northern Benin.

02

and shaped by its historical and sociocultural narratives. For instance, Sudano-Sahelian architecture was the dominant style in the Sahel region, which cuts across northern Nigeria, Niger, Chad, Mali, Senegal, Burkina Faso, Chad, Cameroon, and Mauritania. This architectural style consists chiefly of Sun-baked earthen bricks, typically rendered in mud plaster. Flat roofs generally characterized the buildings, and in some instances, large structures like mosques and palaces had logs protruding from the walls and turrets, serving as scaffolds for periodic maintenance. Examples of these buildings include the Great Mosque of Djenné and the Sankore Madrasah in Timbuktu (one of the oldest universities in the region). Variants or substyles of this form of architecture include the Tubali, which is defined by tall adobe walls adorned with intricate relief ornamentation, sometimes rendered in vibrant colors. This style is specific to the Hausa people, and it is commonplace across northern Nigeria, Niger, and other areas inhabited by people of Hausa ethnicity. The Ancient Kano City Walls (Kofar Na'isa) and the Palace of the Emir of Zazzau in the ancient city of Zaria are examples of buildings built in this style.

The architecture in the Bight of Benin was altogether different from that of the Sahel region. Though there were several ethnic groups in the Bight of Benin, their architectural styles had similarities, such as the use of adobe walls and thatch roofs; yet, there still existed a few distinguishing features, specific to each ethnic group. The architecture highlighted the individuality of these tribes but also mirrored their social structures, cultural heritage, local customs, and ethno-religious values.

The city of Benin in mid-western Nigeria was once the capital of arguably one of the most advanced tribal states in West Africa—the Great Benin Empire. The influence of the Benin Empire is believed to have almost covered the area from present-day southern Nigeria to Ghana. The architecture in the Benin Kingdom typically consisted of red earthen walls with roofs of palm leaves. The palaces had large open courtyards, and the roofs rested on massive earthen or wooden columns, sometimes covered with brass carvings. The exterior walls had deep horizontal ridges running the breadth of the buildings. Unlike other settlements of the time, the city was planned and designed with precision, exhibiting urban fractal patterns uncommon for an African city. A 1691 eye witness account attributed to a Portuguese ship captain, Lourenco Pinto, describes it as follows: "The great

03

Benin where the king resides is larger than Lisbon; all the streets run straight and as far as the eye can see. The houses are large, especially that of the king, which is richly decorated and has fine columns. The city is wealthy and industrious. It is so well governed that theft is unknown, and the people live in such security that they have no doors in their houses."

The arrival of Europeans in West Africa permanently altered the course of indigenous architecture across the region through slavery and

Beyond the destruction of native architectural heritage in the violent conflicts that heralded the global slave trade, the arrival of Europeans in West Africa also contributed to the architectural landscape of the region.

04

colonialism. Beyond the destruction of native architectural heritage in the violent conflicts that heralded the global slave trade, it also contributed to the architectural landscape of the region. Firstly, the European traders erected European-styled architectural monuments—mostly classical Greco-Roman-style buildings—to service their enormous commercial enterprise in the area. For instance, in 1482, the Portuguese built Elmina Castle on the western coast of Ghana—one of several forts built by Europeans across the region. The castle had luxurious living quarters with beautiful views of the sea, but the basements housed subterranean dungeons where thousands of slaves from across the region were imprisoned in squalid and inhumane conditions, before being transported to the Americas by ship. The conditions in these chambers were so horrific that many died in them. Although the castle was not designed to be a slave port—it only became one after the Dutch captured it in 1637—it served this purpose so well that it is difficult to believe it was constructed for any other reason.

Another example of the architectural influence of the slave trade was exerted by former slaves who returned to Africa from Brazil. They settled in cities along the west coast, bringing with them valuable architectural skills, which made it possible to replicate Brazilian baroque architecture, in the creation of a genre of architecture called Afro-Brazilian. All over Lagos Island, the influence of this architectural style is still visible.

Among the most prominent Afro-Brazilian buildings in Lagos are Water House, Holy Trinity Church, and the Shitta-Bey Mosque, and, until it was demolished in 2016, Casa Fernandez. This architecture style is also popular in Ghana, Togo, and Benin. In Liberia, former slaves created another genre—Americo-Liberian architecture, a neoclassical architecture influenced primarily by the antebellum buildings in the southern states of the US. In Sierra Leone, former Creole slaves brought back an architectural style influenced by the colorful wooden homes in the West Indies. All over the region, there are imprints of different architecture styles conceived by former slaves.

The Architectural Legacy of Colonialism in West Africa

There is a consensus across Africa that colonialism significantly curbed the development of traditional African architecture on the continent. Violent conflicts between the locals and colonial interlopers preceded the colonial era in West Africa and devastated the cultural heritage of the area. Thriving cities were destroyed, as was the case with ancient Benin City, which was razed to the ground by British soldiers in 1897. The magnificent palace at Abomey in present-day Benin met a similar fate at the hands of French invaders. All over West Africa, colonialists reduced native architectural edifices to rubble. Sadly, communities were rarely able to rebuild what was lost, and several decades of colonial occupation made this even less attainable, as the loss of cultural heritage meant that people had nothing to build on when the colonialists left.

Post-Colonial Architecture in West Africa

As national independence swept across West Africa, it is ironic that the first set of native post-independence leaders in the region did very little to revive indigenous architecture, especially at a time when African patriotism was at its apogee across the continent. Even as these new national leaders set about dismantling other vestiges of colonial legacies on the continent, they were happy to move into the palatial colonial mansions left behind by the colonialists. Consequently, the post-independence era led to a boom in colonial architecture. Considered to be aspirational, it was a preference for most of the continent's nouveaux riches, who replicated the style across the region. Before long, even low-income communities started building houses that adhered to the morphologies of colonial architectural styles. They tended to be constructed using cement blocks, with deep verandas and overhanging eaves, and corrugated zinc or tin sheet roofs secured by steel posts.

This period also saw growth in modernist architecture; the Soviet constructivist style was a favorite for West African leaders at the time and it became the style of choice for government offices, university campuses, and other public buildings in the region. In some cases, the local authorities wanted to replicate the designs of specific buildings they had seen in Europe. An example is the National Theatre in Lagos, modeled on the Palace of Culture and Sports in Varna, Bulgaria. Some West African states even had European architects on their payroll. In Ghana, several Eastern European architects worked at the Ghana National Construction Corporation, which was responsible for the design and construction of several public buildings in Ghana.

Neo-Vernacular Architecture

Despite its towering influence in the precolonial era, African vernacular architecture largely failed to develop beyond the earthen wall and thatch roof architecture. It, therefore, remained unattractive to homeowners across the continent who associated it with poverty and ruins. Thus, the neglect of indigenous architecture on the continent naturally resulted in a shortage of skilled people knowledgeable in the art of building traditional African architecture.

Unfortunately, the architectural curriculum on the continent barely acquaints local architects with enough knowledge or the design skill set to propagate this style. Design schools teach students the history and theory of classical European architecture styles such as gothic, baroque, and even modern European architecture, but there is little focus on African vernacular architecture.

City authorities on the continent still have reservations about vernacular architecture. Development control departments in city councils, even in big countries like Nigeria, are still ill-equipped to arbitrate over traditional architecture building plans and it is difficult to get building permits for this type of construction. Unfortunately, incidences like the collapse of Kunlé Adeyemi's Makoko Floating School have given further ammunition to opponents of neo-vernacular African architecture. However, in the last decade, a growing number of vernacular

04 Elmina Castle on the Ghanaian coast. Built by the Portuguese in 1482, it was the first European trading post on the gulf of Guinea.
05 The National Arts Theatre in Lagos, Nigeria, which was inspired by the Palace of Culture and Sports in Varna, Bulgaria.

Design schools teach students the history and theory of classical European architecture styles but there is little focus on African vernacular architecture.

Contemporary West African Urbanism: Opportunities and Emerging Challenges

In the last 15 to 20 years, the urban landscape in West Africa's major cities has significantly changed. Capitalizing on the region's newfound economic prosperity and political stability, these cities are now embarking on massive urban development. Slums are giving way to skyscrapers, boulevards, and shopping malls. Several West African cities are funding "purpose-built" megacities that mimic similar developments in Europe and the US. Regional governments and private developers regularly commission "Starchitects" from all corners of the globe to design buildings and even redesign city master plans, or create brand new ones. No country in the region is exempt from the skyscraper race; from Lagos to Abidjan, Takoradi to Abuja, the story is the same. Construction across the region is widespread, with new neighborhoods being designed and built from scratch, while old ones are modernized. One such brand new city is Nigeria's Eko Atlantic, sprouting from a reclaimed four-square-mile (ten-square-kilometer) strip of land on Lagos's Atlantic coast in southwest Nigeria. The city, touted to become Nigeria's new financial hub, is expected to be called home by at least 200,000 people, who will live, work, and play here.

architecture projects have been realized on the continent. Today, a handful of African and foreign architects are pushing the boundaries of traditional African architecture by combining traditional methods, local materials, and modern design techniques and materials to create impressive contemporary vernacular architecture. Architects like Diébédo Francis Kéré and a few other outliers have demonstrated the versatility of contemporary African vernacular architecture over the last decade with designed and built projects, ranging from schools and hospitals to communal spaces and private homes.

06

07

Although these developments have birthed world-class buildings across the region, they have done little for local architects, because many of these projects were conceived in design studios in London, New York, or Amsterdam with minimal local involvement. In some instances, the role played by local architects is to merely append their licensure seal to the planning application to fulfill statutory requirements. Most Western-trained architects see design commissions in Africa as low-hanging fruit, and they are pouring into the continent in search of work. It is no coincidence that some of the most celebrated architecture in West Africa today was designed by Western-trained architects. In spite of their allure, some of these urban makeovers have left a trail of socially fragmented communities, especially in cities where low-income settlements were demolished to make way for upscale constructions. This approach has further deepened the already vast social class divisions in the region and has the potential to create enormous social problems in the future.

Overall, the region has made tremendous progress over the last few decades: Eko Atlantic city and similar developments across the region embody the vaulting ambition of West African states. Growth has been slow and challenging, but it undoubtedly demonstrates a commitment to move beyond Africa's painful past and become a global force.

These developments must continually adapt to meet the needs of the region's rapidly growing population and the challenges of twenty-first-century placemaking. It is critical that they prioritize the social well-being of the inhabitants and be environmentally conscious to ensure that natural resources are preserved.

06 Kunlé Adeyemi's Makoko Floating School, which collapsed following strong weather after being decommissioned for several months.
07 Construction on the Eko Atlantic project, which is being built on reclaimed land off the coast of Lagos in Nigeria.

Mathias Agbo Jr, is an architectural designer and design researcher, who runs a small design-build consultancy—MACA Design Studios in Abuja, Nigeria. He also periodically publishes discourses on African architecture and urbanism; his bylines have appeared in notable architecture and design publications around the world. He has also contributed book chapters to a couple of upcoming books on African architecture and urbanism.

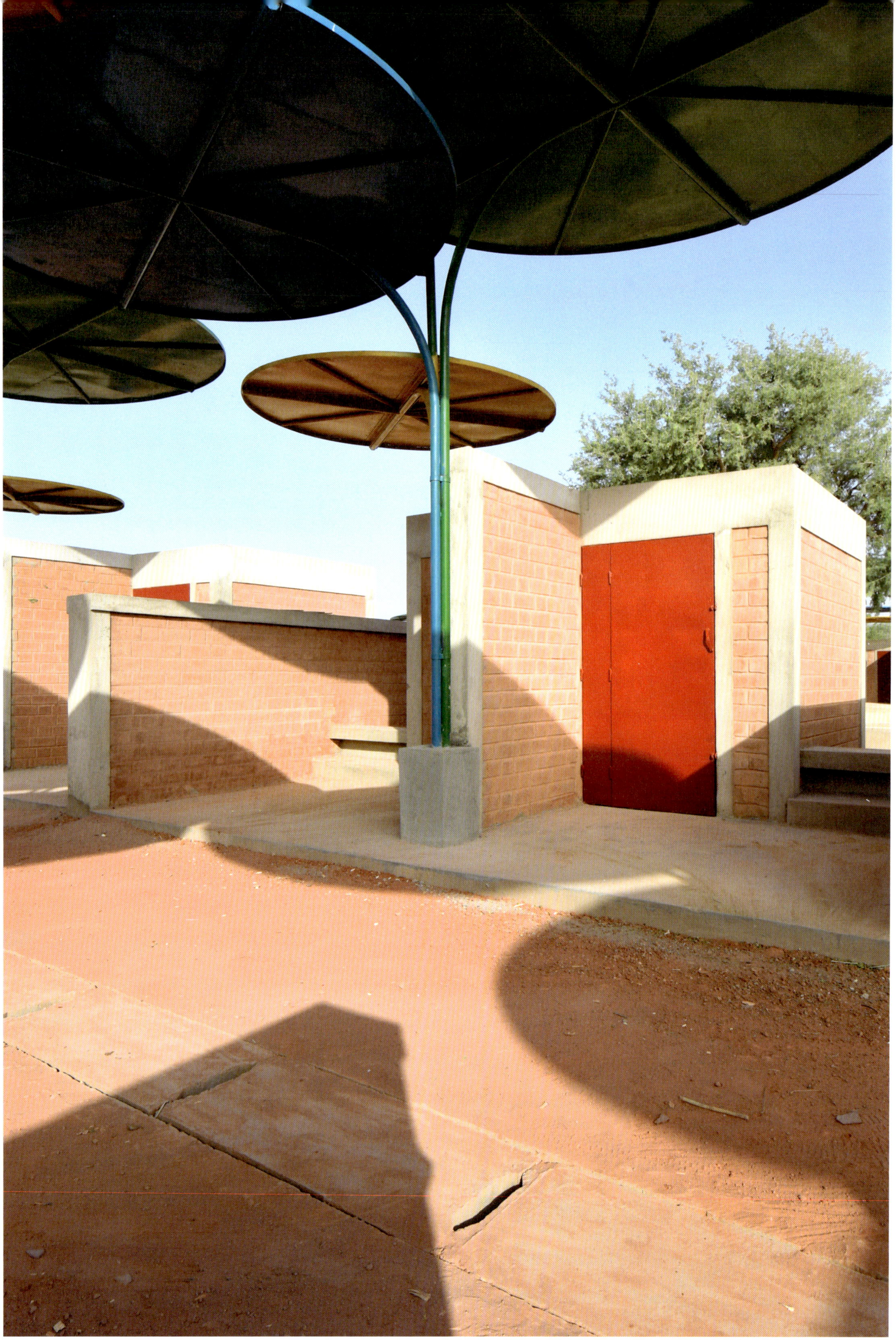

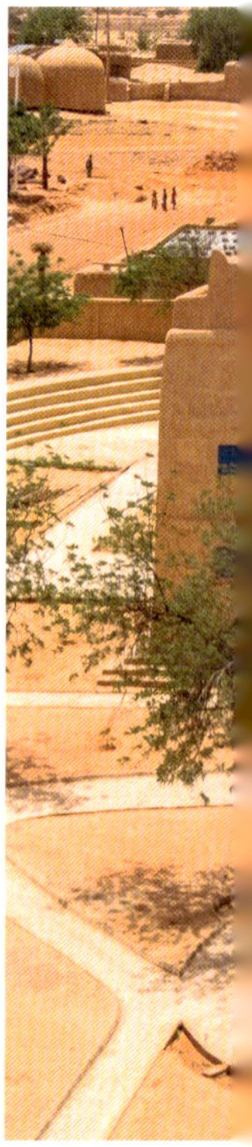

Niamey / Niger

Atelier Masōmī

Mariam Kamara began her career in computer science but, now well established in the field of architecture, she is commited to improving the lives of fellow Nigeriens.

"Design that sustains people" is the slogan of Atelier Masōmī, the architecture studio founded by Mariam Kamara in her hometown of Niamey in Niger, West Africa. It's an apt reference to her practice of architecture, which prioritizes the users of the buildings she designs. Her process constantly questions what matters to them most socially, economically, and culturally.

"Taking the time to uncover the way people network, communicate, and socialize with each other opens up new and exciting design possibilities," Kamara says of her style. She's also acutely aware of the economic consequences of every decision she makes. "What we build, the choices we make in terms of form, materials, and so on have direct economic implications," she states. The fact that her work is focused in Niger, one of the poorest countries in the world, makes this even more pertinent. "I feel a responsibility to be mindful of these choices by trying to import as little as possible, and to use as many local skills as possible to keep costs low."

It may come as a surprise that architecture is Kamara's second career—one she launched in 2013, after graduating from the University of Washington with a master's degree in architecture, a year before founding Atelier Masōmī. Her previous master's in computer science from New York University led to a thriving career in software development, but Kamara's impulse to serve the people in her home country overshadowed her tech-industry success. "I went into architecture knowing what I wanted to do with it, and that was a huge advantage," she says of entering the profession in her 30s. "It made me zero-in on classes, professors, and resources that were relevant to the

> Mariam Kamara explores contemporary realities and proposes attainable, low-cost solutions that help maintain a cultural way of life using materials, knowledge, and skills from the region.

type of architecture that I ultimately wanted to do and the challenges that interested me."

Her particular interest is a form of sustainability that is focused on the local context of what she terms an "economically emerging nation." She explores contemporary realities and proposes attainable, low-cost solutions that help maintain a cultural way of life using materials, knowledge, and skills from the region.

After living in the US for 15 years, she now divides her time between the States and Niger, where she first gained prominence for Niamey 2000, a culturally appropriate modern housing solution for a city undergoing exponential growth. She undertook the project as one of the founding members of united4design, a global collective of architects. It won an *Architect Magazine* R+D Award in 2017.

They built six homes on a site intended to accommodate just two houses, increasing the land's habitable potential, and they used compressed-earth bricks rather than expensive concrete to reduce construction costs. Tall towers and apartment blocks would have been out of place amid the one-story structures predominant in the neighborhood, so density was increased by reducing the typical building footprint and going up one level. Although this was a new approach for buildings in Niamey, the concept was informed by residential buildings in precolonial cities such as Zinder in Niger, Kano in Nigeria, and Timbuktu in Mali, all sprawling urban centers where intertwined homes of two or three levels existed. As with precolonial dwellings, Niamey 2000 is designed to maximize privacy in a Muslim environment while maintaining a robust connection with the street.

Kamara's reverence for Niamey's streets and the way citizens use them led her to design the Artisans Valley, a new public space project that is expected to break ground in 2020. Conceived as a promenade that leads to the National Museum, the layout will draw citizens and visitors to an area that is currently abandoned, unlit, and considered dangerous by creating a safe public environment bustling with activity.

Atelier Masōmī

Page 66: At the Dandaji Regional Market, "avenues" of brick stalls are lined with posts topped with flat metal disks. Set at different heights, they mimic the trees that might line streets in cooler climates, and that are so difficult to grow in such an arid desert country as Niger. Finished in bright colors, the disks complement the colorful market goods on display.

69

Pages 67–71: In creating a new mosque at the Hikma Religious and Secular Complex in Dandaji, the architect skillfully reinterpreted the architecture of the old mosque for the twenty-first century. The design makes use of the latest compressed-earth brick technology, and the rectilinear styling is resolutely contemporary.

Atelier Masōmī

Although adobe (clay) is the most accessible traditional local building material, compressed-earth bricks possess all the same advantages (such as being cooling and fire retardant), but they are more resistant to the elements and require less maintenance.

The design incorporates a series of perforated semicircular structures of compressed-earth blocks, inspired by the cylindrical granary buildings traditional in rural Niger. The curved niches they create will house artisan boutiques, food vendors, and play spaces, with an amphitheater also forming part of the plan. It's Kamara's way of using architecture to make spaces more inclusive within a pedestrianized street setting, because "the street belongs to everyone," she says.

Kamara's use of compressed-earth bricks is a consistent element in her designs. "Concrete is widely used by default in urban centers," she says, "and one can definitely feel how warm spaces get in such buildings compared to dwellings in the countryside made of adobe, which makes them significantly cooler." Although adobe (clay) is the most accessible traditional local building material, compressed-earth bricks possess all the same advantages (such as being cooling and fire retardant), but they are more resistant to the elements and require less maintenance. Therefore, they are her preferred material in this partially arid, scorching hot country.

Kamara utilized them in Niger's village of Dandaji, where she was commissioned to create a permanent market to replace the weekly one that existed around an ancestral tree. This important tree is preserved in the vibrant Regional Market design, which integrates thermal comfort for artisan retailers. Kamara's team modeled the design for the new market on the area's traditional market architecture of adobe posts and reed roofs, but they used compressed-earth bricks for the walls and recycled colored metal for the overhead canopies, which are elevated at different heights and offer protection from the Sun while also promoting natural ventilation.

"I feel lucky that I love all types of architecture of all scales and contexts," says Kamara. "I love the craft itself... the creative process, and looking at a brief and figuring out what to do with it. As long as I can bring a certain ethos to it in terms of sociopolitical awareness, material, and context sensibility, I am happy." For Dandaji's Hikma Religious and Secular Complex, Kamara again turned to its users. Shaping a derelict mosque into a library and building a new mosque alongside it, Atelier Masōmī's intervention brings secular knowledge and religion into direct communication while responding to the local reality of illiteracy by encouraging learning in a welcoming, accessible environment.

The remodeling of the mosque paid respect to the architectural legacy of the area by calling on the original structure's masons to join the renovation team. They brought the building back to its former glory while passing their skills on and learning about erosion-protection techniques and new material technologies.

"The original masons had a lot to teach the 'contemporary' ones," Kamara says. "This doesn't happen automatically in general construction. Traditional masonry is transmitted from generation to generation within specialized families in villages and traditional towns. They tend to work in rural areas, while their city-dwelling counterparts generally work with concrete and steel, making multistory buildings. Typically there is no cross-pollination between the two, so that dialogue was fascinating on the project."

Atelier Masōmī regularly calls on traditional masons, weavers, and metalworkers to form part of its construction teams. "The process of collaborating with local artisans reinforces the power of ideas," says Kamara. "I try to understand what they can do on a fundamental level and what their skills are, and together we always try to stretch that in a mutual exchange. I learn from their techniques and approaches, and they have the opportunity to practice their skills, building things that no one has ever asked them to do before. It is a lot of fun."

"The process of collaborating with local artisans reinforces the power of ideas. I try to understand what they can do on a fundamental level and what their skills are, and together we always try to stretch that in a mutual exchange."

Kamara's efforts to produce architecture that speaks to its African context has been recognized internationally, and she has been invited to exhibit at the Milan Triennale and African Mobilities in Munich. In 2019 she was a Prince Claus Laureate, and she was mentored by leading architect Sir David Adjaye as part of the 2018/19 Rolex Mentor and Protégé Arts Initiative. "Being mentored by Adjaye is helping me develop greater confidence in the direction I have chosen," says Kamara of her user-centric leaning. "I believe architecture is about people," she reiterates. "That is what separates it from visual arts like sculpture, for example. I don't understand how we can make architecture without focusing on the communities of humans who will be using it, living in it, making memories in it."

Opposite page: Central to the architect's design for the Artisans Valley project in Niamey is the injection of a traditional form—the circular granary shape—into an urban landscape. The intention is to confront issues of "rural" vs. "urban," "African" vs. "contemporary," and "local" vs. "Western" that often divide the country's architectural landscape.

Above: For Niamey 2000 housing project, the architect hit on a design in which each of two units is arranged back to back. They tessellate in such a way that they are completely closed off from the street, but have private terraces and courtyards within.

Prototype School Floats on a Lagoon

The Makoko Floating School in the Lagos Lagoon, designed and built by Kunlé Adeyemi's architectural practice NLÉ, became a beacon of hope for the rapidly expanding Nigerian city. Conceived as a prototype in collaboration with the Makoko waterfront community, which lives on the lagoon in homes raised on stilts, it demonstrated a new way of addressing the growing needs of flood-ravaged parts of Africa.

Addressing the impact of climate change and urbanization, the Makoko Floating School offered a sustainable solution to increased rainfall and flooding in coastal cities. Three tapered levels stood on a base of recycled plastic barrels, creating a buoyancy system with a low center of gravity that ensured stability in strong winds. The open-plan ground level served as an assembly and play area, while the enclosed floor above accommodated up to four classrooms, and as many as 100 adults. The top-level provided a partially enclosed workshop. Customizable according to the community's needs, the 33-foot-high (10-meter) A-frame "watercraft" could adapt to varying water levels and tidal changes, meaning it was still usable during flooding and storms.

The structure, decommissioned after four years of use, used renewable energy from photovoltaic cells on the roof to recycle organic waste, and harvesting rainwater in a catchment system made it a viable ecological construction method for developing cities.

"We aim to provide sustainable solutions to the environmental, infrastructure, and human challenges posed by this century," says the architectural firm. By using builders from the community, and local bamboo and timber from a nearby sawmill, NLÉ ensured the authenticity and integrity of the development. "We want to create more social, political, and economically responsible interventions for people who make their homes in cities," the studio explains of its aversion to invasive and costly land-reclamation on Africa's coastline. "This is an opportunity to think, build, and live differently."

Architect Kunlé Adeyemi / NLÉ
Project Floating School
Location Makoko / Nigeria

NLÉ wishes to develop its Floating School concept further, to create a series of modular houses based on the same design.

The structure used renewable energy from photovoltaic cells on the roof to recycle organic waste, and harvesting rainwater in a catchment system made it a viable ecological construction method for developing cities.

Floating School

Ultimately, the plan would be to create entire floating communities based on the concept, complete with municipal and public buildings, as well as houses and schools. The Floating School project explores the concept of independent floating structures constructed of primarily local materials.

77

Architect Ramos Castellano Arquitectos
Project Terra Lodge
Location Mindelo / Cape Verde

Simplicity Defines an Island Hotel

Terra Lodge on Cape Verde's island of São Vicente was an old colonial house on the edge of the island's historic center. Mindelo-based Ramos Castellano Arquitectos transformed it into a hotel with 12 bedrooms and a suite, linked to the rooftop of the original house by a bridge, creating a space to enjoy al fresco breakfasts and beautiful sunsets.

Separate volumes were designed to fit in with the style of the surrounding buildings, and they are set into the terrain at different heights to avoid creating a single imposing form. "Each block has a different view of the city and the bay," explain studio directors Moreno Castellano and Eloisa Ramos, who designed the verandas to reduce the impact of direct sunlight. "Partially enclosed gridded timber frames provide protection while allowing guests to enjoy the views," they say. They also needed to block out the strong winds that sweep in from the Sahara Desert. Cross-ventilation provides passive air-conditioning, and the lime-plastered white walls offer solid protection from the Sun, wind, and sea spray.

The lack of resources on the island led to simple and yet innovative solutions. Rain only falls in August, so water is recycled for irrigation, and photovoltaic panels take advantage of the sunny climate to generate electricity. The construction materials are untreated, conforming with the simple aesthetic predominant on the island, and almost every element has been handcrafted by island residents, ensuring a circular economy. Natural timber, walls built using stone sourced from the site, and gates constructed from old oil barrels demonstrate the eco-conscious concept behind Terra Lodge, securing what Castellano references as "the equilibrium between human intervention and nature."

The lime-green walls of the original colonial building make for a standout feature on a hillside that is otherwise a jumble of ocher and terra-cotta-hued volumes.

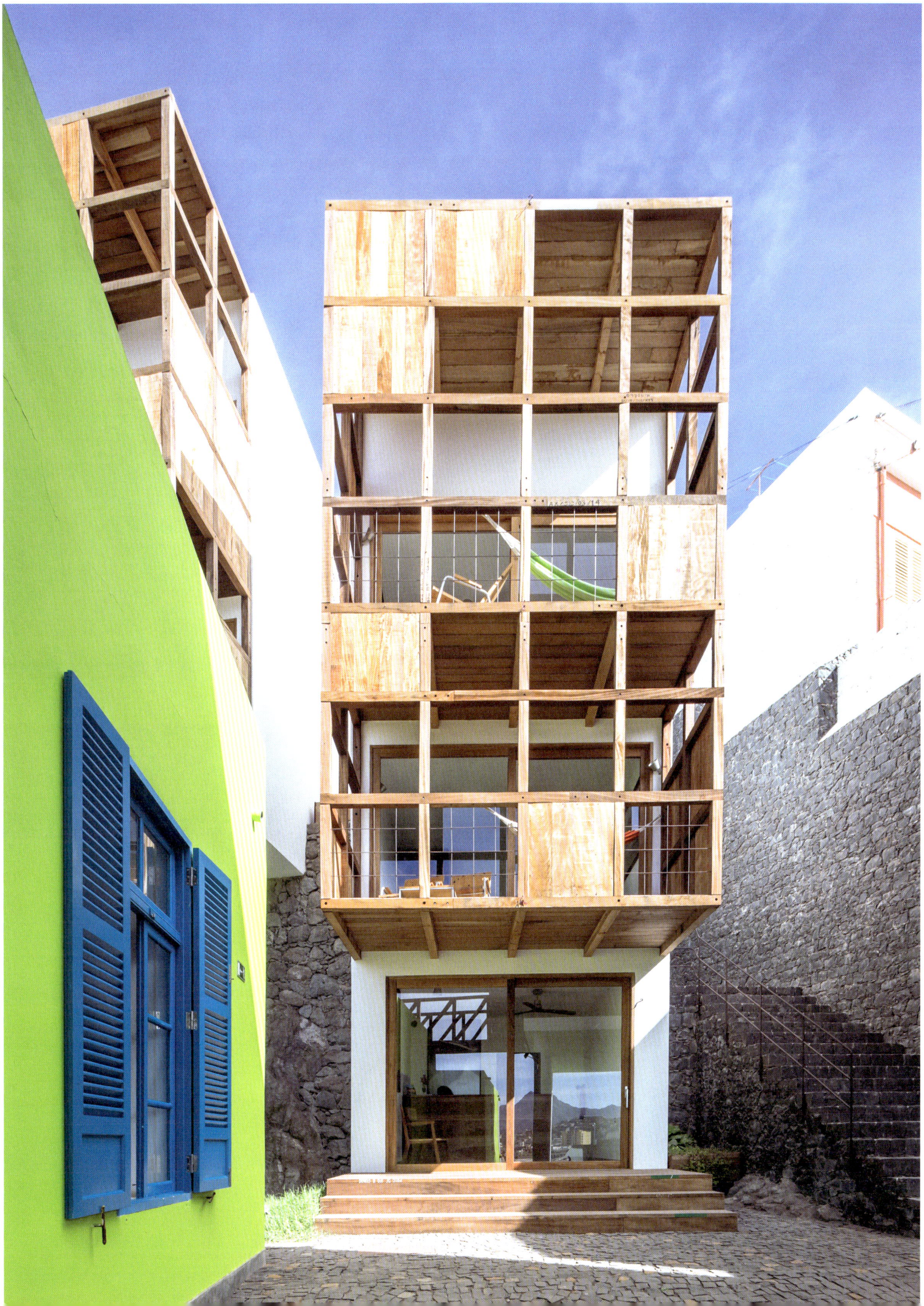

Terra Lodge

The construction materials are untreated, conforming with the simple aesthetic predominant on the island.

The individual units in the hotel complex, with their crate-like verandas, are set against a framework of local mountain stone, rooting them firmly in the hillside. The vibrant green of the original colonial building is offset by the more earthy tones of the woodwork and stone; it also serves as a fitting backdrop for the vegetation.

Terra Lodge

The verandas cantilever out above the ground floor of the hotel.

84 Terra Lodge

The wooden box-like facades of each unit provide double-height verandas for the rooms within. Select panels are filled in to reduce exposure to direct sunlight.

85

A Community Builds a School for Change

James Mitchell and Tatu Gatere founded Orkidstudio with "the simple belief that architecture can inspire change for people and communities." Since then, 52 percent of the workforce it has employed have been women whom they train in bricklaying, carpentry, and metalwork.

The Kenya-based organization was, therefore, the obvious choice to design the Swawou Girls' School in Kenema, Sierra Leone, which provides free learning facilities for up to 120 disadvantaged young girls from the area.

True to its ethos, Orkidstudio employed 70 people from the local community. "Building collectively brings communities together, supports local economic growth, empowers, instills pride, and leaves a legacy that reaches far beyond completion," say Mitchell and Gatere.

Shuttered openings provide ventilation and a way of controlling the amount of sunlight entering the classrooms, which is essential in the hot climate. The floating metal roof offers additional ventilation, while its angled gradient directs monsoon rain into a series of water-collection channels below. A woven ceiling beneath the roof helps to reduce the sound of the rain to avoid it distracting the students from learning.

Classrooms at Swawou are larger than those usually found in Sierra Leone, and they have been arranged to form a sheltered courtyard and outdoor spaces that encourage social interaction. There are gardens in the open courtyards, and the school girls participate in maintaining these.

Orkidstudio's philosophy is: "By creating spaces that are well lit, properly ventilated, and comfortable to be in, we can help improve public and user health and well-being beyond the building."

The Swawou Girls' School offers new opportunities to a group of young women, and it is a beacon of hope in their world.

Architect Orkidstudio
Project Swawou Girls' School
Location Kenema / Sierra Leone

87

Swawou Girls' School

The land immediately surrounding the school buildings serves as a play area for the girls, while the central courtyard functions as an assembly point.

90   Swawou Girls' School

Shuttered openings provide ventilation and a way of controlling the amount of sunlight entering the classrooms, which is essential in the hot climate.

The school comprises four simple single-story brick buildings framing an inner courtyard. There is room for six classrooms, a computer room, a kitchen, and a school office. Inside the school's rooms, both decor and facilities are pared back. Surfaces are left as bare brick or concrete, and rooms are decked out with lines of painted wooden desks.

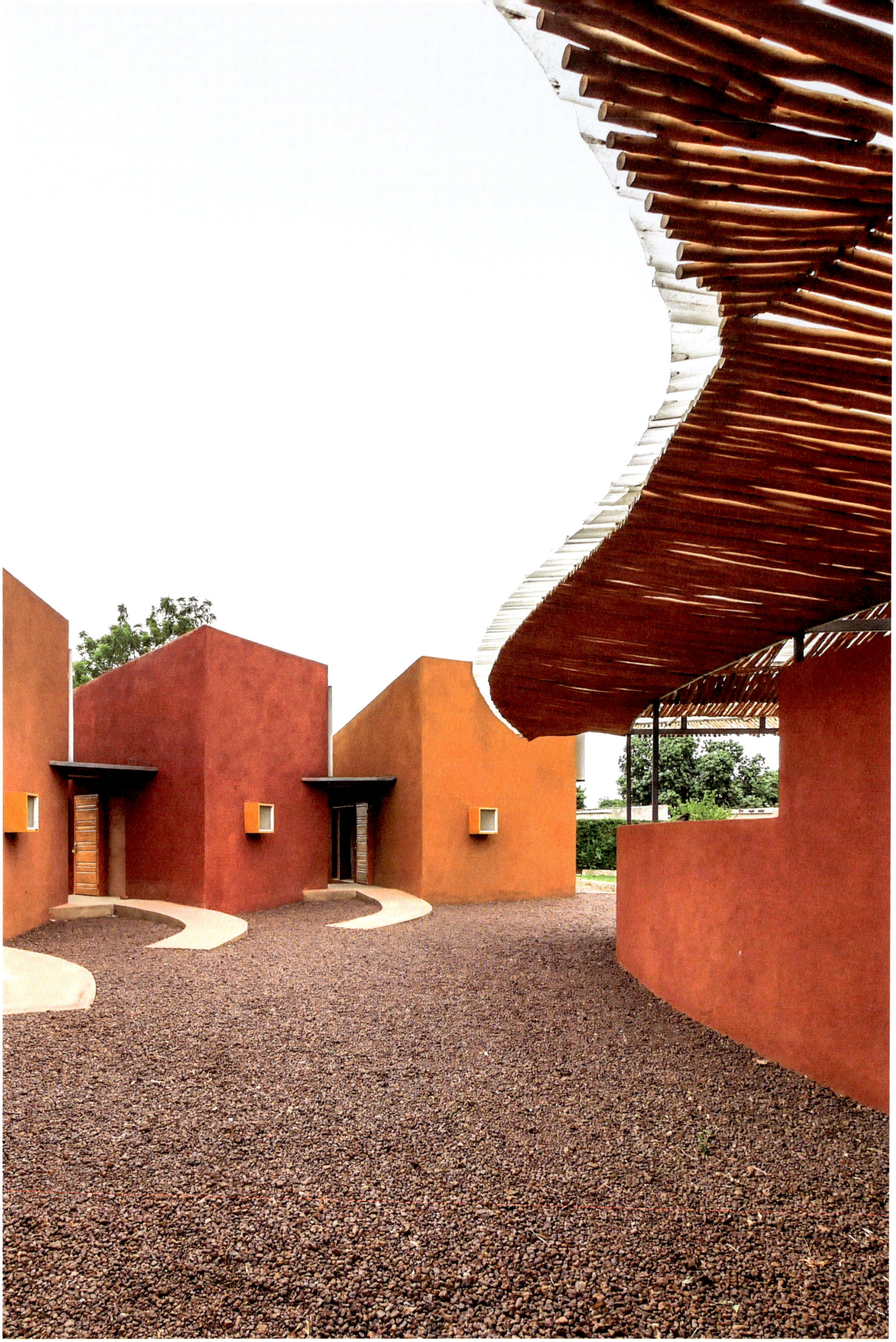

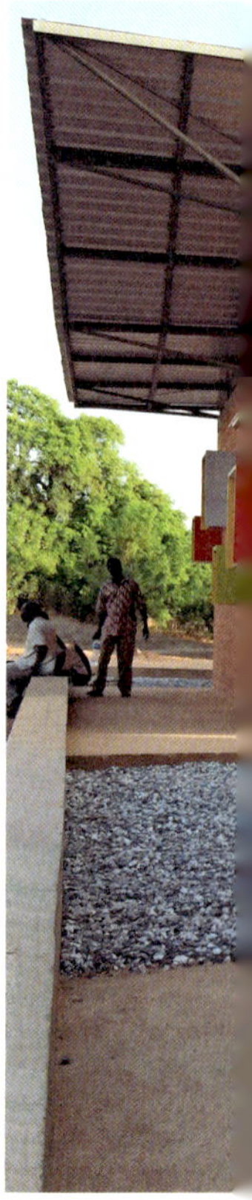

Berlin/Germany

Kéré Architecture

Now based in Berlin, Kéré rose to prominence with the prestigious Serpentine Pavilion commission. But some of his most noteworthy buildings are those in his home country of Burkina Faso.

Trees from Burkina Faso have informed some of Berlin-based Burkinabé architect Diébédo Francis Kéré's recent works in the US and UK. His installation for the 2017 Serpentine Pavilion in London was inspired by a tree in Gando, the village where he grew up, where members of the community meet to reflect on their days. For his 2019 installation at the Coachella music festival in California's Colorado Desert, Sarbalé Ke, Kéré found inspiration in the baobab tree, whose trunk hollows as it ages. His ancestral roots are clearly close to his heart.

Growing up in Gando as the eldest son of the village chief, Kéré was one of very few children afforded the opportunity of being educated outside the village, where there was no electricity or running water. Gaining a scholarship for a carpentry apprenticeship in Germany, he went on to study architecture in Berlin, graduating from Technische Universität (TU Berlin) with a vision: to give back to the community that had supported him.

"I started my architecture career with the desire to build a school for my people that would result in little maintenance and few running costs," Kéré explains of the Gando Primary School project he began while he was still at university, for which he obtained private funding, and that won him the Aga Khan Award for Architecture in 2004.

In a study that has become his standard operation, he looked at the resources available in the area and used them to their full potential. Kéré invented a new way to build mud bricks by hand with local soil that would not be compromised by the region's rainfall; this enabled him to avoid using concrete, which is commonly used in the rural village even though it is expensive and keeps the scorching heat trapped inside. He also designed long overhanging tin roofs set away from the ceilings to encourage air circulation while protecting the buildings from the elements, making the learning environment much more comfortable, with minimal resources.

Sustainability is high on Kéré's agenda and is a subject he speaks passionately about whenever he has the opportunity to teach. He has a permanent teaching post at his alma mater in Berlin, and has also lectured at Harvard Graduate School of Design, the Swiss Accademia di Architettura di Mendrisio, and Yale School of Architecture.

"My team and I are constantly exploring material," he goes on to explain of his studio, which fluctuates between 11 to 16 people, depending on commissions. "No matter where we build, we look at locally available materials, and we favor things that are abundant, but overlooked or discarded." Sarbalé Ke was made from plywood and steel, which are widely available industrial materials in that part of California, while Xylem, his pavilion for the Tippet Rise Art Center in Montana, is constructed from dead wood from the region. Projects in Burkina Faso—such as Lycée Schorge Secondary School in the city of Koudougou, and the Centre de Santé et de Promotion Sociale, a basic healthcare facility in Laongo—employ locally mined laterite stone shaped into bricks.

"In addition to identifying these materials, I am interested in employing them to create surprising effects," adds the architect, who, in 2009, was one of the five winners of the Global Award for Sustainable Architecture.

In the Gando Library, which is currently under construction as part of the broader vision for the Gando Primary School, earthenware pots and eucalyptus create fascinating visuals. The pots, made by women in the village, were sawn in half and cast into the ceiling, forming playful shade patterns and allowing natural light and passive ventilation to enter the building. The eucalyptus used for the screen—viewed as an invasive plant in Burkina Faso because its intense water absorption leads to desertification—shades the study area

"My team and I are constantly exploring material. No matter where we build, we look at locally available materials, and we favor things that are abundant, but overlooked or discarded."

more effectively than it would if it were growing as a tree. Eucalyptus screens are also used to create spaces for circulation and gathering, which are an integral part of Kéré's designs. Although social spaces are ingrained in his heritage, he views public space as something that "should be valued highly within any community."

"Growing up, for me these [public spaces] were village squares, the shade of a tree and the semi-public areas within the compounds of people's homes," he explains of the gathering areas in Burkinabé culture. "It is within public spaces that we learn to be with one another, take communal decisions, navigate around each other, meet, or simply be aware of each other's presence." Such spatial notions inspire all his projects—be it in the Camper Store on Barcelona's Rambla or the Songtaaba Women's Center in Gando. "Ideally, there is no hierarchy within them," he says. "Everyone breathes the same air and has the same right to be there."

In the same way, he prefers not to make distinctions between "Western" and "African" influences on his work.

Pages 92–93: The Léo Surgical Clinic and Health Center in Burkina Faso includes accommodation flanking a common courtyard. Designed as a modular system, the units are made from compressed-earth blocks and topped with a roof of corrugated-metal sheeting that is suspended away from the ceiling to allow heat to escape.

Opposte page: Two years after the completion of the Gando Primary School, it became apparent that an extension was badly needed to service the educational needs of the region's children. With support from surrounding communities, the School Extension was built. Community members personally trained in modern construction techniques by Francis Kéré aided the build.

Above: Windows are arranged asymmetrically at the health center in Laongo. This is to allow those admitted to the center to be able to see views of the landscape whether standing, seated, or confined to a bed. Similar consideration for visitors sees the inclusion of shaded courtyards for gathering and waiting.

"I tend to avoid such a clear distinction when thinking about my path. We always bring with us experience and knowledge. I arrived in what we may call the 'West' with a young man's lifetime's worth of learning. I then added to my personal toolbox the experience gained through living elsewhere and learning a new language and system, as well as my formal training at the TU Berlin. I used this mix to form my particular understanding of the architectural craft in order to build in my hometown. You can add to that the many identities and origins present in my team, shaping my studio. It is a lot more multilayered than the supposed dichotomy of Africa and the West would have it be."

Connection and community are part of the fabric of Kéré Architecture. In Burkinabé projects, this means people from the surrounding areas are employed to

Above: Marking the fiftieth anniversary of the independence of Mali, the national park in Bamako commissioned Kéré Architecture to develop new amenities, such as a restaurant and sports center. Rendered in local natural stone, a characteristic of the design is a large overhanging roof that serves to shade the facades, protecting the interior and surrounding spaces from the hot sun.

Opposite page: Kéré Architecture employed several methods and materials to keep temperatures low inside the Lycée Schorge Secondary School. Besides using compressed-earth bricks, known for their thermal-mass capabilities, the design features wind-catching towers, a massive undulating ceiling, and a secondary facade of wooden screens.

Kéré Architecture

"I arrived in what we may call the 'West' with a young man's lifetime's worth of learning. I then added to my personal toolbox the experience gained through living elsewhere."

Above: At Dano Secondary School, a small complex comprising three classrooms, a computer room, and office space, natural ventilation is achieved by means of slits in the suspended ceiling, the incline of the corrugated metal roof, and the shuttered windows. This is a more sustainable solution than typical Western models of construction, which necessitate air-conditioning in this part of the world.

Opposite page: The plan for Gando Primary School included the provision of six houses for teachers and their families. Each house is based on an adaptable module that is roughly the size of the traditional round huts typically found in this region. Single modules were combined in various ways to create each home.

Diébédo Francis Kéré's buildings forge a sense of ownership, pride, and identity for the people they serve, profoundly connecting them with the structures and their ongoing maintenance.

assist in construction, in what is seen as the "labor of community" and the architect's commitment to social inclusion.

Kéré's belief in his profession's ability to help communities shape their future is not an idle philosophy—it's one he's invested in since beginning work on the Gando Primary School. "It was my desire to apply the knowledge from my architectural studies to my hometown, but as there were little resources and I needed all the help I could get, I asked everyone to assist in whatever way they could," he says. His buildings forge a sense of ownership, pride, and identity for the people they serve, profoundly connecting them with the structures and their ongoing maintenance. Based on the training that resulted from the project,

a building company has been established in the area, providing work for 100 to 200 builders, welders, carpenters, and bricklayers, depending on the demand. Many have become sought-after experts whose skills are requested at other building sites in Burkina Faso and beyond.

Kéré founded the Kéré Foundation at the same time as launching Kéré Architecture, and the independent fundraising entity helps to fund schools, clinics, and housing where there is a need. "The Kéré Foundation is sustained through donations from generous individuals who believe in what we do," explains its founder, who also personally contributes to it with means resulting from his work as an architect. "The Kéré Architecture structure works closely with the Kéré Foundation in providing design services, and may at times do work at a reduced rate, if capacity allows, but cannot finance [the projects]. So rather than compromising my work, I decide whether my studio can take on a social project I greatly believe in, with little or no budget, when those are proposed to us."

Kéré's influence in his homeland has brought much-needed attention to architecture as an instrument for social upliftment. "Before my work there, construction tended to be seen as something done by big corporations or the government. But structures like the Gando Primary School and Lycée Schorge have shown that we can envision and build our own infrastructure and shape the buildings around us."

Aspirations for his home country continue to drive his practice; this is explicit in Kéré Architecture's design for the Burkina Faso National Assembly and Thomas Sankara Memorial Park in the capital city of Ouagadougou. During riots in 2014 when the president was ousted, the parliament building was destroyed. Again, a tree informed Kéré's approach to the

Above: Although in keeping with the same material palette as the surrounding buildings—compressed-earth blocks made with local clay—the library building at Gando Primary School takes on more of an organic elliptical shape reminiscent of the traditional vernacular housing in the region. Its position on the site shelters the school yard from dusty easterly winds.

"In places that have been held back for a wide range of reasons, it is important to have visions and hopes, and to plan for a future that is ambitious."

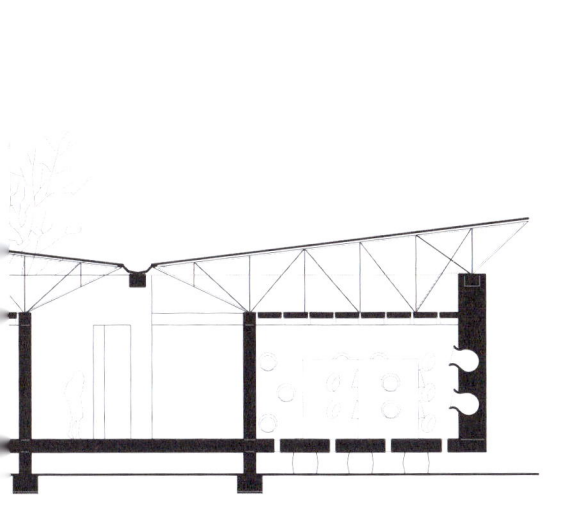

new building. The design takes its cue from the *arbre à palabres,* or tree of discussion, where village elders gather to discuss matters of importance while being observed by the community. A massive tree grows from the structure, where a 127-seat assembly hall lies, and the public can circulate around it. Outside, the tree's foliage integrates with a terrace that overlooks the city (symbolizing citizens climbing above the politicians underneath).

For Kéré, a project such as this, which is pending funding from the Burkinabé state, is an important exercise, whether in the design or construction phase. "In places that have been held back for a wide range of reasons," he says, "it is important to have visions and hopes, and to plan for a future that is ambitious."

Above: In creating a center for Gando's Songtaaba Women's Association, Kéré Architecture ensured the group would have a sheltered space for its activities as well as dry storage for grain and other goods. Raising the building on a series of concrete *pilotis* also keeps goods safe from water damage and rodents.

Multiple Personalities for a School Hall

Architect Localworks
Project Multipurpose Hall
Location Mannya / Uganda

This multipurpose school hall in the Ugandan village of Mannya demonstrates that built spaces can be adapted to suit different needs without unnecessary effort and cost. The versatile circular structure acts as an assembly hall, performance venue, and dining area for 650 students. It was designed by Localworks, a young practice based in Kampala, Uganda, specializing in the design and implementation of innovative "green" architecture in rural East Africa.

Open to the exterior, but covered with a hovering metal roof, the building presents as an amphitheater. It follows the sloped gradient of the land, forming three tiered levels for ideal viewing of the stage, and its curvature enhances interpersonal connection. The simple stage shares a wall with an enclosed kitchen at the rear, alongside storage space and an office. Meals are served in the auditorium, where 9-foot-wide (2.7-meter) steps allow for the comfortable placement of dining tables and benches, and facilitate transitions according to pupils' needs.

Partially recycled, locally available clay bricks, tiles, and slate clad the tilted reinforced-concrete columns holding up the roof, in decorative layers. The wedge-shaped roof planes attached to these columns are installed at two different angles, allowing sunlight to enter softly through narrow triangular strips of translucent material. The roof serves other purposes: 90 percent of its surface area provides concealed rainwater harvesting, and the sound baffles (made from locally available hemp fabric) suspended underneath strengthen the acoustic quality of this outdoor venue cost effectively.

Other considerations related to the environment include solar chimneys in the kitchen to facilitate natural ventilation in this hot part of the country. These openings also welcome natural light into the kitchen. Fuel-efficient firewood stoves with built in water heating play an equally valuable role in reducing electricity consumption.

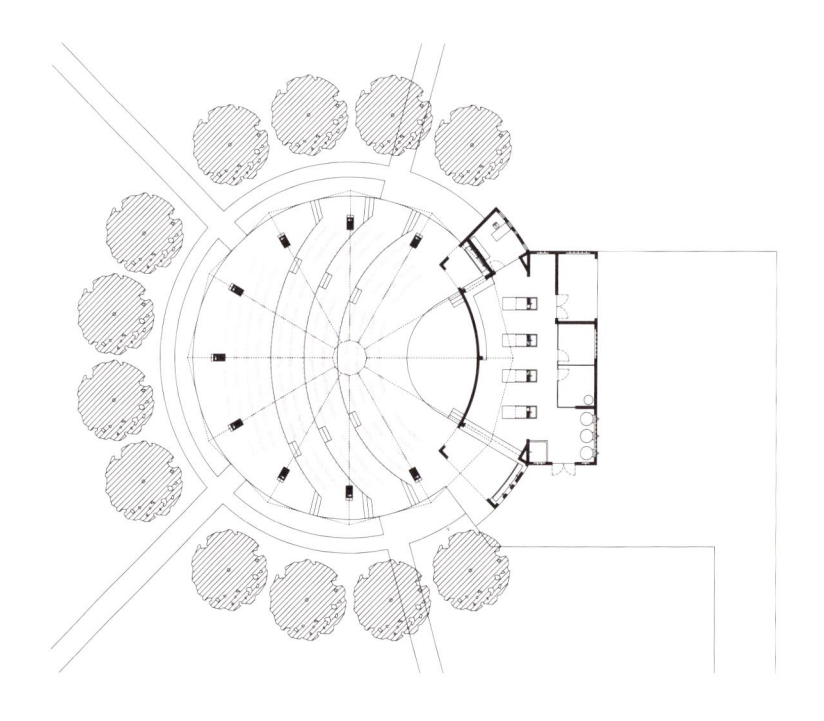

The simplicity of the design belies the dual use of many of its features: the amphitheater steps that are wide enough to accommodate canteen seating, a roof that shields from bright sunlight while concealing a rainwater harvesting system, and a kitchen wall that provides a backdrop for the stage.

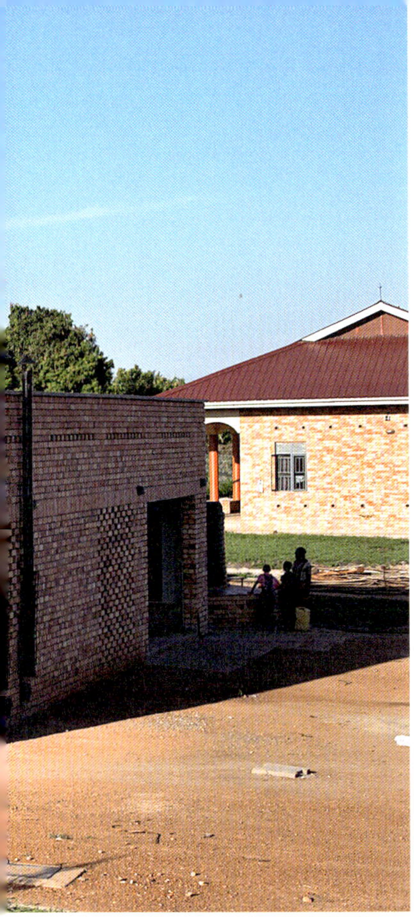

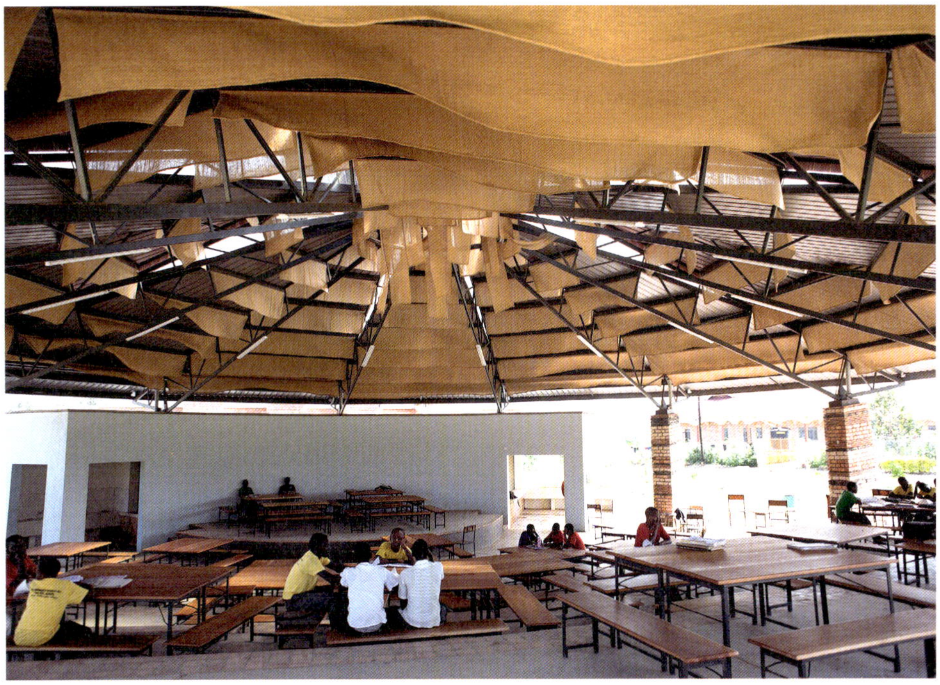

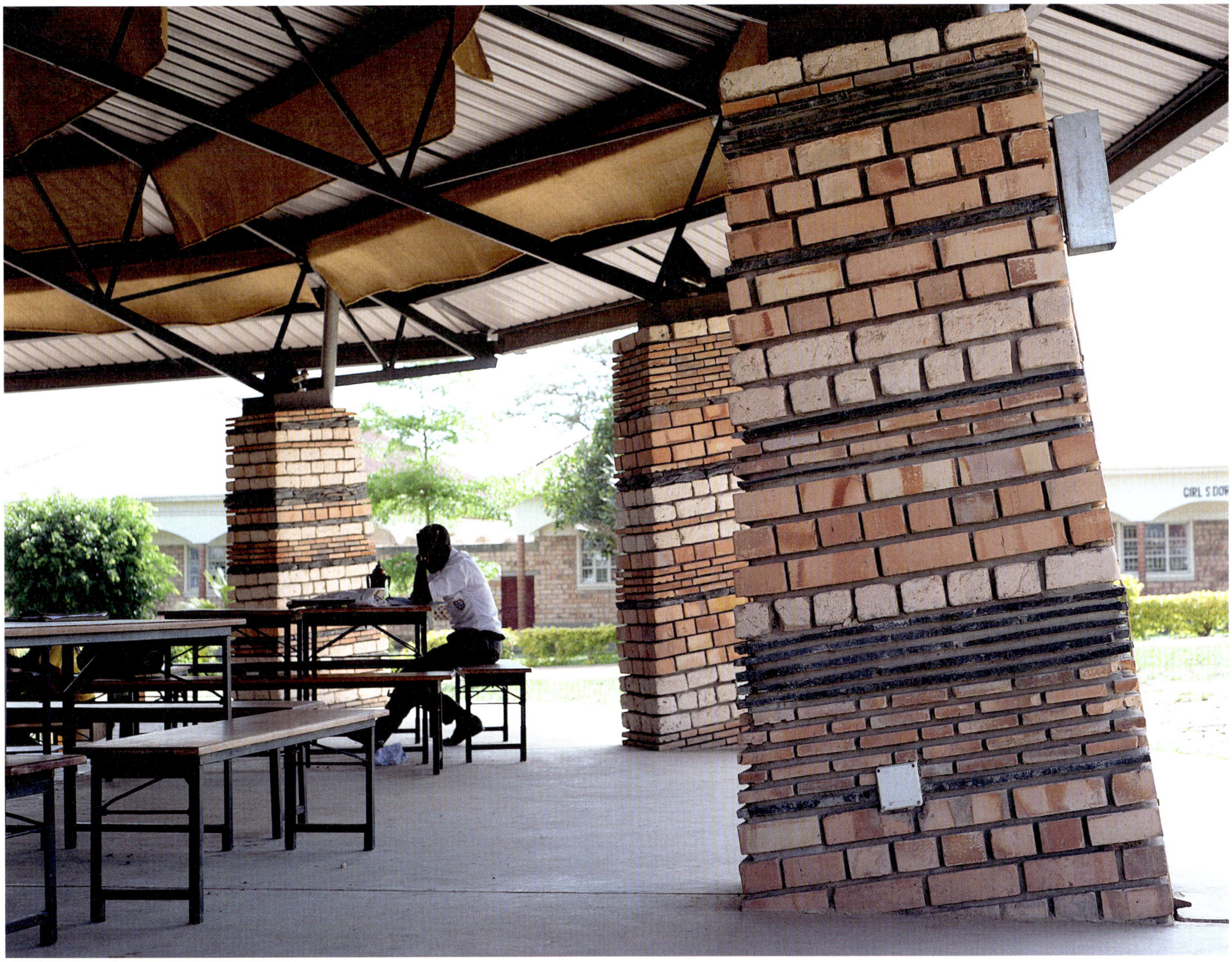

The architects have conceived of every possible use for the amphitheater, by day and by night, ensuring that it provides the local community with the widest range of services possible in a relatively small space. The design is quite literally rooted in the local environment, emphasized by the use of natural local materials and the fact that the main structure works organically with the natural slope of the land.

Multipurpose Hall

The building follows the sloped gradient of the land, forming three tiered levels for ideal viewing of the stage, and its curvature enhances interpersonal connection.

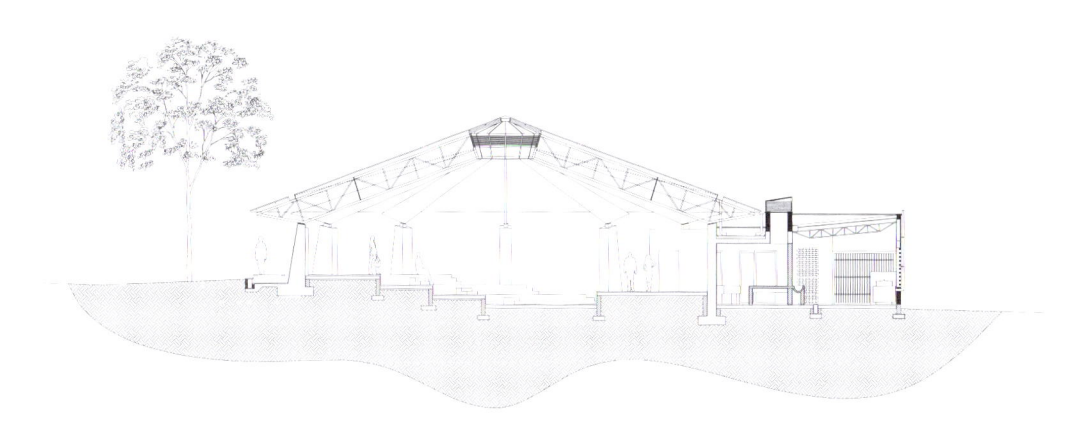

The Architecture of Mexico's Evolving Identity

A rich pre-hispanic culture, the Spanish invasion and its own modernist tradition have all influenced Mexico's built environment. Its thriving architectural scene introduces contemporary building with a sense of returning to its ancestral roots.

01

Mexico is often afflicted by an ailment known as *malinchismo.* It is a derogatory term that originates from the treachery of an indigenous Nahua woman known as La Malinche or Malintzin, who sided with the Spanish invaders in the sixteenth century and served as interpreter and aide to the conqueror Hernán Cortés. Particularly prevalent in the built environment, the accusatory term *malinchista* is applied to structures that emulate first-world buildings. Mexican architectural heritage from the colonial period and revolution is highly regarded and protected by the state, but pre-Hispanic architecture, modernism, and particularly vernacular buildings are seldom recognized in the same way. While foreign architects and scholars readily acknowledge the heritage of Mexican architecture, it has been a challenge for Mexicans to recognize it themselves.

In 1961, German émigré architect Max Cetto wrote: "True, in the first quarter of the [twentieth] century, Mexico had no pioneer of the caliber of a Gaudí, Perret, Henry van de Velde, or Wright; but in the people themselves the joy of creative art is

02

01/03 Pyramid of the Magician in Uxmal, Yucatan, Mexico.
02 Mosaic mask, from the 15th or 16th century, of the deity Quetzalcoatl. A mask like this one, was reportedly given to Hernán Cortés by Moctezuma II.
04 Church of Santa Prisca de Taxco, constructed in the Baroque style in the 1750s in Guerrero, Mexico.

03

present in such abundance that, within a generation and without direct influence from the outside, Mexican architecture became fluent in the idiom of our age." He concluded, "our modern buildings need not fear comparison." A history of combining stylistic choices under the premises of colonialism, imperialism, and even socialism created an incomparable woven landscape, which has informed the present architectural landscape.

Today, Mexico is facing more than just identity issues. In September 2017, earthquakes caused considerable damage in Oaxaca, Morelos, and Puebla. Hurricanes and flooding are a constant threat to the entire nation of Mexico, and there is an urgent need for shelter and housing. Reconstruction and preventive measures are pressing, especially given the uncertainty of climate change.

The Search for Mexican Identity

Architect Fernanda Canales established her firm in 2002 and is one of the most important voices in contemporary Mexican architecture. She has studied the complex history that influenced her country's buildings. In her comprehensive volume *Architecture in Mexico, 1900–2010* (Arquine, 2013), she writes: "Mexican cities have been built on the basis of destruction: the center of New Spain erected over the ruins of Tenochtitlan, the late-eighteenth-century neoclassical city created over Baroque treasures, the liberal country of the nineteenth century overlying the viceregal heritage, the modern twentieth-century metropolis tearing down everything, and the twenty-first century now refusing to recognize twentieth-century buildings as a legacy worth protecting." This destruction-based process is off-putting. As is the lingering question, "What if we were more like a first-world country?" Nonetheless, it is hard to understand the complex context of Mexican architecture in the twenty-first century.

Until the 1920s, the Mexican national identity in architecture remained a work in progress. A decade after the revolution, a miscellany of European influences remained. Monumental government buildings, baroque catholic churches, city plazas, grand mansions, and gardens, together with a gridded urban plan in the capital, were the result of the long Iberian occupation. Following the overthrow of dictator Porfirio Díaz in 1911, the architects guild rejected the French neoclassical style that had been installed together with a sort of "Haussmannization" of Mexico City during the rule of Archduke Maximilian of Austria in the late nineteenth century. However, the question remained as to what modern Mexican art and architecture might become.

04

05

In 1921, Minister of Education José Vasconcelos established a government-funded program to push education, labor, and culture forward through the arts and industry—an initiative that would later be referenced by the Works Progress Administration in the post-Depression US. Under this program, Mexican patrimony was recognized with an element of pride, and the revolution became the subject of study and artistic expression, particularly in the muralist movement. Institutional buildings expressed their "Mexicanness" through the representation of indigenous heritage and the triumph over New Spain in monumental murals or stone mosaic murals, and three-dimensional wall surfaces that became known as *integración plástica* in some of the first functionalist buildings.

The advent of Mexican modernism as such was recognized by architecture historian Ramón Vargas Salguero through the work of José Villagrán García, who in 1925 completed the Granja Sanitaria, a research and vaccine production facility that for the first time joined the modern concept of hygiene with the budding functionalist architecture style. Other explorations in functionalism and significant influence from Corbusian concepts are most evident in the "University City" of the National Autonomous University of Mexico (UNAM), developed in the 1950s by Mario Pani, José Villagrán García, and Enrique del Moral, among others. Their unique vision included the artistic representation of Mexican history and culture through *integración plástica*. Artist and architect Juan O'Gorman, who built the first rationalist home in Latin America in 1929, was one of the most influential proponents of this movement. In 1951, he finished the central library at UNAM with a 40,000-square-foot (3,700-square-meter) natural-stone mosaic mural. Architecture historian Louise Noelle describes this period: "The concern was to achieve a local expression that, without abandoning rationalist precepts, offered a new path for shared creativity."

05 *Representación histórica de la cultura*, mural by Juan O'Gorman on the facade of the library, National Autonomous University of Mexico (UNAM).
06 Colonial-era street near to Plaza Borda in Taxco, Guerrero.
07 The Museo Rufino Tamayo in Mexico City, designed by Abraham Zabludovsky and Teodoro González de León.

Mexico / Central America

International Panorama

A seminal moment in history occurred when Mexico City was selected to host the 1968 Olympic Games. It was a source of pride for the entire country, a coming-out party, in a sense. Architect Pedro Ramírez Vázquez was named artistic director by president Gustavo Díaz Ordaz, who told him, "what matters is the image the country will give to the world of its organizing capacity; that we can do it, and we can do it well. It is, therefore, an issue of image before the whole world. What is needed is efficiency." Amid the civil rights movements and student protests happening in Mexico and all around the world, the desire to project a good image above all else remains a burden for Mexican culture.

With increasing population growth, particularly in the capital, which is home to over 21 million people, lack of housing has always been a critical issue. Both Centro Urbano Presidente Alemán and Conjunto Urbano Nonoalco Tlatelolco, built by Mario Pani in the late 1940s and early 1960s, respectively, were the first high-density developments known as *multifamiliares*. Noelle states, "Its zigzag plan is a formal and conceptual reference to Le Corbusier's *redent* form in the Ville Contemporaine (1922)." Unfortunately, today, the concept of the *multifamiliar* has transformed into poorly constructed high-density developments that focus primarily on quantity, in an effort backed by the government to build shoe-box-style homes with almost complete disregard for living conditions.

06

During the 1980s and 90s, a generation of architects like Ricardo Legorreta, Abraham Zabludovsky, Teodoro González de León, and Agustín Hernández worked toward an aesthetic that was uniquely Mexican, referencing pre-Hispanic architectural elements. Their singular expression was monumental and solemn (like the Museo Tamayo and the Auditorio Nacional by Zabludovsky and González de León), with an incomparable majestic energy (Legorreta's coastal hotels, or Hernández's futurist vision for the Heroico Colegio Militar, or Hernández's sister's Folkloric Ballet School).

07

Institutional buildings expressed their "Mexicanness" through the representation of indigenous heritage and the triumph over New Spain in monumental murals or stone mosaic murals.

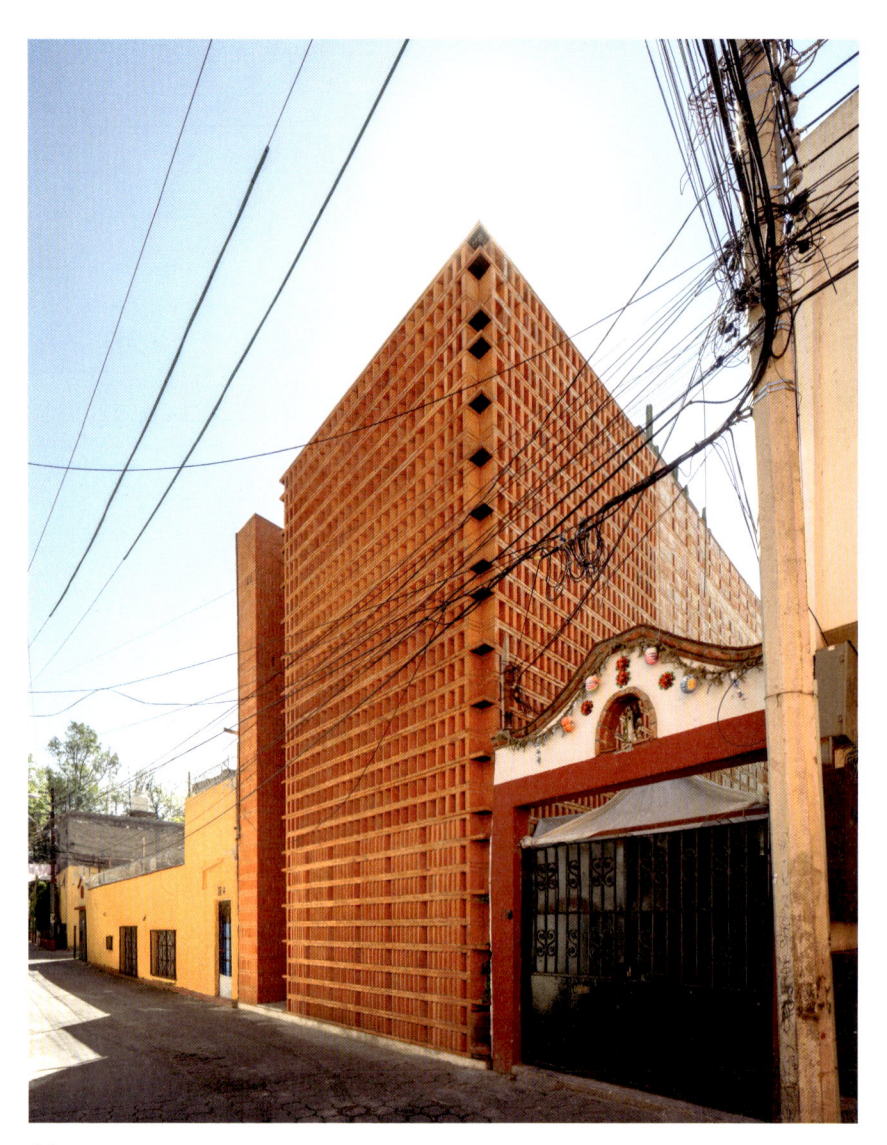

08

Contemporary Issues

Like Fernanda Canales, other architecture practices today are acutely aware of this background and its underlying issues, although it has seldom been an approachable subject. Reactions are evident through sustainable social housing models, from those by Tatiana Bilbao Estudio and Frida Escobedo to TACO; the reconstruction of disadvantaged communities seeking optimal environmental conditions, like the work of Comunal in Tepetzintan; singularly adaptable institutional buildings like the Pátzcuaro courthouse by Mauricio Rocha and Gabriela Carrillo, and the Teotitlán del Valle Cultural Center by PRODUCTORA; and the focus on transforming the urban landscape through the study of the country's past, like Alberto Kalach's proposal to bring back the original lake beds of Mexico City.

Some Mexican architecture practices in the twentieth century explored the values ingrained in vernacular architecture. It is particularly evident in the late work of Luis Barragán, who constantly referenced the traditional homes of his native Guadalajara and adapted similar construction processes in his own architecture. Architect Óscar Hagerman, author of the essay "Design in the Service of Mankind" (1979), has spent most of his life studying the typologies of traditional Mexican architecture in Chiapas, Puebla, Jalisco, Michoacán, Oaxaca, and Guerrero while working with farmworkers and indigenous families in rural Mexico to build schools, clinics, and social reintegration centers. Similarly, new practices like TACO and Comunal are strong advocates for marginalized communities. The use of elements like compressed earth by architects Tatiana Bilbao and Frida Escobedo has proved vernacular references go beyond stylistic choice. Instead, materials are chosen based on what has the least environmental impact.

Founded in 2015 in Mexico City, Comunal is led by architect Mariana Ordóñez Grajales and architecture scholar Jesica Amescua Carrera, who describe their work as a "participatory social process" that aims to preserve vernacular typologies in rural districts. One of their most important projects is the Social Reconstruction of Habitat, which after the earthquakes of September 2017 focused on rebuilding and preserving the ways of living of the Mixe people of Oaxaca, without disregarding quality and functional design. Likewise, Mérida-based TACO is a multifaceted family practice that works with local materials and construction methods to create versatile spaces that consider everything from climate to local customs.

An important characteristic that relates to *malinchismo* is the way colonial and neoclassical architecture is, at times, revered to the extent that it becomes intimidating. Contemporary architects have approached the need for welcoming public spaces through the construction of pavilions that are open to the public and built around human interaction. Canales's Museo Abierto (Mexico City, 2018) was a temporary open-air museum where the visitor became part of the exhibition through a series of transitional patios. The reactivation of public space like TACO's Parque la Rejollada in Yucatán, which sits over a former *cenote*, or sinkhole, that collapsed into itself, now serves as a meeting place for local

08   A live/work space for a photographer in Mexico City designed by Taller Mauricio Rocha and Gabriel Carrillo.
09–10   The "Satellite Towers", concrete sculptures designed in collaboration with Luis Barragán, constructed in the north of Mexico City.

Mexico / Central America

> Mexico's cultural wealth has been cultivated for centuries. There is something in human nature that makes us return to our roots—in a cyclical manner, through phases of discovery an innovation.

09

residents. Tatiana Bilbao Estudio's Capilla Abierta (2010) is an open sanctuary built along the Ruta del Peregrino (Pilgrimage Route), part of a masterplan that included, among others, works by Ai Weiwei, Christ & Gantenbein, and Alejandro Aravena.

Mexico's cultural wealth has been cultivated for centuries. There is something in human nature that makes us return to our roots—in a cyclical manner, through phases of discovery and innovation, we remind ourselves we have been there before. Eventually, we come to terms with our problems by looking back to our ancestors for answers. Today, there is growing instability of multilateral institutions and large-scale migration crises, exacerbated by populist and isolationist attitudes worldwide; architecture and design practices have shifted and now confront the need to adapt and respond. Mexico's complex and layered history cannot be ignored. It is a crucial part of what the country is today. It is what helped it strengthen and rise from the rubble over and over again.

Natalia Torija Nieto is a Mexican-born, Kyiv-based art and architecture writer. She was previously Content Director at *PIN–UP* in New York and has collaborated with The Met, Nakashima Studio, Judd Foundation, and Noguchi Museum. Her writing is published internationally, including in *PIN–UP*, *apartamento*, *Travesías Media* and *The Calvert Journal*.

10

111

Camouflaged and Contextually Conscious

Architect PRODUCTORA
Project Centro Cultural Comunitario Teotitlán del Valle
Location Oaxaca / Mexico

Projects by Mexico City-based architectural studio PRODUCTORA always start with an analysis of the context of the site. For the design of the Centro Cultural Comunitario in Teotitlán del Valle, PRODUCTORA focused on the way the plot relates to the surrounding village in the Mexican state of Oaxaca.

The practice developed a very defined geometric shape split into two volumes to fit the property. They take up less than 20 percent of the land, leaving vast spaces for a public plaza and gardens to encourage citizen participation and movement. Pedestrian routes subtly connect the building with the village and allow easy navigation.

The main three-story edifice looks out to the village square. It houses a museum exhibiting traditional textiles from the region. A second double-story volume contains the municipal library and a service zone.

Both buildings have double-slab sloping roofs and 12-inch-thick (30-centimeter) concrete walls. Automated openings create a passive ventilation system that responds to the hot climatic conditions of the area. This regulates the temperature inside to provide a comfortable environment without the need for air-conditioning.

In keeping with the low-lying, neutral vernacular of the village houses, the structures have sober facades with natural hues and basic materials. The stone paving of the public areas provides an additional link to similar elements found throughout the village.

A dominant visual signifier is the pigmented concrete of the walls, imprinted with vertical wooden planks. The textured tonality complements the locally sourced orange brickwork and locally produced clay tiles and timber frames. These materials melt into the village landscape allowing the building to become part of a greater cultural dialogue.

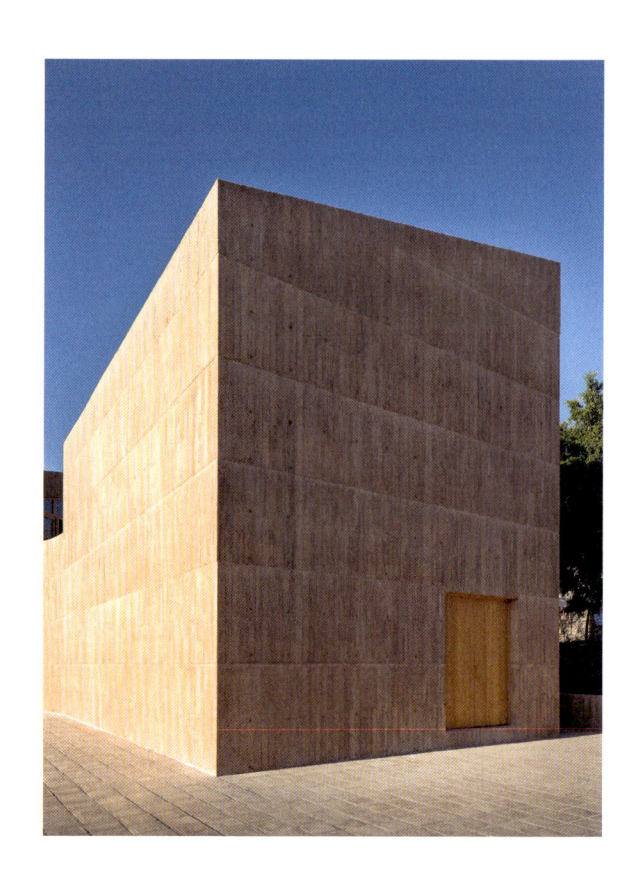

The minimal palette of locally made materials allows the building to sit comfortably and unobtrusively within its surroundings, and yet its strong geometric lines move beyond the more vernacular style of adjacent buildings.

113

114

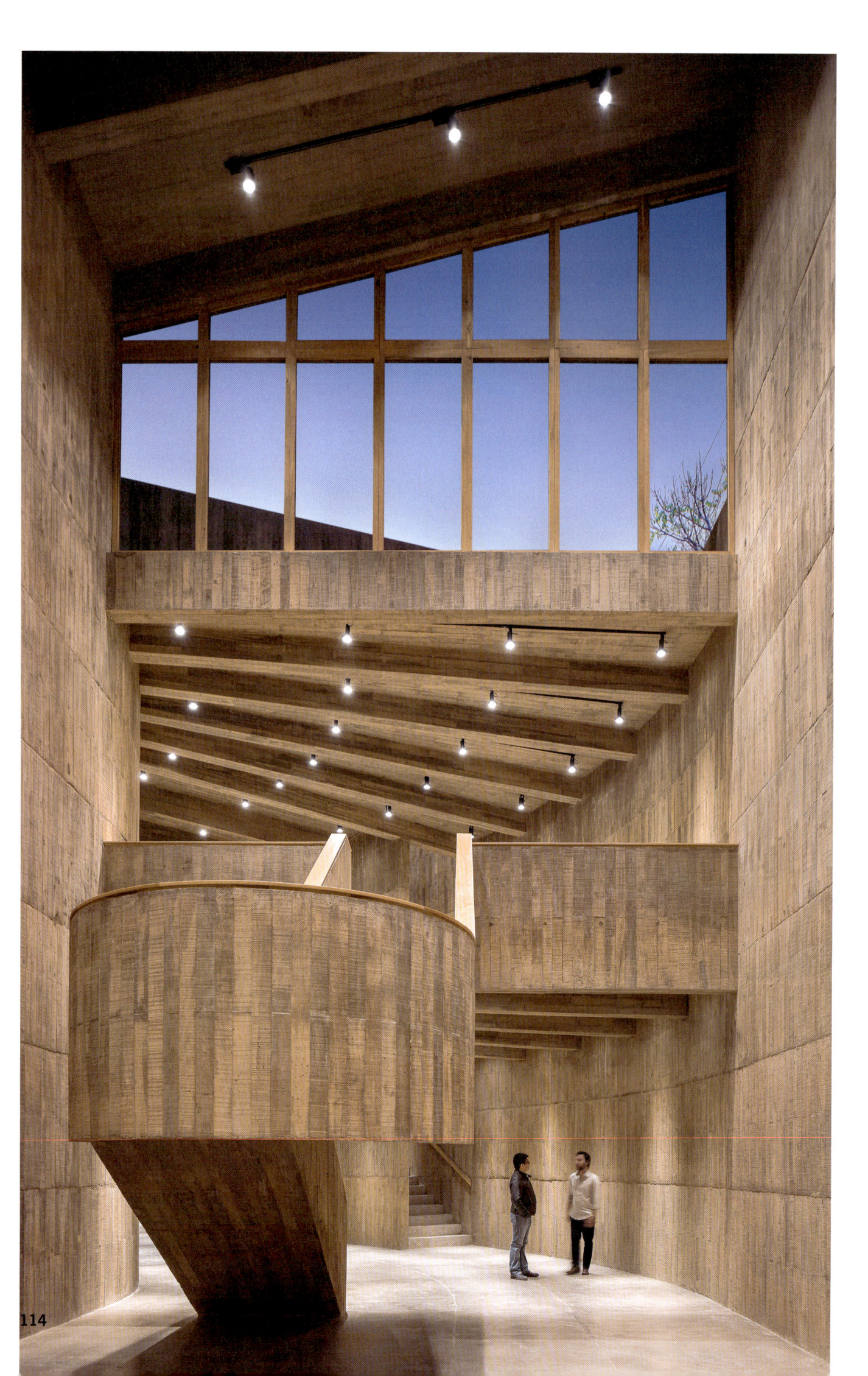

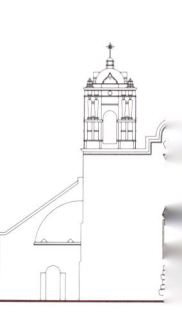

The textured tonality complements the locally sourced orange brickwork and locally produced clay tiles and timber frames.

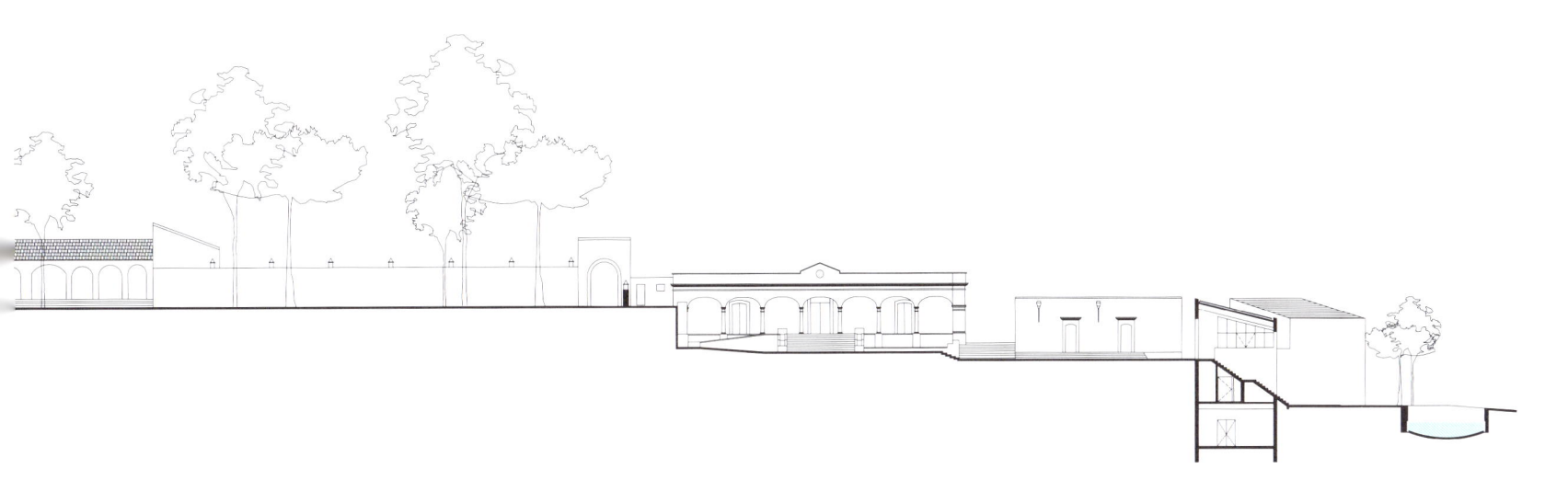

The soft, earthy colors of the exterior continue inside, providing both a neutral backdrop for exhibiting the museum's collection and a calming ambience for quiet study. A cross-sectional drawing of the site shows how one-third of the building is submerged belowground to allow for a spectacular triple-height space within.

115

Centro Cultural Comunitario Teotitlán del Valle

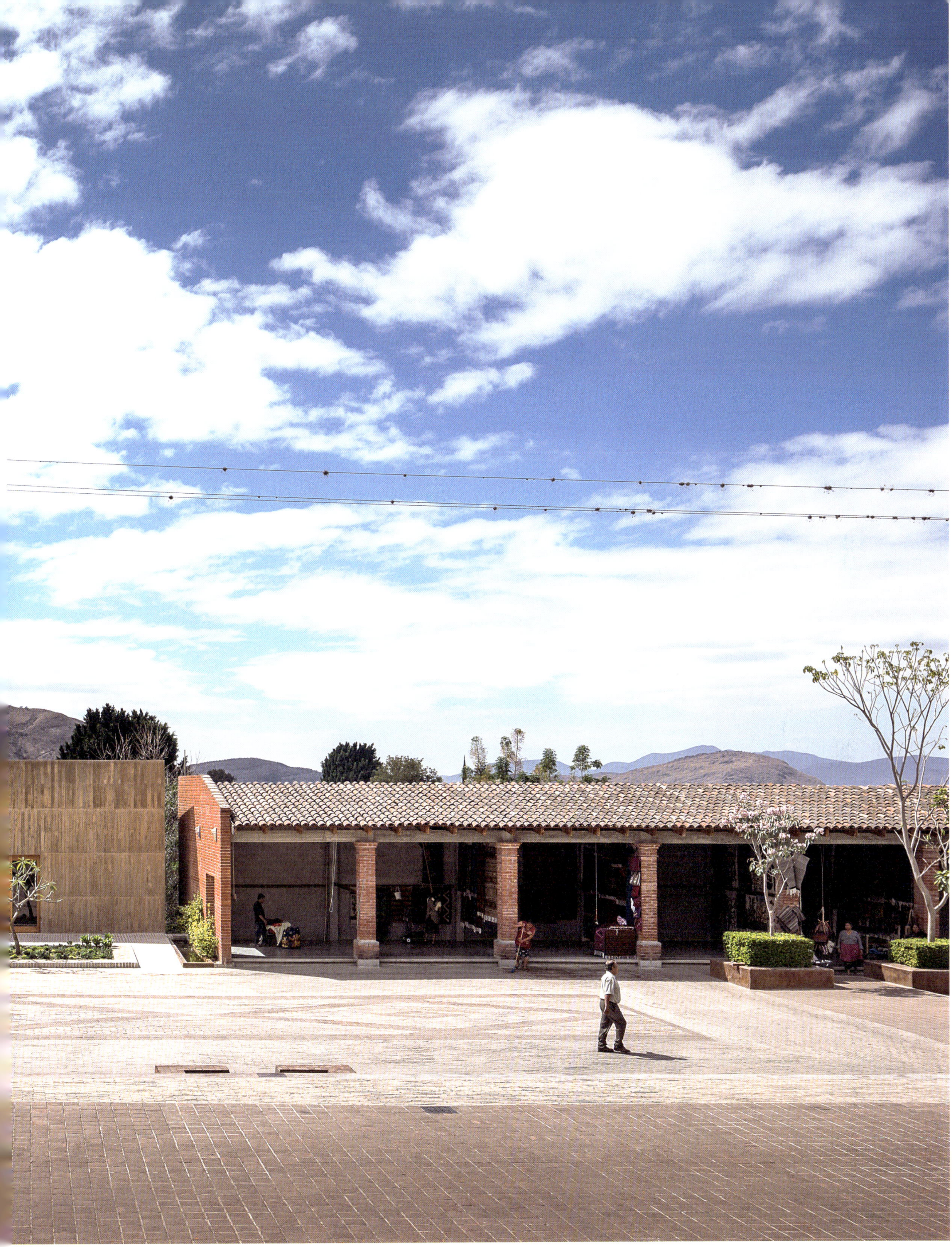

New Life is Built into a Forest

Architect Taller Héctor Barroso
Project Entre Pinos
Location Valle de Bravo / Mexico

"Because architecture needs to live, the natural environment is as important as the architecture," says Mexico City architect Héctor Barroso Riba of Taller Héctor Barroso.

Barroso Riba demonstrated this sentiment with a residential complex in Valle de Bravo, where he designed five weekend houses that have become part of the site's topography. Six separate volumes make up each home. These structural forms are unobtrusively connected with short passageways, and they are interspersed with vegetation.

"This draws the architecture closer to human scale," explains the architect. "It also means that the sense of a group of houses is lost," he says of the design, which is replicated for all five houses. Extensive views of the gardens merging with the pine forest to the south provide a focal point, and the central courtyard, formed by the void between the six volumes, creates an intimate feel.

The non-linear composition of the separate volumes allows movement through the houses in a free-form sequence inviting exploration. Light, shadow, and nature's sounds create different experiences at various times of day—whether residents are curling up in enclosed spaces or basking in the openness of more exposed areas.

Each volume operates almost independently, as there is no architectural hierarchy. One of the bedrooms and the living, dining, and kitchen areas are on the lower level, directly connected to the outdoor environment. The upper levels include three additional bedrooms, offering cocooned spaces with framed forest views.

The use of local materials such as locally produced bricks, certified wood from the area, and soil extracted during excavations root the buildings into the landscape. The muted color of the soil used on the walls ensures the houses blend in with the forest and exist as part of its living language.

This well-considered design leaves the lasting impression that the development has been here for decades—almost as if the trees have grown in the spaces between the volumes and not the other way round.

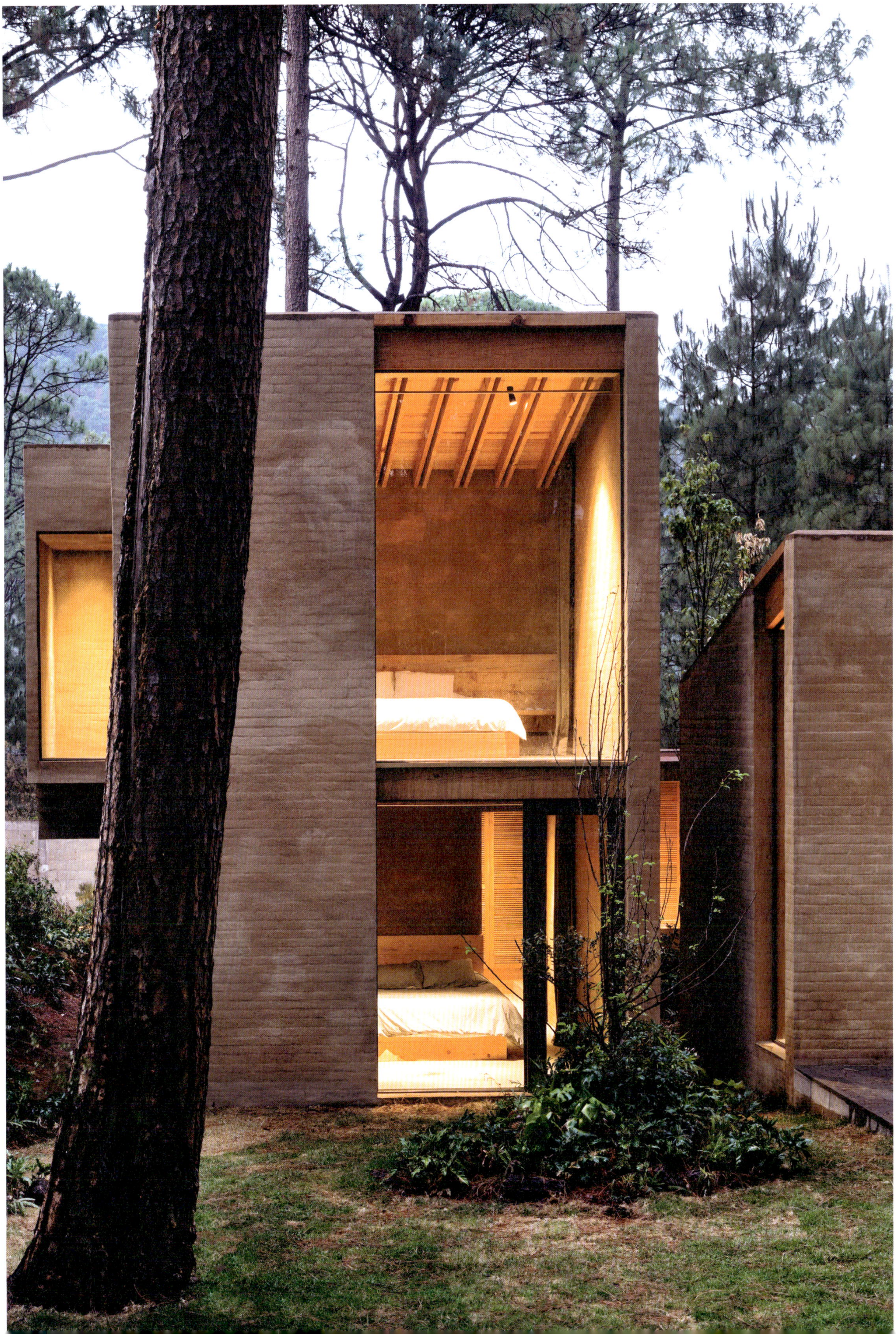

The non-linear composition of the separate volumes allows movement through the houses in a free-form sequence inviting exploration.

The architect has taken great care to match interior colors to those of the exterior and to tones that have their origins in the surrounding soil and pine trees. The timbers that make up kitchen cupboards and seating areas all blend together seamlessly.

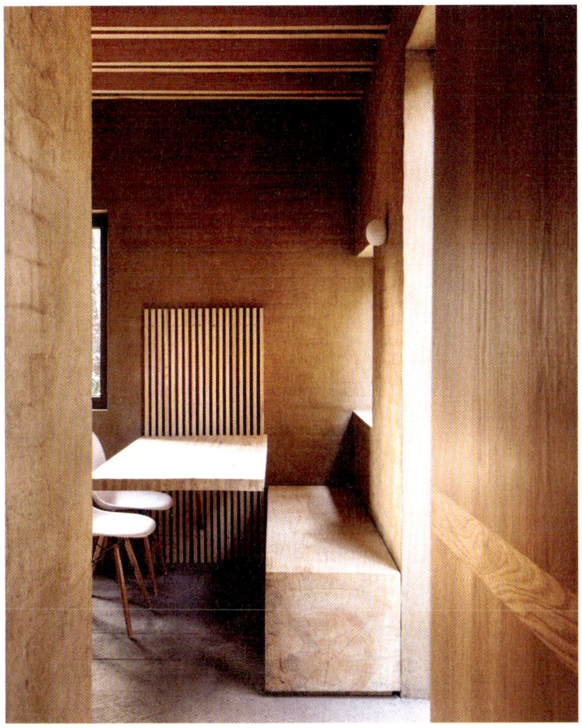
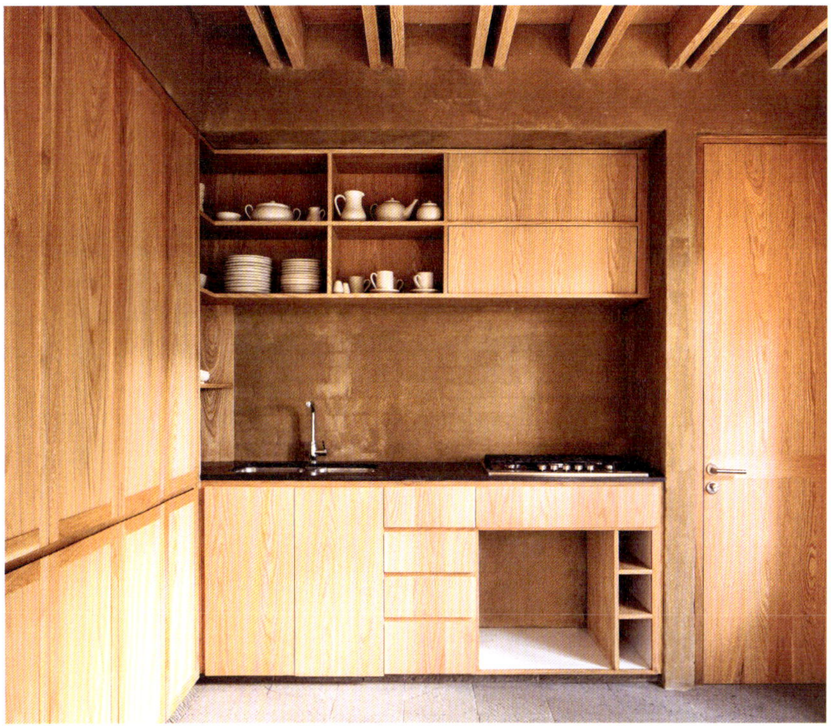
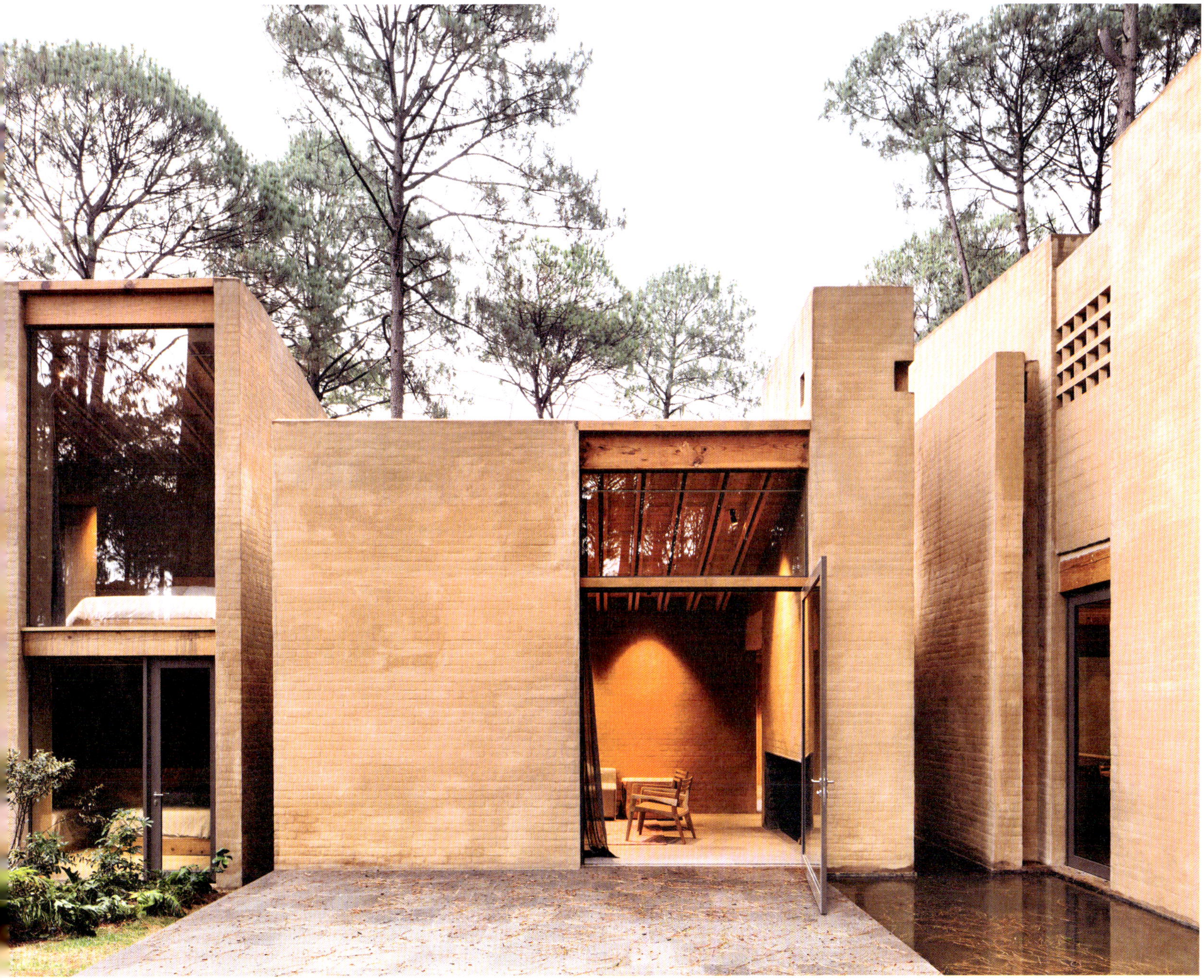

Inside the houses, furnishings are typically simple and rustic, in a range of muted earthy tones—chunky wooden side tables, timber headboards for the beds, lightweight armchairs with woven or cane seating, and textiles devoid of decoration.

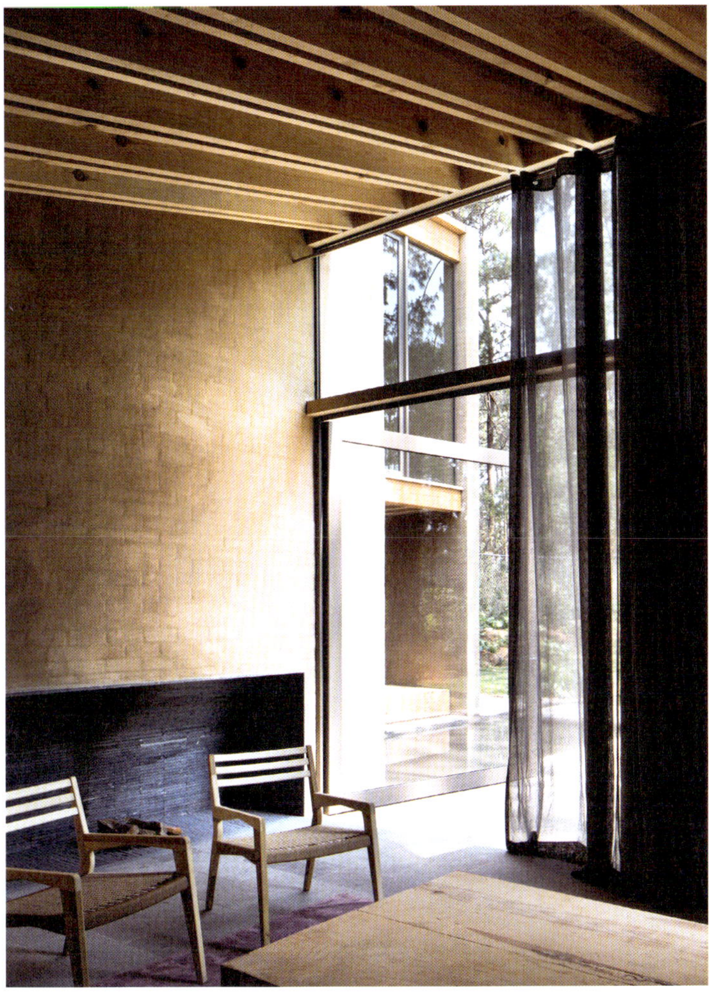
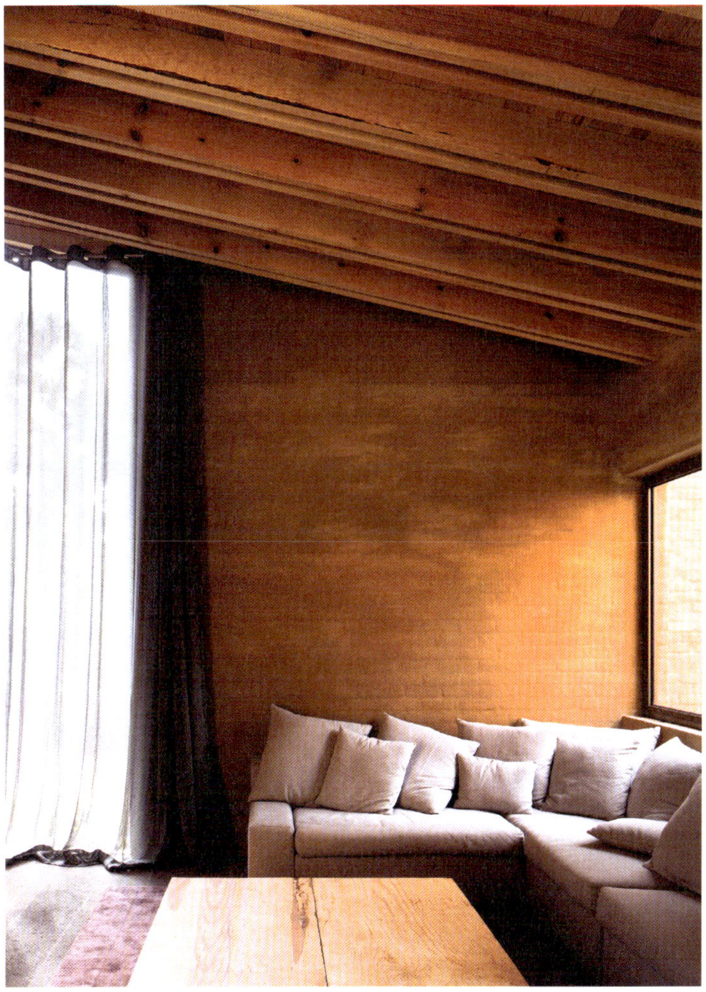
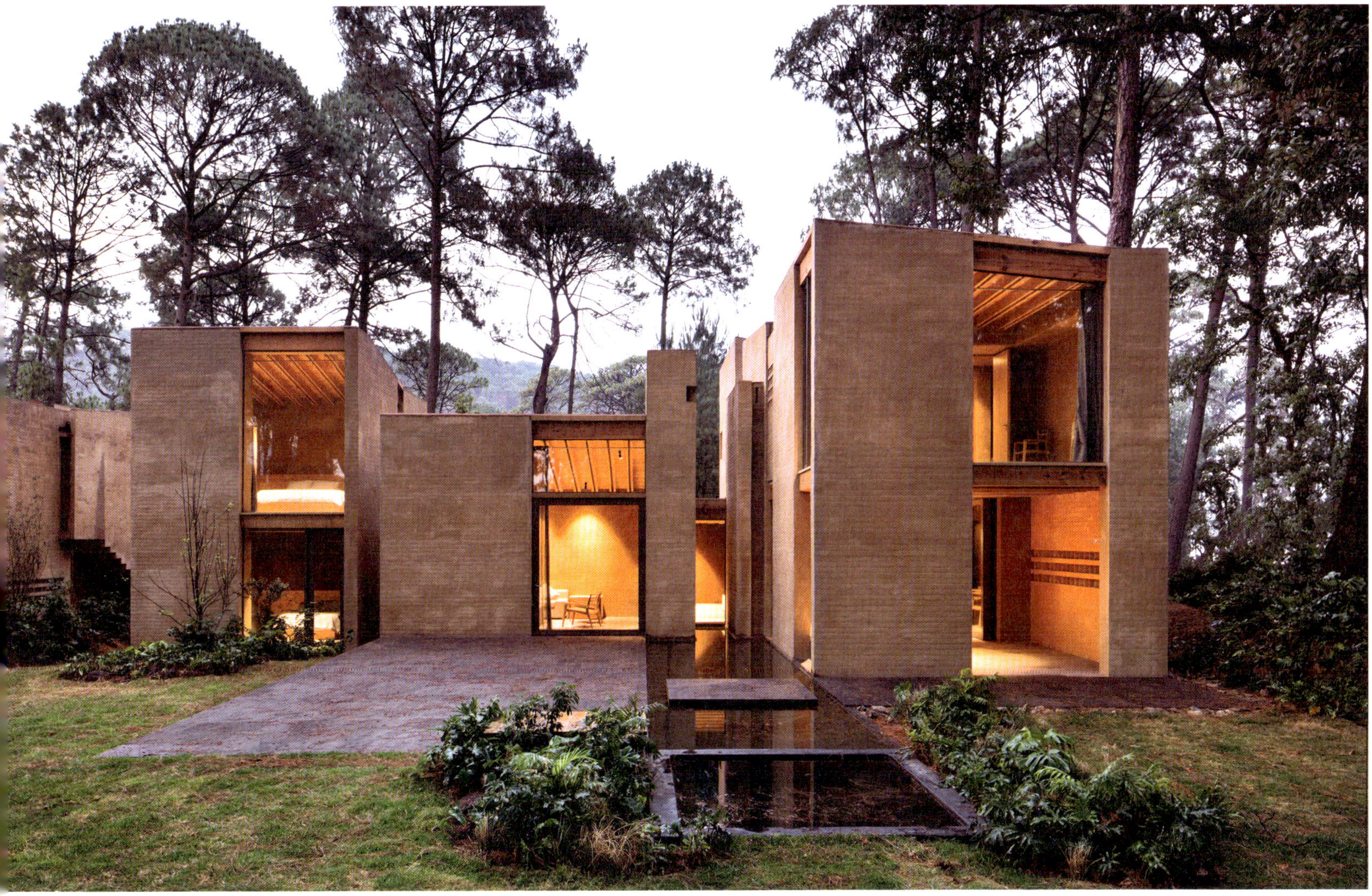

Entre Pinos

Each house is oriented to gain the most from the changing position of the Sun.

Trees Inform a House of Pavilions

Architect Fernanda Canales
Project Casa Bruma
Location Valle de Bravo / Mexico

There was one rule for the development of Casa Bruma, a house in the remote forested area of Valle de Bravo in Mexico: all of the existing trees had to be kept. This uncompromising brief led to the unorthodox approach adopted by architects Fernanda Canales and Claudia Rodríguez, who designed what Canales describes as an "exploded house."

A series of nine independent rectangular pavilions are oriented around a central stone courtyard to maximize morning and evening sunlight. They also take full advantage of the verdant views without needing to disturb the trees.

Although completely private, the structures maintain a close relationship with one another. Covered walkways connect specific adjacent volumes, such as those containing the kitchen, dining room, living room, master bedroom, and children's room—all located on one side of the circular courtyard. The two guest bedrooms, service room, and garage, which are not connected, shape the opposite periphery.

The courtyard thus becomes a converging point for human interaction, closing itself off from the natural surroundings and heightening the experience of each volume opening up to the landscape opposite.

A cleverly placed discreet walkway, which leads to the main entrance and then into the courtyard, is a path of discovery, as each step reveals another volume. The visual identity is expressed simply in the five materials used throughout the project. Concrete, especially mixed with black pigment, is employed for the low-maintenance walls, while wood, stone, metal, and glass integrate the structures into the environment.

Each volume exists at a level that accords with its typography, so the rooftop terraces and gardens are at different heights. The sculpting of this multidimensional house into the landscape blurs all lines new and old, affording the property timeless stature.

An aerial shot and the plan of the site reveal the locations of the nine buildings in relation to one another around the courtyard, and the varying presence or absence of physical links between them.

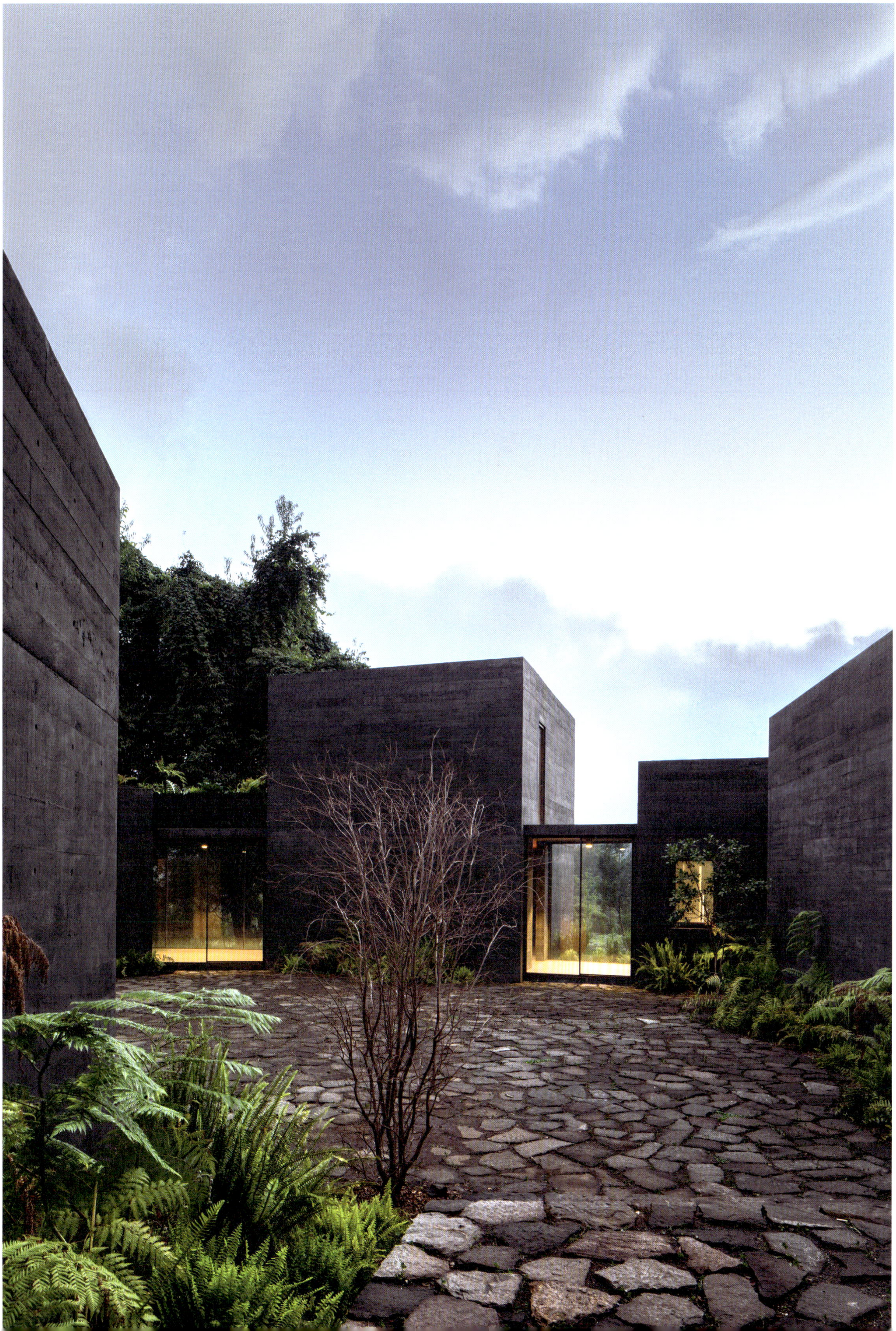

There is a marked contrast between the "closed" sides of the buildings, with their stark rough-cast concrete surfaces, and the "open" sides, where generous windows allow in the unspoiled landscape beyond the development.

128 Casa Bruma

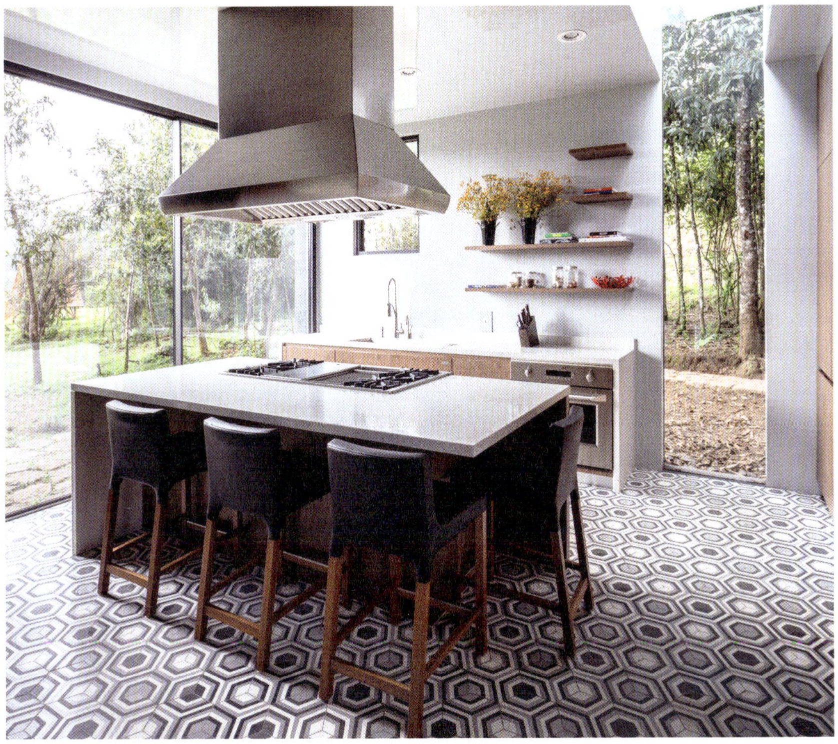
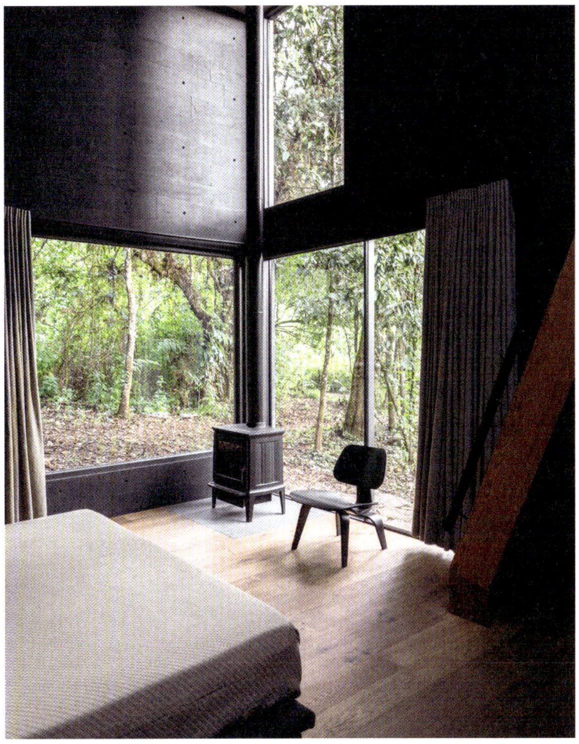
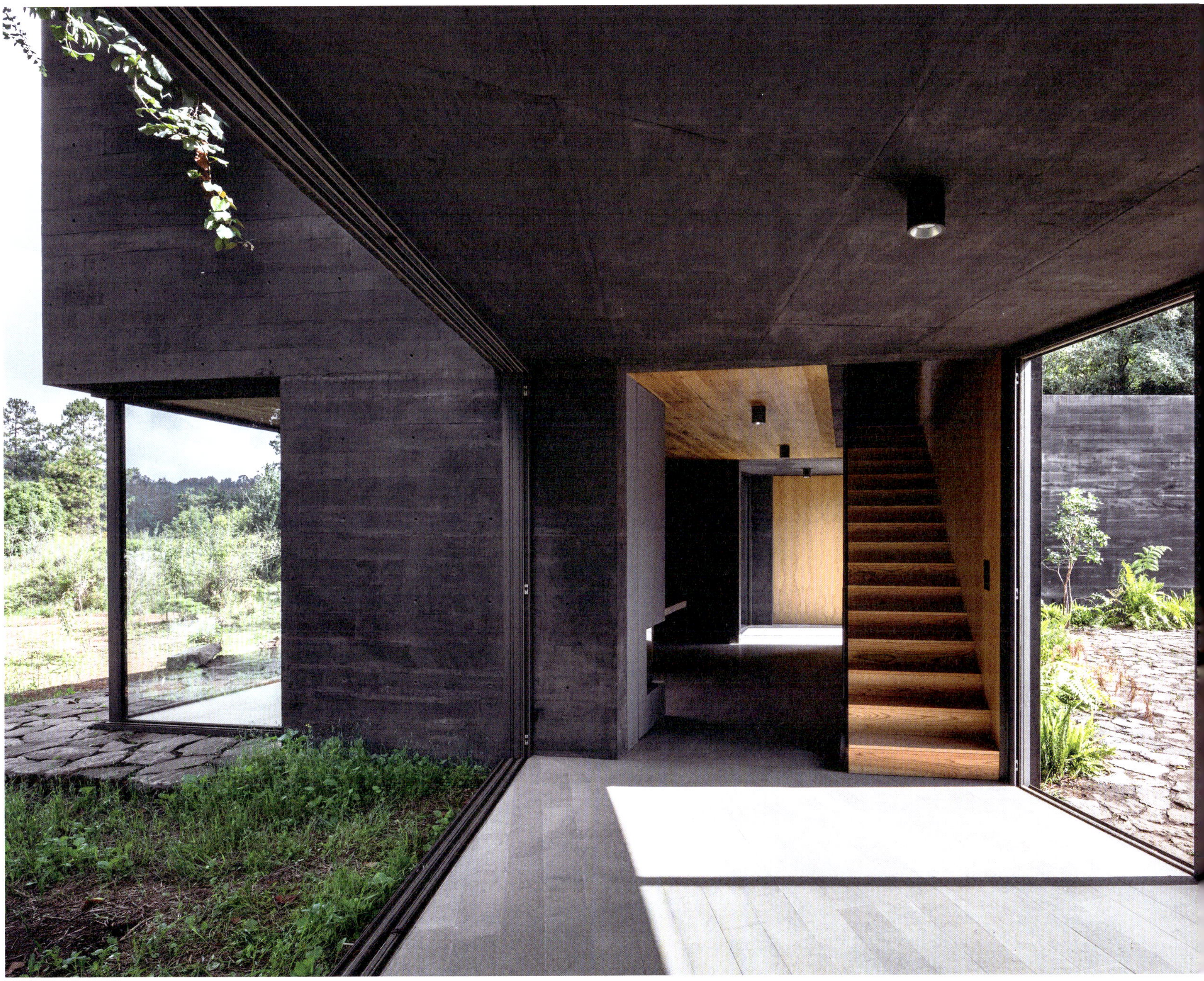

Concrete, especially mixed with black pigment, is employed for the low-maintenance walls, while wood, stone, metal, and glass integrate the structures into the environment.

The relatively small scale of the individual buildings, their unobtrusive facades, and the vegetation sprouting from their roofs help the development to blend into the environment—something that will become more successful with age.

An Office Invites Both Work and Play

Architect TACO (Taller de Arquitectura Contextual)
Project Pórtico Palmeto
Location Merida/Mexico

Merida-based multidisciplinary Mexican studio TACO (Taller de Arquitectura Contextual) adheres to a philosophy of maintaining conscious contextual sensitivity in the spaces it develops. Pórtico Palmeto was conceived to have an identity that roots it to its Yucatan setting. The multifunctional building, primarily housing an architecture studio, allows nature to maintain a strong presence in this palm tree-brimming location in the suburb of Cholul.

By integrating the natural and constructed environments, Pórtico Palmeto is a versatile structure that facilitates an alternative way of working and interacting. More akin to a domestic setting, the building also hosts socio-cultural activities, opening it up to the public.

The structure fuses the Mayan hut vernacular with the tranquility and sobriety of Franciscan convents from Mexico's colonial period and the functionality of Yucatan haciendas that accommodated work and living space. The result is a large double-story building attuned to its sun-soaked surroundings. The cross-ventilation, high ceilings, and zenith openings allow heat to escape. The roof, cast with waterproof concrete, is thermally insulated with polystyrene panels to maintain cooler temperatures.

Local construction methods employing blocks, joists, and cement slabs create imposing features. Floors, made of white concrete and "eco-crete" joints that release moisture from the ground, blend seamlessly with the pathways of the garden esplanade. Burnished stucco, colored to match the site's earthy tones, covers the walls and ceilings.

The portico is covered with locally manufactured bamboo panels. It can be completely open or closed, controlling insulation while offering privacy, security, and safety from prevailing hurricanes. The entrance leads to the work and relaxation areas, and a central patio with a cantilevered staircase to the top story and roof terrace.

Pórtico Palmeto sits within an already established palmetum in Merida, southeast Mexico. The site originally served as a "green lung" for the Mayan colonial community that was established here.

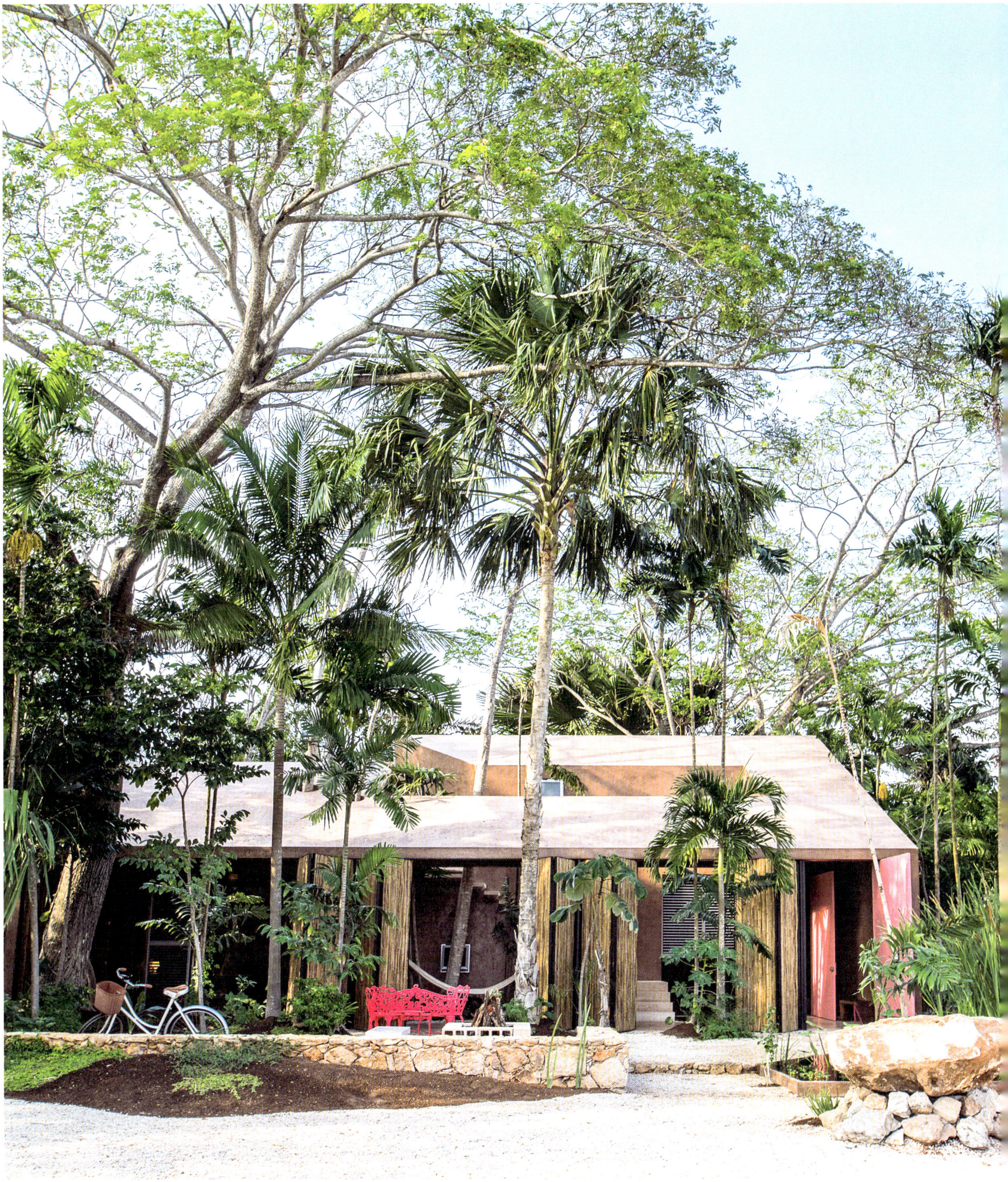

The cross-ventilation, high ceilings, and zenith openings allow heat to escape. The roof, cast with waterproof concrete, is thermally insulated with polystyrene panels to maintain cooler temperatures.

Beds of vegetation within the portico area emphasize the conscious desire of the architects quite literally—to "plant" the development within its natural surroundings. The rose and copper tones of the stucco find echoes in doors and furnishings. They reflect the warm tones of the local architecture as well as those of the surrounding landscape.

Pórtico Palmeto

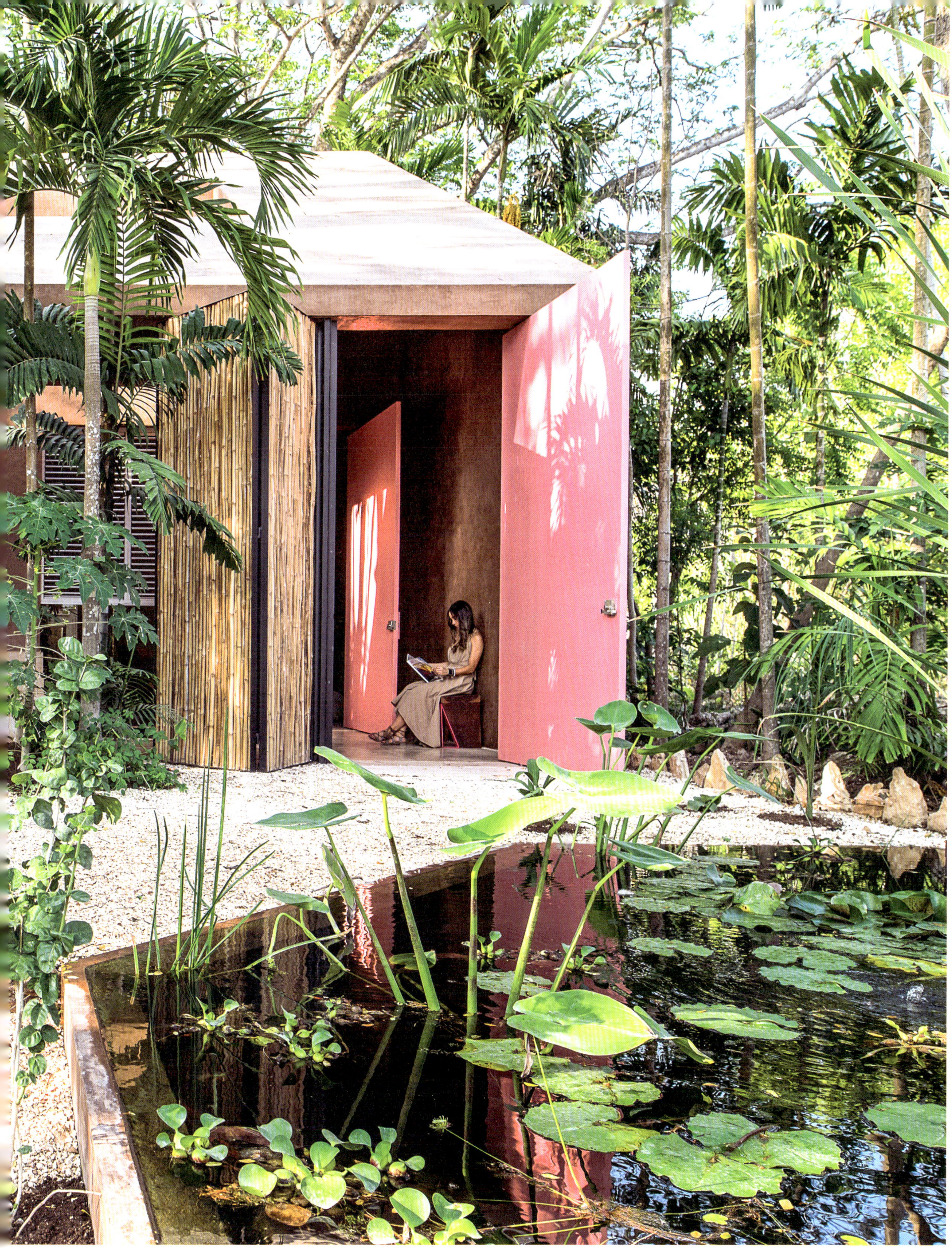

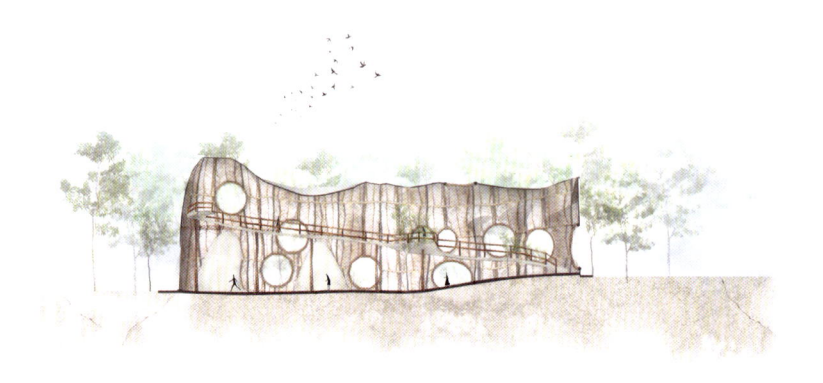

Nature Calls for Artistic Expression

SFER IK Museion by Roth Architecture is an interdisciplinary creative space in Tulum, a coastal town on Mexico's Yucatan Peninsula. Jorge Eduardo Neira Sterkel, the self-taught architect behind Roth, built the intriguing structure on his eco-conscious Azulik resort.

Art, nature, local materials, and traditional techniques coexist in this unconventional structure that resists the definition of "gallery" because it is entirely devoid of straight lines. Designed to be sensitive to the natural environment of the site, SFER IK stands on stilts that allow wildlife to pass beneath it, and trees grow through its curved walls. The vegetation is wholly integrated with exhibitions of art and sculpture, and the verdant landscape can be appreciated through numerous circular windows and gaps in the walls and roof. These perforations allow dappled light to interact with the building and give the impression that it is a living organism.

The floors are laid with a material that resembles concrete, contrasted with bejuco, a flexible vine that grows abundantly in the Yucatan jungle and has been used by Mayan artisans for thousands of years. A traditional method of weaving these vines has also been employed for the walls, where it is combined with chechen wood, which is resistant to rot and termites, and softer wood from the abundant local chaca tree. A fiberglass canopy covers and protects the structure.

Guests are invited to enter barefoot, which heightens the sense of imbalance when walking along the undulating floors and ramped walkways. The intention is to encourage visitors to explore mindfully and allow themselves to become immersed in nature and art.

The SFER IK philosophy succinctly conveys this concept: "We believe that art is a bridge to the sacred. To cross it, it is necessary to lose control, to let go and surrender to the experience."

Architect   Roth Architecture
Project   SFER IK Museion Tulum
Location   Tulum / Mexico

Natural vegetation is integral to the organic design of the gallery space.

At SFER IK the combination of vegetation, shifting light patterns, curvaceous forms, and contrasting materials provides visitors with a deeply immersive experience.

SFER IK Museion Tulum

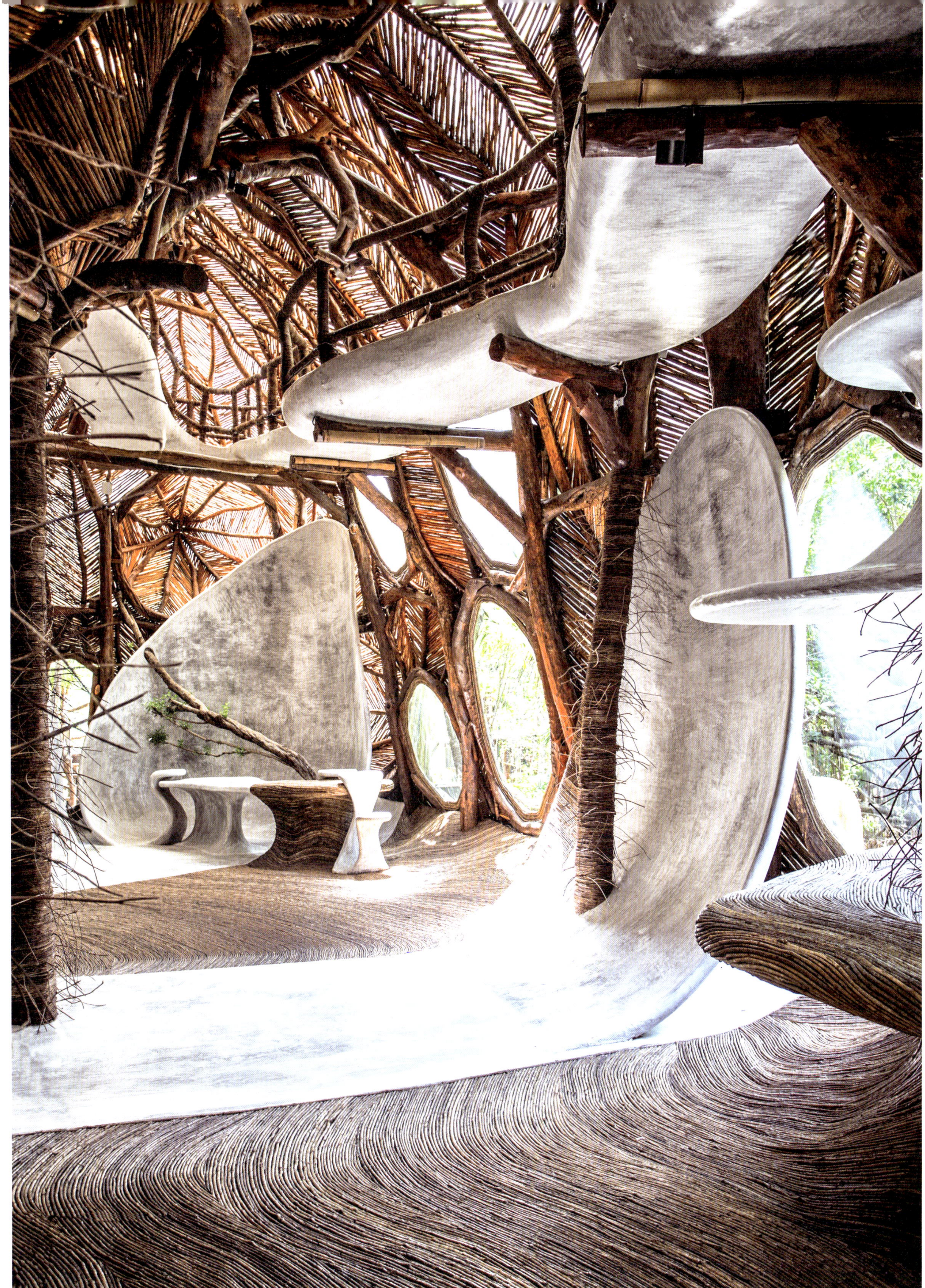

SFER IK Museion Tulum

Guests are invited to enter barefoot, which heightens the sense of imbalance when walking along the undulating floors and ramped walkways.

A ramped walkway wends its way through the gallery, allowing visitors to walk through the space at different levels. The ramp also provides access to a terrace.

Community Buy-In Makes Homes Relevant

Architect   Comunal
Project   Social Housing Production
Location   Sierra de Puebla / Mexico

Mexico's National Housing Commission changed its regulations for awarding federal subsidies to limit the use of traditional materials and construction processes, meaning that this social housing project had to be reconceived. Comunal, a socially geared architectural studio based in Mexico City, had already built a version of these homes with the rural community of Tepetzintan, in Puebla, but they had been constructed with local bamboo, straw, palm, reeds, and wood, so the design needed to modified in order to receive funding.

Comunal always works closely with the communities benefiting from its projects. For this project, it joined forces with two local indigenous cooperatives to determine a way forward that would maintain the integrity of the people the houses were designed for.

"We firmly believe in our profession as a tool to improve the quality of life in communities through processes that trigger autonomy, empowerment, and self-sufficiency," say Comunal's directors Mariana Ordóñez Grajales and Jesica Amescua Carrera. "For us, architecture is not an object; it is an open, participatory social process that allows villagers to express their ideas, needs, and aspirations, placing them at the center of projects and decision-making."

By utilizing panels of non-native giant timber bamboo (*Bambusa oldhamii*), they created a prefabricated modular system that reduces assembly time to a week, avoiding high labor costs. A plant fiber used to make coffee sacks (ixtle) and a thin layer of mortar coat the bamboo, and an EcoLam sheet made from food-grade aluminum waste with thermal, acoustic, and antibacterial properties protects the interior.

The 750-square-foot (70-square-meter) homes are modeled on the customs of the local Nahuatl people, so the kitchens have permeable walls that allow the smoke from indoor fires to escape. The hallways are designed for drying coffee beans and corn, and they feature an altar that acts as the center point of the home.

Each structure relies on low-cost modular bamboo infill panels and roof trusses that sit on, or between, concrete-block walls and bamboo piers. Sections of intricate brickwork offer additional support and ventilation. The corrugated-metal metal panel roof allows for the essential capture of rainwater on-site.

145

Comunal always works closely with the communities benefiting from its projects. For this project, it joined forces with two local indigenous cooperatives.

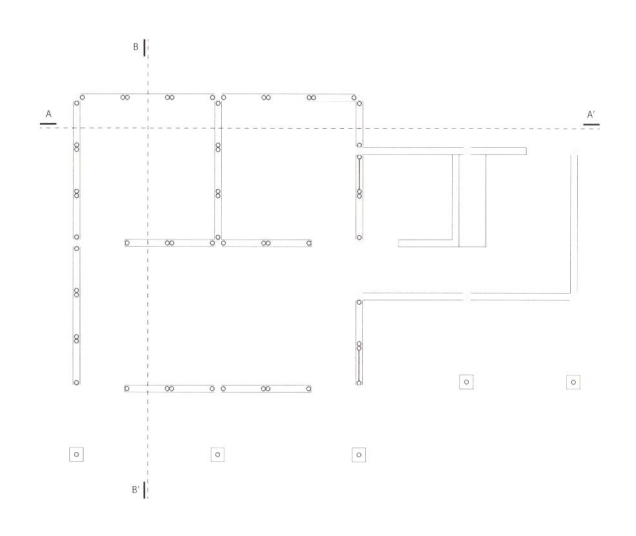

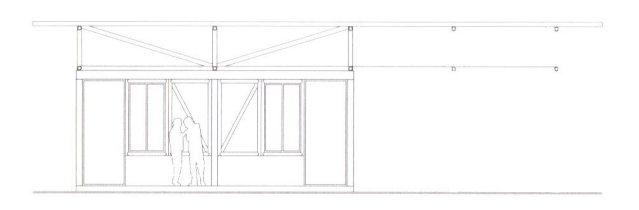

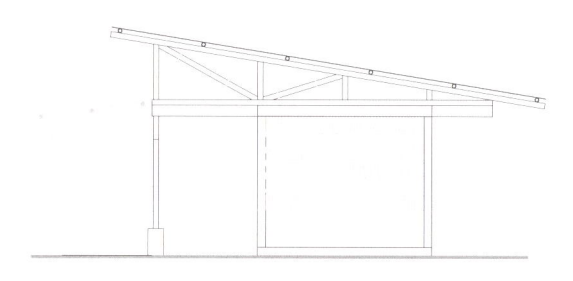

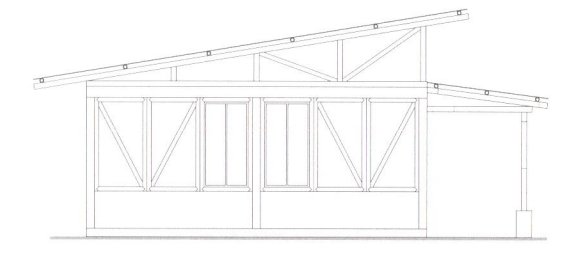

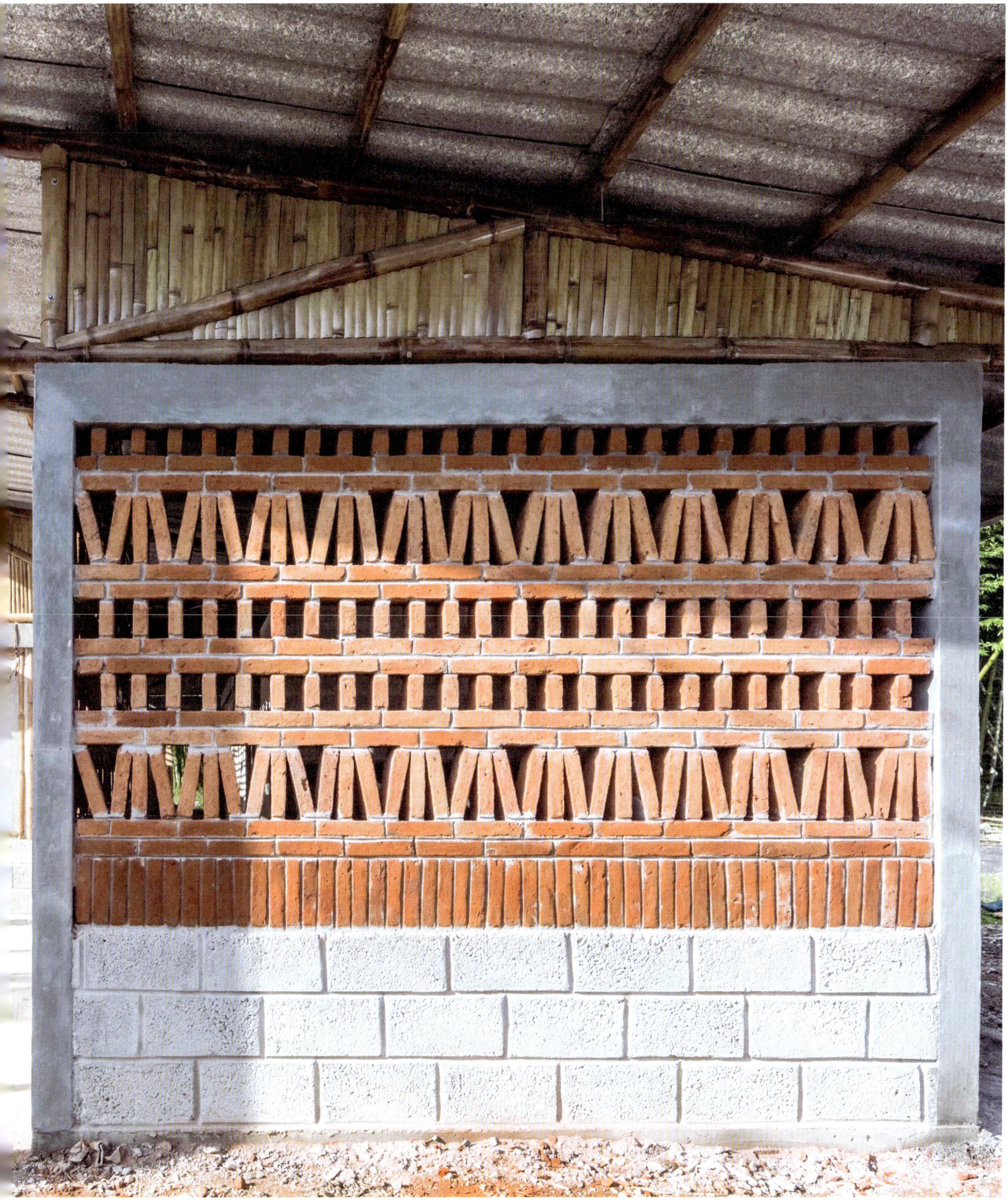

Architect TAX (Taller de Arquitectura X)
Project Torre 41
Location Mexico City / Mexico

Relating an Urban Park to a City Tower

Mexico City's TAX (Taller de Arquitectura X) defines itself as a "lab, greenhouse, and learning team that questions, explores, and redefines space." Under principal architect Alberto Kalach, this group of innovators developed an office tower that illustrates its methodology by relating a multistory building to a park adjacent to it.

Torre 41 was conceived to be a back door to the verdant playground of Chapultepec Forest, the city's green lung. Challenging the less-conscious approaches to urban planning haphazardly scattered in the neighborhood, Torre 41 presents itself as an echo of the forest. The glass facade reflects images of the treetop canopy and allows uninterrupted views from the interior while providing the office spaces with abundant natural daylight.

Two structural concrete walls unite the glass walls, forming a rhomboid shape designed to fit the geometry of the tight, oblique-angled plot. At night, the diagonal steel structures that cross the glass for support are even more pronounced, transforming the building into a sculptural light installation.

Without proposing to be a "green" building, Torre 41 exists as one. Plants are growing on all levels—from the parking garage to the rooftop garden, where shrubbery appears to blend into the park's leafy scene. The triple-volume atrium contains an interpretation of a nursery, continuing the discourse with the park while absorbing the noise of the busy street with water fountains and an acoustic wall.

Avoiding the contemporary trap of glass architecture that is closed off to the outside and requires electrical air-conditioning, this structure begs to be opened up. The glass panes open and shut to create a bioclimatic cross-ventilation system, and simultaneously offer office workers the opportunity to have a more immediate connection with nature.

Inside the building, concealed lighting follows the framework of the steel structures that support concrete floor slabs. After dark, they create a geometric light display from the bottom of the tower to the top.

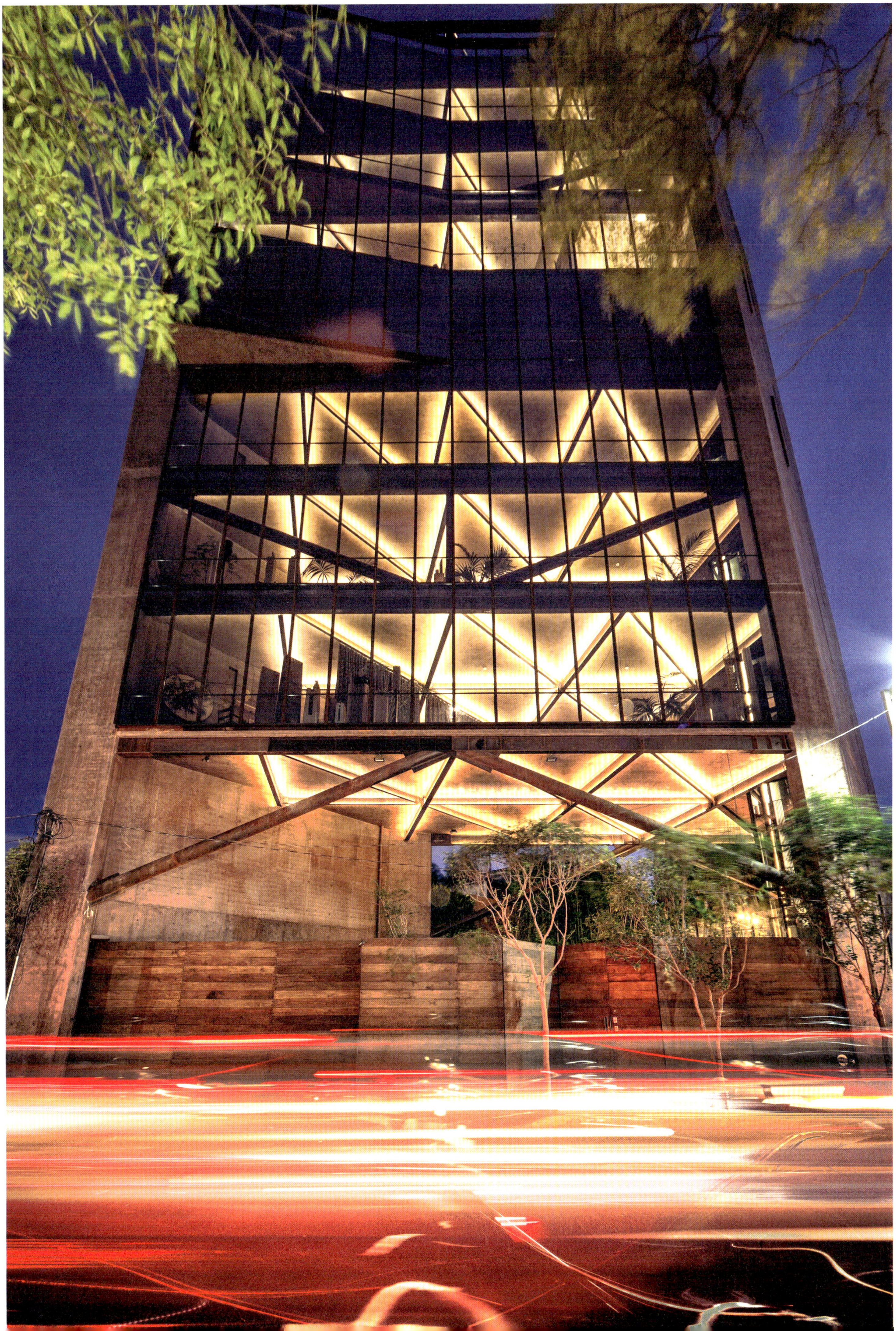

At night, the diagonal steel structures that cross the glass for support are even more pronounced, transforming the building into a sculptural light installation.

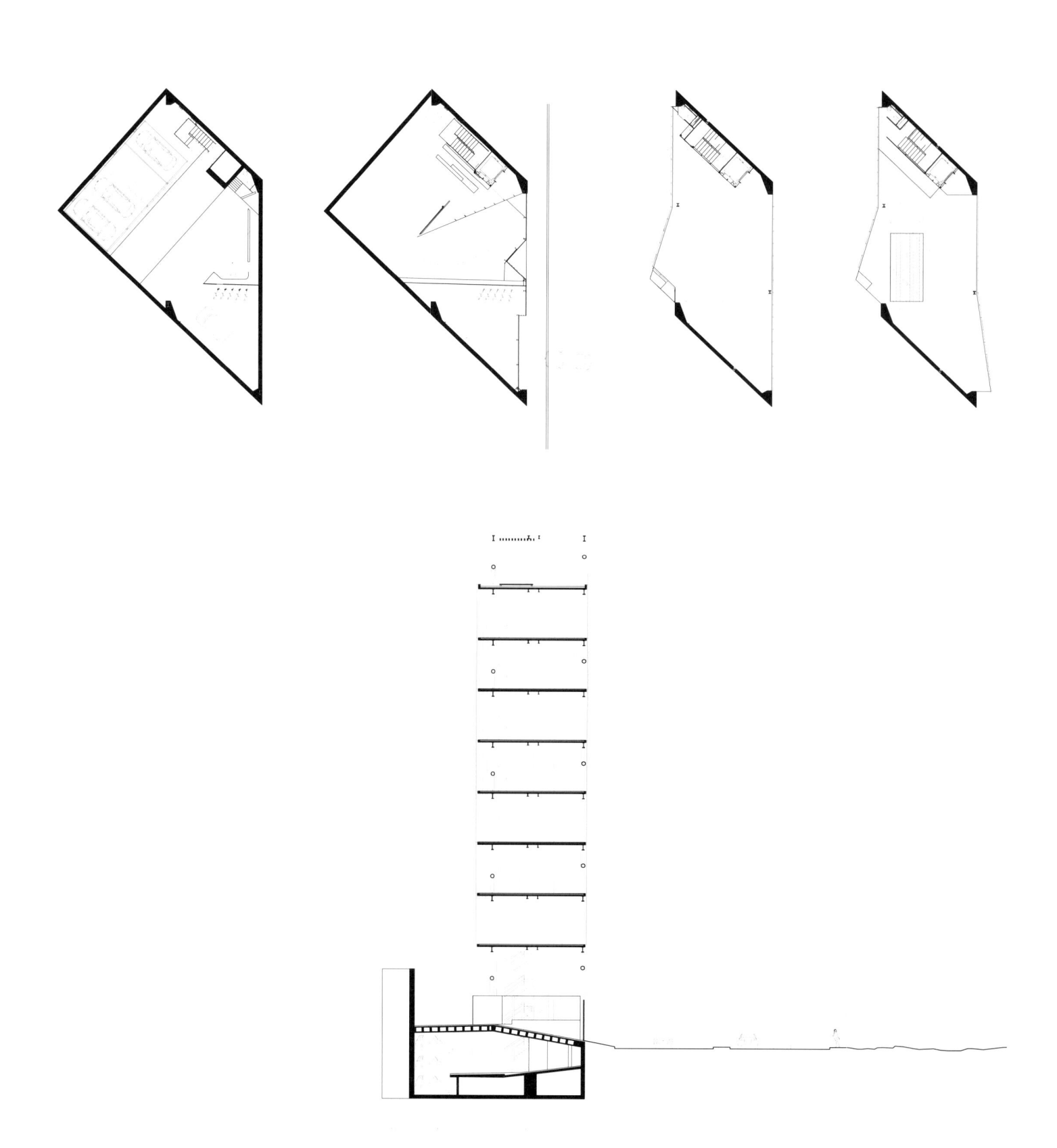

Plans of the project show how the building has, essentially, a rhomboid footprint. The short parallel sides are huge concrete slabs that support the fully glazed longer parallel sides with the aid of sturdy steel structures.

150   Torre 41

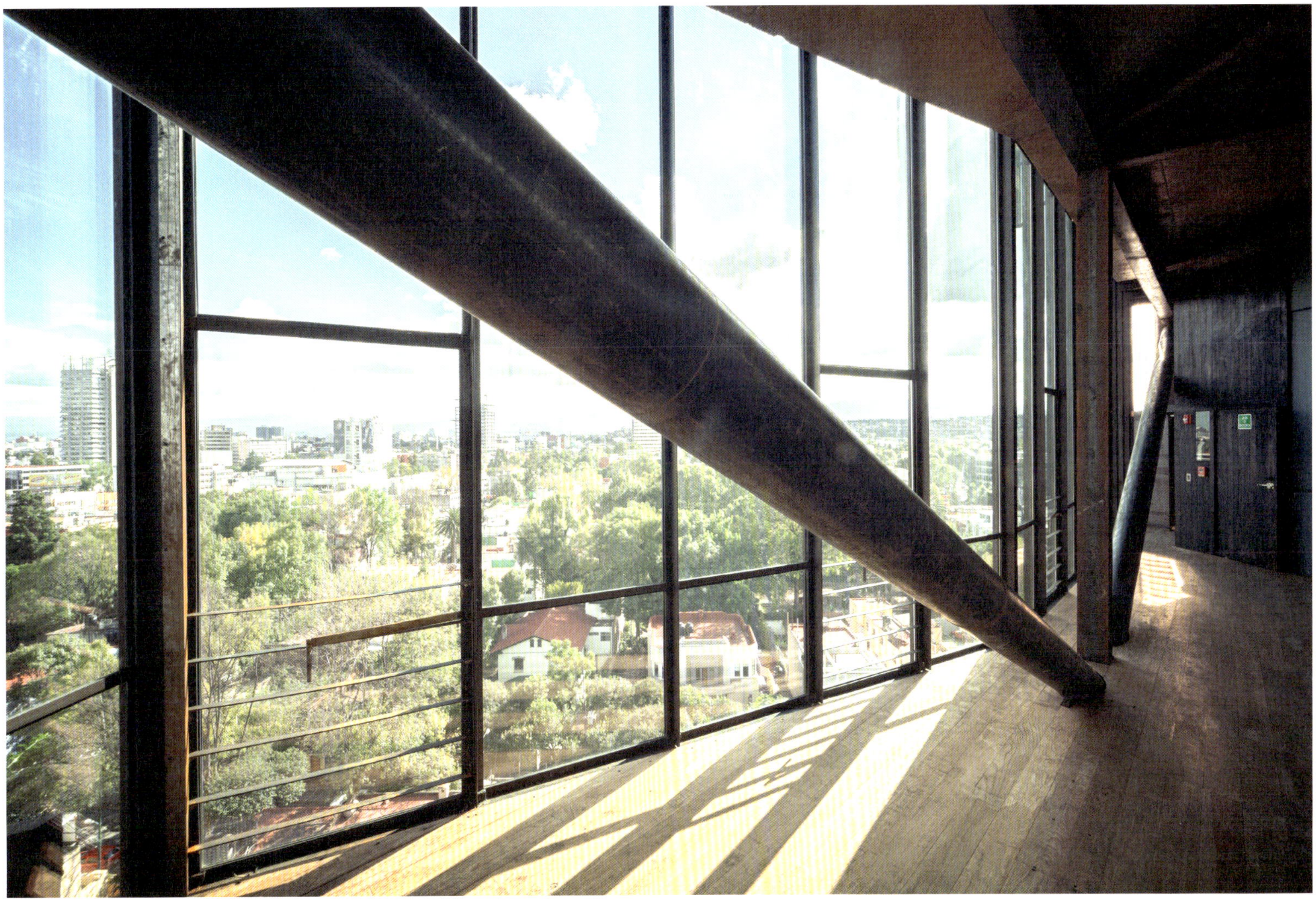

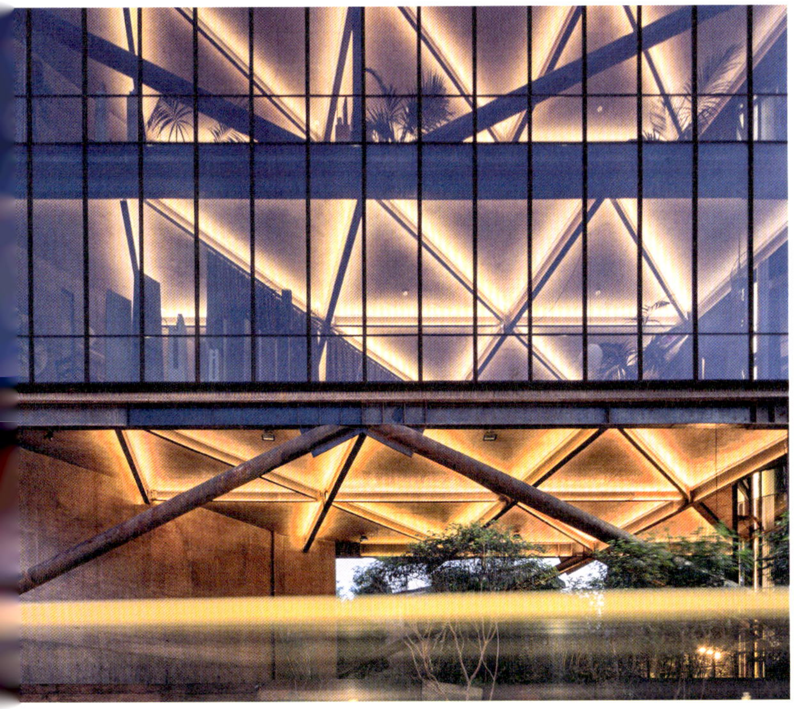

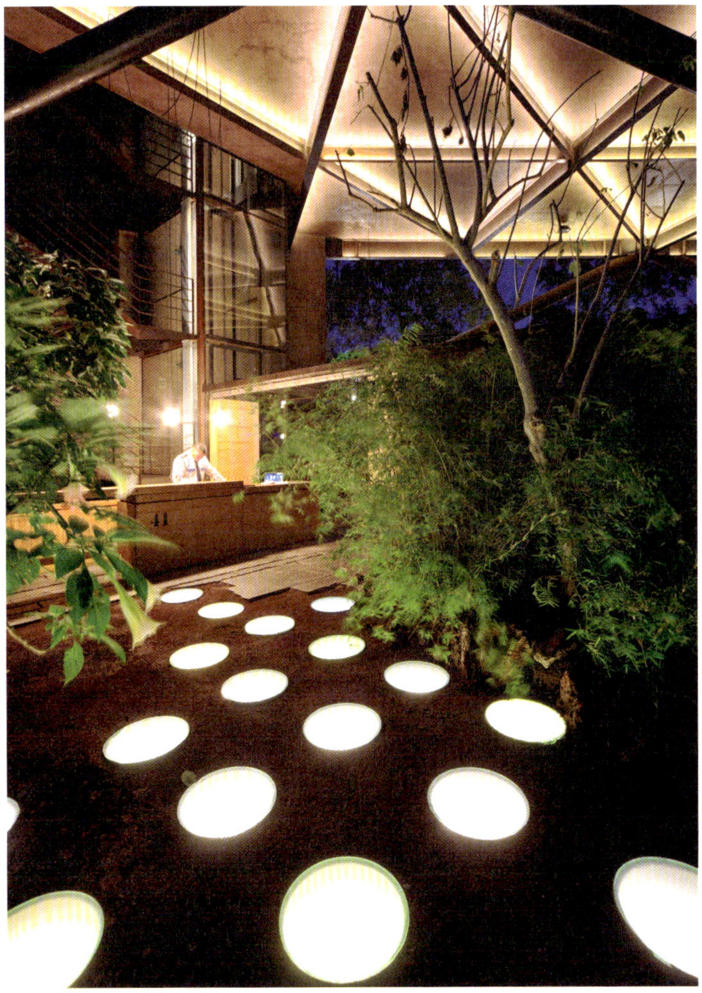

Lush planting is integral to the scheme, not only for its sound-absorbing effects on the ground floor, but up high, too, where the vegetation represents a continuation of the forest canopy beyond.

152   Torre 41

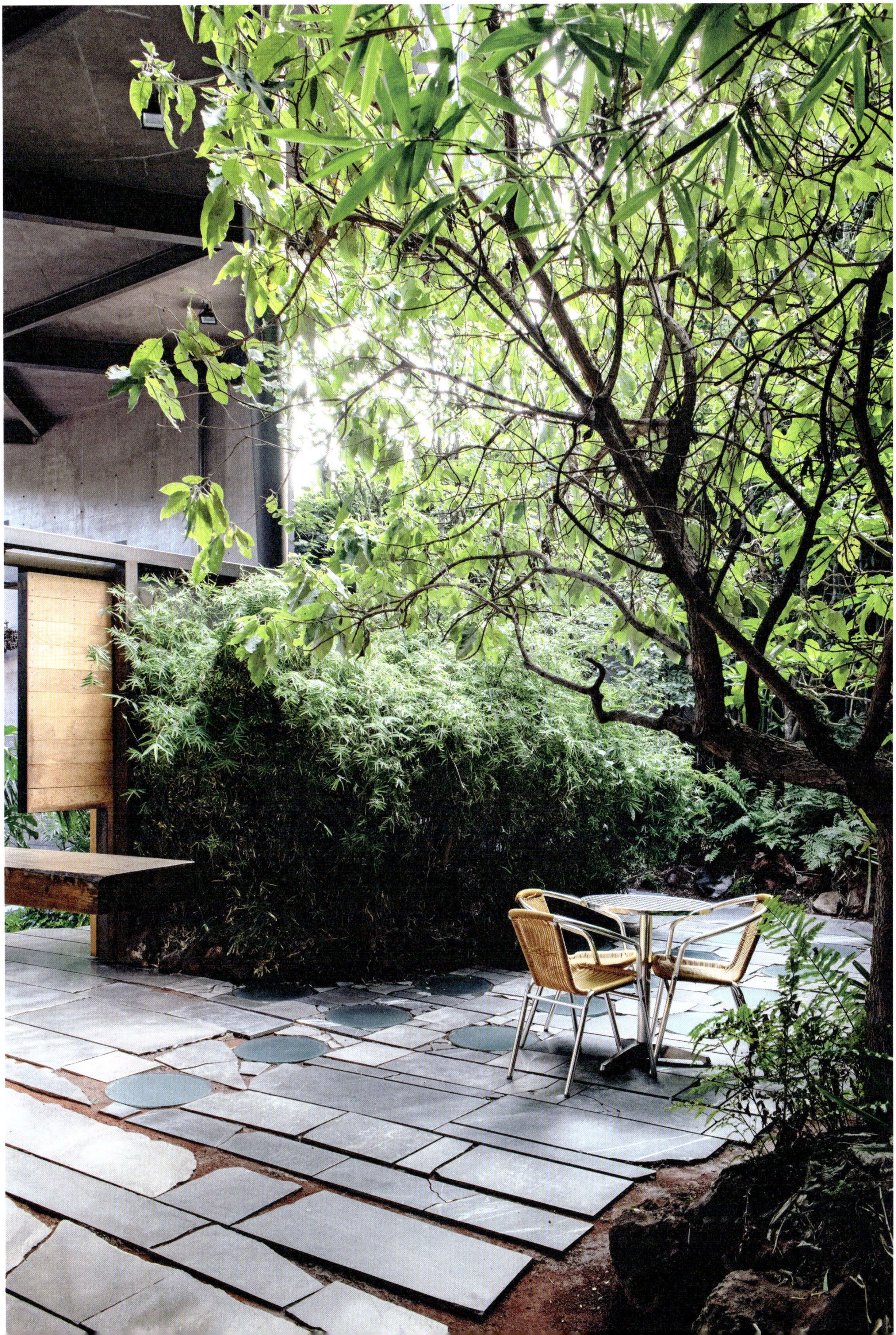

154

Frida Escobedo

This Mexico City-based architect creates buildings to live many lives. As the social context around it evolves, so too does the building, just like the city she grew up in: expressive, adaptable and, above all, never finished.

"Architecture is a very generous discipline," says Frida Escobedo of her chosen profession. "It allows you to do so many things." The Mexico City architect would know. Conceptual thinker, teacher, biennale participator, researcher, and designer, Escobedo is making the most of her calling. In 2018, she became the youngest architect to design the annual Serpentine Pavilion in London's Kensington Gardens (and only the second woman after Zaha Hadid). Her eponymous studio's noteworthy building projects include revitalizing Acapulco's 1950s Boca Chica Hotel with architect José Rojas and designing a series of stores for skincare brand Aēsop. Her accomplishments led to her being honored as an International Fellow of the Royal Institute of British Architects in 2019. She has been a visiting professor at various universities, including the Harvard Graduate School of Design and the Architectural Association of London. She has worked on several prototypes for social housing, and she is working on a book about rethinking the ruin in a contemporary way.

Although Escobedo has been working for herself since graduating with a degree in architecture and urbanism from Universidad Iberoamericana in 2003, her master's degree in art, design, and the public domain at Harvard set her on her current trajectory. Escobedo was inspired by lecturer Erika Naginski's theories of public space and her understanding of history through fragments, never to be grasped as a finished whole. It instilled more confidence in her own opinions. "Architecture is not just about commissions you get from private investors, institutions, or the government," she says. "It's about how you think about space."

> Escobedo delves beyond site-specific notions of physical permanence, placing greater emphasis on the social context that her projects exist within and acknowledging that it will evolve.

Escobedo delves beyond site-specific notions of physical permanence, placing greater emphasis on the social context that her projects exist within and acknowledging that it will evolve, allowing the architecture itself to transform over time. "This is how buildings get to live different lives," she states.

It follows her notion that architecture is always unfinished—an idea ingrained in her Mexican psyche. In Mexico, she lives alongside historical monuments and pre-Hispanic ruins. Such social and cultural dynamics further illustrate her theory of architectural layering. "In downtown Mexico City there might be a colonial building adapted with a modernist structure that has become a jewelry shop and may evolve to become a phone shop. The architecture is modified, creating layers. It's richer and more alive, and allows the past to be present."

Escobedo adds her own coating, on top of these layers that represent precise moments in time, that she hopes is "a little more porous." Her designs interact with previous versions of the environment, and they are open to aging and transforming.

When she won the competition to reimagine La Tallera, late muralist painter David Alfaro Siqueiros's historic house and studio in Cuernavaca, her vision was to overlay it with a new facade, rearranging the murals in the courtyard and creating a striking entrance. "It was about shifting preexisting spaces and adding things to activate the space," she explains of opening the museum up to create a more dynamic entrance.

Even when working on new builds, her multilayered approach still persists. In such cases, Escobedo produces neutral and flexible structures that allow people to adjust spaces as they see fit. She attributes this methodology to having grown up in Mexico City, where people adapt spatial parameters and combine styles to maximize the occupiable area. "Most of Mexico City is self-constructed. It is not a city made by architects," she explains. "It's a very expressive form of architecture."

Pages 154–155: At La Tallera in Cuernavaca, the reorientation of two murals—once overlooking a private courtyard and now framing the entranceway—has achieved a dual purpose. As well as opening the complex up to the public, the murals also serve to separate the gallery building from the original house, which now functions as a base for artists in residence.

Above: Escobedo's renovation of the Boca Chica Hotel in Acapulco sought to reinvigorate the 1950s charm of the complex. The design employed a range of materials, from rough concrete flooring to plastics, to breathe new life into public spaces. A 1950s mint green graces the balconies and the waterside deck.

Above and opposite page, left: A residential project at Mar Tirreno, Mexico City, sees dwelling units divided between two volumes on either side of an open-air, corridor-like patio. The patio serves as a transitional space, between the bustling street and the family home, while doubling as a gathering place for residents.

Opposite page, right: The studio's work creating practical low-cost housing centers on developing units that rely on sustainable practices such as the collection of rainwater, the best orientation for the capture of natural daylight, and reducing the number of internal walls—all to lower initial building costs and long-term household expenditure.

Frida Escobedo

For the Mar Tirreno residential complex in Mexico City, she expanded the built environment by "folding" balconies inward to form quiet, sheltered terraces, increasing the level of privacy while optimizing the natural light inside. Rather than a typical apartment block, these residences present as multistory patio houses where people can make the most of indoor and outdoor areas.

Escobedo protected this intimacy by using breeze-block walls that offer views from the interior but restrict overlooking. It's a building method she enjoys for its ability to "seal but also reveal." Similarly, at La Tallera, a fresh veil-like skin was wrapped around the old building, but gaps provide glimpses of the original structure.

Her design for the Serpentine Pavilion also employed breeze blocks, allowing the surrounding landscape to penetrate the space inside. "It was a temporary structure, and if it moved to another city, it needed to absorb the context and incorporate the landscape, so something closed didn't make sense," Escobedo explains.

Context is sometimes more subtly expressed, such as in the Aēsop Park Slope store in Brooklyn, where Escobedo's team incorporated walls of tessellating bronze-colored bricks handmade in Mexico's Oaxaca region. Instead of using a style of tile historically employed in Brooklyn, she opted to look to the present moment, when talk of territory and US-Mexico relations are high on the agenda. Escobedo took the opportunity to create a metaphorical bridge in the conversation by using soil from her country to build on her neighbor's land. "It was an almost playful thing to do and shows that collaboration creates beautiful results," she says.

Social issues are a preoccupation, and her studio worked with the Mexican Institute of the National Fund for Workers' Housing for nearly five years to make such housing more appropriate for family living. They did this by densifying abandoned neighborhoods, creating mixed-use ground-floor activations, restoring plazas for community use, and developing prototypes for rural housing that could then be incorporated into urban environments.

Her interest in the way people live led her to develop a course at Harvard Graduate School of Design around domestic spaces and the hierarchy that exists in the built environment. She is particularly interested in domestic labor. She cites examples of middle-class housing in Mexico: "We have two types of residents—the people who own the homes, and the live-in domestic workers who are invisible. It's important to address this and to understand how architecture has contributed to this situation. In Mexico City, this social dynamic is so embedded that we sometimes forget that it is not necessarily appropriate or even normal."

She also seeks to counter what she sees as unnecessary urban sprawl and ego-centric developments that have little regard for the environment. "I wish we could build less new architecture and start using more of what we have, and redistributing it," she says. Her concerns include how water will be provided over the next 10 years, how mining can be reduced, and the way that territory is defined. "We have eroded the land to such an extent that the past cannot exist in the present," she says.

But, despite political, social, economic, and environmental disturbances, working in Mexico continues to feed Escobedo's hope for the future. "We're used to working in crisis," she says. "When things are not presented or given to us easily, we become more creative."

Above: The walls of Escobedo's design for Hyde Park's Serpentine Pavilion are composed of ordinary cement roof tiles commonly used throughout the UK. Their arrangement is such that the visitor's views of Kensington Gardens beyond are diffused, becoming little more than a blur of greens and blues.

161

Brazil: Uncertainties and Stabilities

A colonial history, a decades-long dictatorship and an economic recession have all shaped the face of modern Brazil. And yet, the country's sumptuous approach to modernism has yielded some of the world's finest examples of the movement.

01

A 200-foot (60-meter) prestressed concrete slab hovers steadily over São Paulo's landscape. *No Ar* is an intervention by Brazilian artist Laura Vinci that causes a dense fog to rise from the ground, dissipating the structure of the Brazilian Museum of Sculpture and Ecology (MuBE). It reinforces the idea of the large open span and the "stone in the air" so desired by Pritzker Prize winner Paulo Mendes da Rocha, and so representative of Brazilian architecture, while destabilizing the perception of materiality. This seems to be an analogy for the social condition of Brazil, an uncertain and fragile territory tainted by daily aggressions, and yet full of hope for a more just society.

Since Portuguese colonial rule, Brazil has faced a series of adverse circumstances that have created this vulnerability but also offered opportunities for architects. The MuBE, conceived between 1986 and 1995, is an important example. In the 1980s, the military government declined, and democracy was established. The MuBE symbolizes the force of resistance from the modernist movement repressed during the dictatorship because of its liberal ideals.

The Basis for Solid Responses

The desire to create a national identity and modernity emerged in Brazil with the artistic avant-garde of the early twentieth century, and this movement assumed its most revolutionary form in architecture. In the 1920s, Brazilian architect Lúcio Costa and Russian-born architect Gregori

01 The Sao Paolo Museum of Art, designed by Lina Bo Bardi, on Paulista Avenue in Sao Paolo.
02 Oscar Niemeyer in the garden of "Casas Da Casoas", his private home in a suburb of Rio de Janeiro.
03 Oscar Niemeyer's Cathedral of Brasilia, completed in 1970.

02

Warchavchik introduced modernist architecture to Brazil. They had a common desire for purity and simplicity expressed through the use of traditional construction techniques and geometric and abstract plans.

In the mid-1930s, the process of modernization and industrialization accelerated. The construction of the Ministry of Health and Education in 1936 is an important milestone of this period, mainly because of the way the building interacts with the public space around it. Beyond the main volume, which is suspended by 33-foot-high (10-meter) *pilotis,* the structure embodies the ideas of Le Corbusier, who acted as a consultant on the project. A decorative tile panel by Brazilian artist Candido Portinari and landscaping by landscape architect Roberto Burle Marx imbue it with playful and authentic haracteristics.

This combination of social function and individual expression precipitated the rise of the first regional modernist school, known as the Carioca School. Its principal representative was Oscar Niemeyer, undoubtedly one of the greatest proponents of Brazilian modernist architecture. Throughout his career, he explored light and sinuous forms, as well as spatial amplitude and structural expressionism, creating his own architectural language.

In the late 1950s, Niemeyer became chief architect of Brasília, the country's new capital, where he designed more than 25 monumental and government buildings. The first masterplan for the city was conceived by architect and urban planner Lúcio Costa and represented the possibility of a better future, after years of authoritarianism. Together, they intended to create a utopian city where every element was harmonious with the overall design. The innovative and imaginative structures, and the dialogue between the political and social aspirations of the time made it a reference around the world.

However, this approach was questioned by a group of architects from São Paulo from the late 1950s. Led by João Batista Vilanova Artigas, the Paulista School movement included architects such as Paulo Mendes da Rocha, Pedro Paulo de Melo Saraiva, Marcello Fragelli, Abrahão Sanovicz, João Walter Toscano, and Ruy Ohtake, among others. While Niemeyer attempted to resolve the country's contradictions through a harmonious and formal synthesis, Artigas revealed the conflict of this struggle using geometric lines, exposed raw concrete, and a heavier aesthetic.

03

During the dictatorship, Artigas was a member of the Brazilian Communist Party, and his work embodied his political ideologies. The Faculty of Architecture of the University of São Paulo, conceived in 1961, is one of the most archetypal examples of his approach. It is a masterpiece of the brutalist movement and exemplifies the extraordinary juxtaposition of light and weight that Artigas achieved. The structure appears to hang miraculously in the air. The building and the school of architecture inside it suggest a society that favors shared experience over private space.

Although Niemeyer and Artigas are the architects most revered by historians, figures such as Affonso Eduardo Reidy, Carmen Portinho, the Roberto brothers, Flávio de Carvalho, and Rino Levi were also influential in this golden age of Brazilian modernism (1930–1960). The Italian-born architect Lina Bo Bardi dedicated much of her career to intense research on Brazilian popular culture and promoting the social and cultural potential of architecture. She was responsible for several projects that had a major impact in Brazil, including the São Paulo Museum of Art (1968), the Sesc Pompéia (1977), and the Oficina Theater (1984).

Broadening the Discourse

In the 1980s, when the dictatorship and the supposed "economic miracle" came to an end, and the process of establishing a democracy began, Brazil suffered an economic recession and monetary crisis. Subsequent governments attempted to control inflation and stabilize the economy, primarily by reducing investment in social programs. This precariousness, the scarcity of public resources, and the lack of a unifying language led to architects assuming different trajectories to maintain their professional practice, sometimes building on the heritage of modernist concepts and occasionally deigning to criticize them.

Architect Paulo Mendes da Rocha created prefabricated reinforced concrete structures, reminiscent of the structural poetics of the Paulista School. In Minas Gerais, architects Éolo Maia, Jô Vasconcellos, and Sylvio de Podestá built projects such as Vale Verde School (1983) and the Tancredo Neves Tourist Center (1985), upsetting many with their postmodern bias.

João Filgueiras Lima, also known as Lelé, transformed the aesthetics of industrial structures while prioritizing construction efficiency and

04

sustainability. Severiano Mário Porto conceived a unique model of sustainable architecture that combined traditional methods developed by indigenous Brazilians with modern and innovative architectural approaches. The exploration of new materials and construction techniques became more commonplace among architects from the 1990s onward.

Most of the social housing in Brazil focuses on the building itself, without consideration of the specific characteristics of the site.

05

In parallel, social and political issues led to an acute housing crisis. In response, radical initiatives by groups such as Usina-CTAH, a collective of architects and researchers, offered leadership, advice, training, and support to community-led dwelling movements across Brazil.

In the early 2000s, greater economic stability inspired a period of hope and political renewal, and consecutive governments made vigorous efforts to combat social inequality. However, the reality has not changed significantly enough, and homelessness is still a massive problem. One of the most interesting movements fighting homelessness is the occupation of abandoned buildings, such as the Nove de Julho occupation in São Paulo organized by the City Center Homeless Movement. In addition to housing, it is a community center with cultural and educational activities, and a community kitchen. Occupations such as this make us rethink the way we occupy our cities.

The quest for an egalitarian society also requires a critical review that questions the dominance of white male architects highlighted by the history of architecture. In Brazil, organizations such as the Arquitetas Invisíveis (Invisible Women Architects), Arquitetas Negras (Black Women Architects), and Terra Preta Collective—all created by women and linked to issues of gender, race, urban segregation, priviledge, or even access to architecture services—are important in transforming the way architecture is practiced in a country where over 53 percent of the population is not white and more than 63 percent of architects are women.

Architecture as Infrastructure

Contemporary Brazilian architects have learned from twentieth-century architects about the value of architecture for society. The Unified Educational Center (CEU), in São Paulo, is one of the most representative contemporary works of architecture as infrastructure. Since 2003,

04 Casa de Vidro, a Modernist villa designed by Lina Bo Bardi and bulit in Sao Paolo Brazil.
05 Chamber of Deputies Annex and National Congress, Brasilia, Brazil.

While Niemeyer attempted to resolve the country's contradictions through a harmonious and formal synthesis, Artigas revealed the conflict of this struggle using geometric lines, exposed raw concrete, and a heavier aesthetic.

architects Alexandre Delijaicov, André Takiya, and Wanderley Ariza have developed educational complexes in deprived areas that offer a combination of educational, cultural, and sporting facilities. São Paulo currently has 46 CEUs and serves more than 120,000 students of all ages.

Most of the social housing in Brazil focuses on the building itself, without consideration of the specific characteristics of the site. However, two projects subvert this with infrastructure that protects from flooding and landslides. The linear Residencial Parque Novo Santo Amaro (2009) designed by Hector Vigliecca and the urbanization project Cantinho do Céu (2008) by Marcos Boldarini transformed precarious areas while creating public leisure space.

It is increasingly necessary to understand the public dimension of architecture beyond that commissioned by the state. Privately funded projects, with different scales and functions, can have a significant impact on social and urban life. A key example is the recreational center Sesc 24 de Maio, designed by Paulo Mendes da Rocha in association with MMBB Arquitetos, that incorporates an abandoned commercial building. The public dimension is amplified by a ground floor that opens up to the city.

The Importance of the Site

The connection between architecture and site is the second important strategy found in contemporary architectural language and practice. Whether in urban or natural landscapes, the search for an authentic and intimate relationship with the surrounding environment manifests itself in myriad ways, from the suspension of buildings, free access to the ground floor, and varied routes enabling new spatial experiences to the use of local materials and minimal interference with the terrain to reduce environmental impacts, among others.

One of the solutions developed to integrate internal and external environments is known as the "pavilion system." The benefits of this system include avoiding large earth movements and providing spaces with few divisions and external claddings to maximize views of the surroundings. Barra do Sahy (2002), realized by Nitsche Arquitetos in São Paulo, and Vila Rica (2017), by BLOCO Arquitetos, in a rural area of Brasília exemplify this approach.

The 239 House (2016), by UNA Arquitetos, in São Paulo has a more introverted identity. Even so,

06 Downtown Sao Paolo from inside the Praca das Artes.
07 Niterói Contemporary Art Museum in Rio de Janeiro, designed by Oscar Niemeyer.

Whether in urban or natural landscapes, the search for an authentic and intimate relationship with the surrounding environment manifests itself in myriad ways.

Marina Pedreira de Lacerda is an architect and urbanist, who graduated from Mackenzie Presbyterian University. She has a master's degree in Architecture, Technology and the City from the State University of Campinas and a specialization in Strategic Design from Istituto Europeo di Design in Sao Paulo. She works as a professor and as a member of the editorial team of the scientific magazines of Escola da Cidade.

Pedro Vada is an architect and urbanist, who graduated from the Escola da Cidade and is currently a master's candidate at the University of Sao Paulo. He works as an editor and professor, and also develops urban research and projects in both the public and private sector.

it responds to its site, as all of the windows face onto a central courtyard where there is a 50-year-old jaboticaba tree. Similarly, the facade of the Unileão Special Civil and Criminal Court (2016), built by Lins Arquitetos Associados in Juazeiro do Norte, is interspersed with typical *cobogós* tiles that offer privacy while filtering the air and light.

The relationship between building and site is explored through the connection with the ground at São Paulo arts centers Praça das Artes (2012), by Brasil Arquitetura, and Moreira Salles Institute (IMS-SP, 2017), by Andrade Morettin Arquitetos. The structure of Praça das Artes connects narrow streets in the city center with a completely open ground floor. IMS-SP opens to Paulista Avenue with a ground floor that functions as an urban hall. While Praça das Artes alludes to the formal language of Lina Bo Bardi's architecture with its pigmented concrete, the IMS-SP building proposes a new relationship with the city with its self-supporting translucent glass facade.

In Brazil, most of the renowned architects mentioned here understand the fragility of our society. Their work demonstrates ways to fight poverty, violence, and unstable democracy. The singularity of each project is emphasized by the uncertain context in which the architects exist and how they respond to it. With this in mind, it is possible to recognize some common expressions in contemporary Brazilian architecture: a certain identity that, even if sometimes clumsy, reacts to the instabilities of Brazil by seeing architecture as infrastructure and acknowledging its relationship with its environment. The uncertain political, social, and cultural circumstances determine the programmatic, formal, and structural stability of architecture that aims for its spatial strategies to take on another symbolic dimension. This is something that will permeate the mind of many architects in contemporary times.

07

Nature and Material on Exhibition

Architect Arquitetos Associados
Project Claudia Andujar Gallery
Location Brumadinho/Brazil

Swiss-born Brazilian Claudia Andujar photographed indigenous tribes in isolated forest locations, so building a gallery dedicated to her work in the botanical gardens of Inhotim, Brazil, one of the largest outdoor art centers in Latin America, was fitting. The collaborative practice Arquitetos Associados conceived the design. Based in Belo Horizonte, its ongoing research into architecture and its relationship to its surroundings allowed the studio to produce an expressive response to the enveloping forest of trees.

"The main aim of our design was to guarantee harmony between building and environment," explains architect Alexandre Brasil, one of the studio's partners, "considering the best way to integrate it into the forest."

The team achieved this by inserting the building at the highest point of a hill, allowing the sloping topography to dictate the views from every angle. The structure is divided into four volumes—one tucked into the land while the other three hover off the ground, accentuating the views in different directions.

The separate areas facilitate a considered curation of Andujar's photographs, with a pause between them. Corridors connecting these spaces offer visitors verdant vistas and access to gardens and the internal patio. The combination of natural and artificial light adds to the invigorating gallery experience. "We wanted an interplay of light and shadow, with vertical lines that allude to the woodlands around the building," says Brasil.

This idea becomes clear as visitors navigate their way through the vegetation to reach the building. Its limited color palette and materials—bricks, concrete, wood, glass, and stone—play into the natural setting. The double-kiln-fired blocks covering the structure were handmade by local expert Pedro Alves dos Santos. Set in such a way that some stand out in striking lines, they add texture to the walls and mimic the linear pattern on the wooden decking.

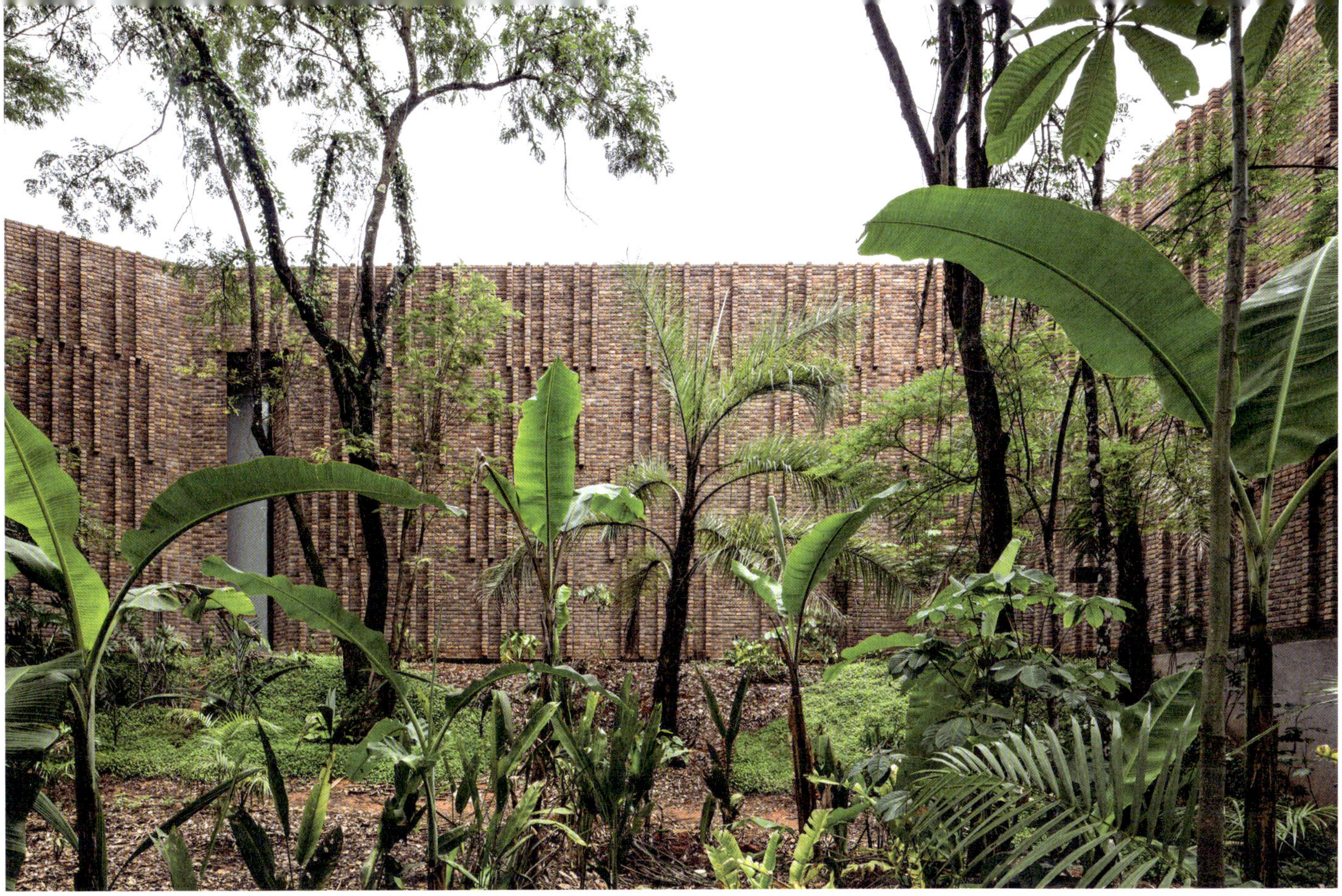

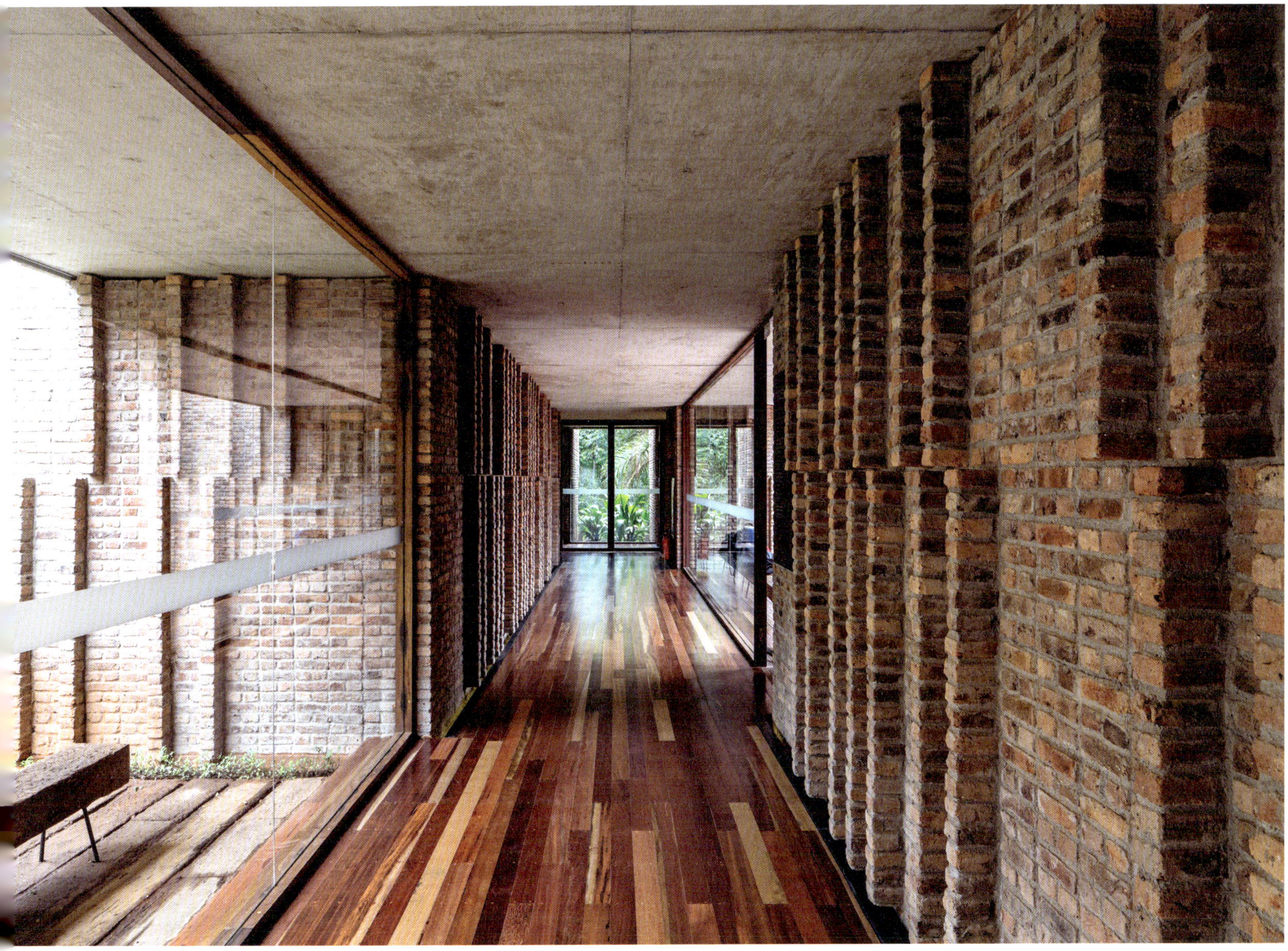

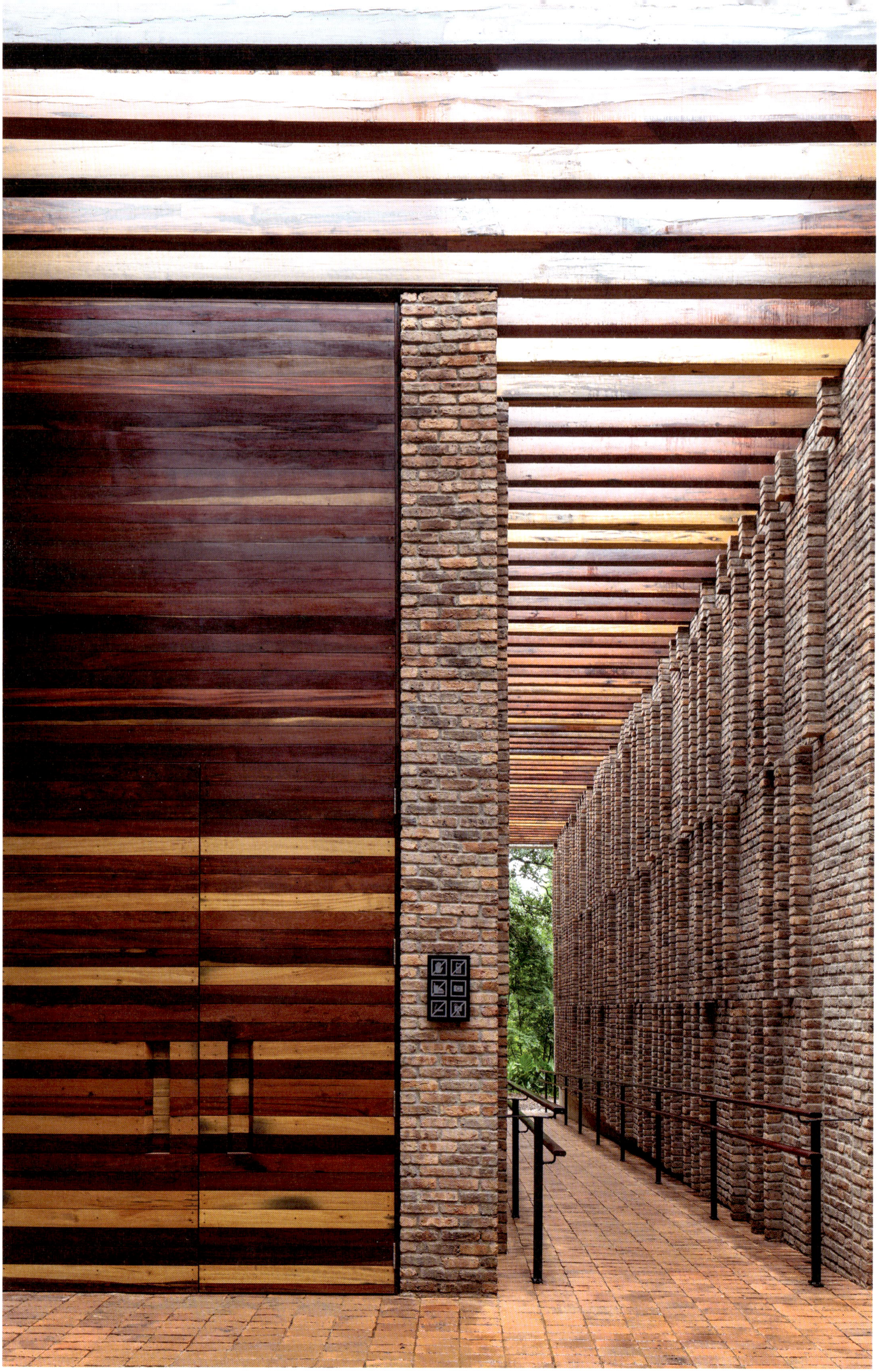
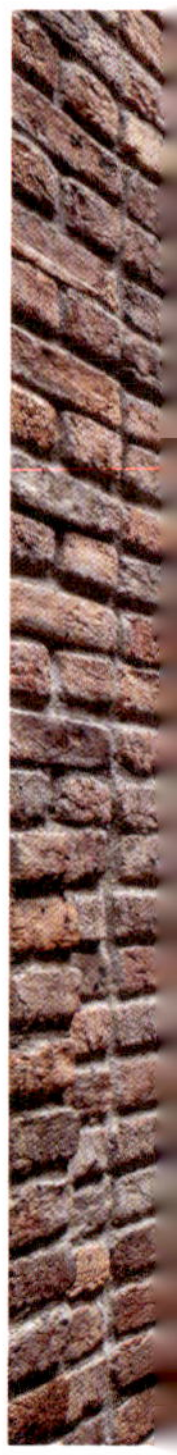

"We wanted an interplay of light and shadow, with vertical lines that allude to the woodlands around the building."

All of the materials have been chosen specifically for the range of natural tones they bring to the finished design—clay tiles, rich timbers, and the red-brown brickwork. They mirror the shifting tones in the barks of the surrounding trees.

In the opening ceremony, Native Americans christened the gallery Maxita Yano, meaning "clay house." The soft colors of the brickwork blend seamlessly with the building's natural surroundings.

Claudia Andujar Gallery

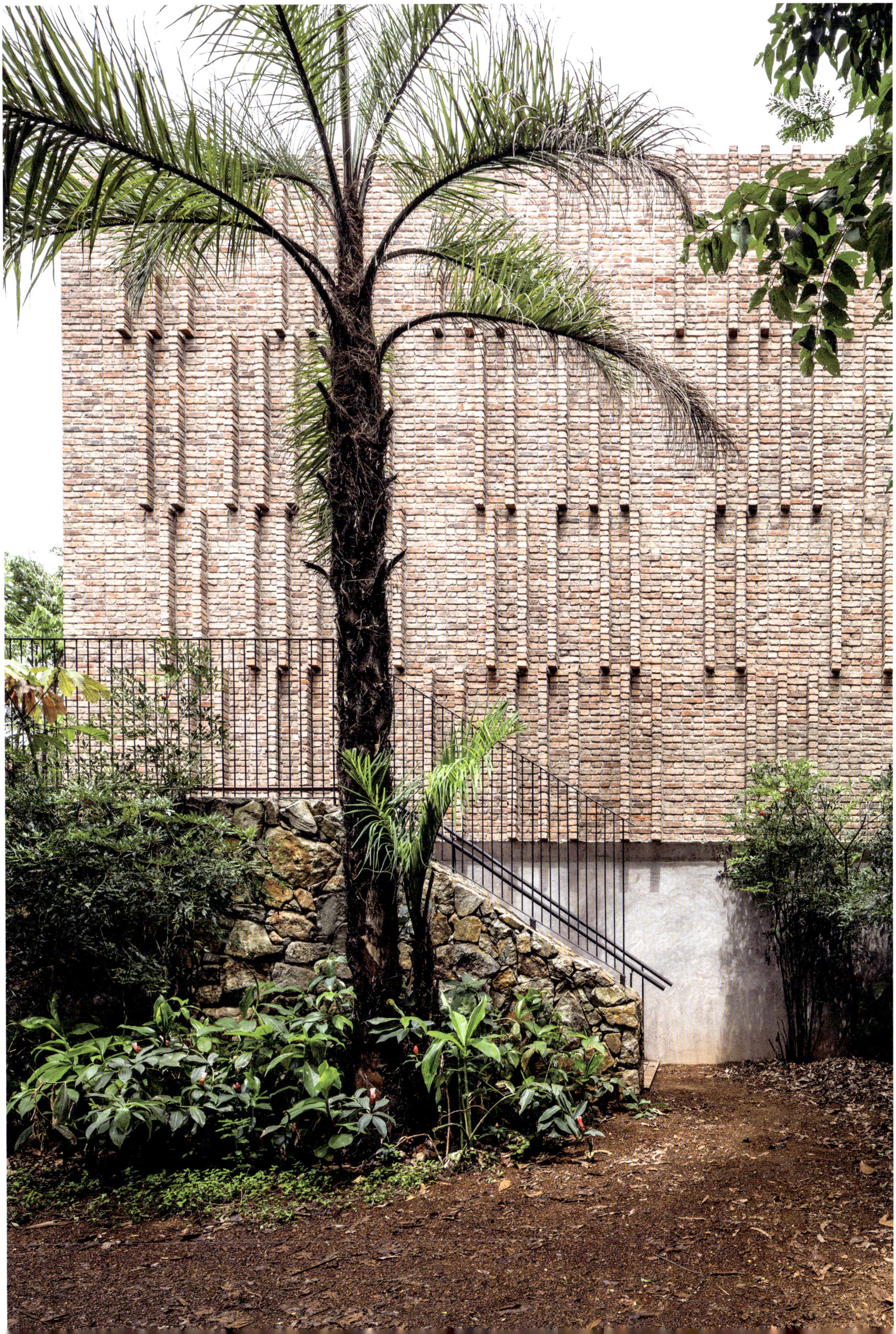

Native Materials Take on New Form

Architect Campana Brothers:
  Fernando + Humberto Campana
Project Zunino House
Location São Paulo/Brazil

Fernando and Humberto Campana, the Brazilian siblings behind design studio Campana Brothers, are committed to using native materials and reviving traditional handicrafts in their practice. Their design for a family home in São Paulo satisfies a brief to blur the distinction between outside and inside using materials and techniques that maintain a continuous dialogue with nature, space, and natural light.

The Campanas sought inspiration from the traditional *oca* structures in Brazil—large indigenous houses covered in bamboo, straw, or palm leaves. Here, they used piassava, a palm fiber originating from the northeast of the country. It shields the interiors from harsh sunlight and adds textural intrigue to the facade.

The long, narrow plot required a rectangular structure that would capture as much natural light as possible. Each of the four levels are treated individually with flooring that showcases various species of salvaged wood. Above an expansive first-floor garage, the second-floor living room has hardwood floors reclaimed from the house that was previously on the site. Above lies the guest and children's bedrooms, with wooden flooring from a *futsal* court in Minas Gerais. The floor of the master suite on the top story is laid with timber from a farm in Londrina. Sunlight streams through a transparent section of the roof, and it leads to a private terrace shielded by mandacaru cacti, commonly used for fencing in the Brazilian countryside.

The home's open staircase is flanked by a voluminous leather-clad bookshelf that leads from the first floor to the top story and acts as the spine of the building, around which everything revolves.

Outside, the focal point is the perimeter wall, which is painted in green and covered with climbing fig, making the house appear to float like an island in a pool of greenery.

Throughout the design are juxtapositions of modernity with tradition and nature—to the front of the house, the facade coated in grass and, to the rear, smooth plastered walls with plate glass and a metal grid-like balustrade.

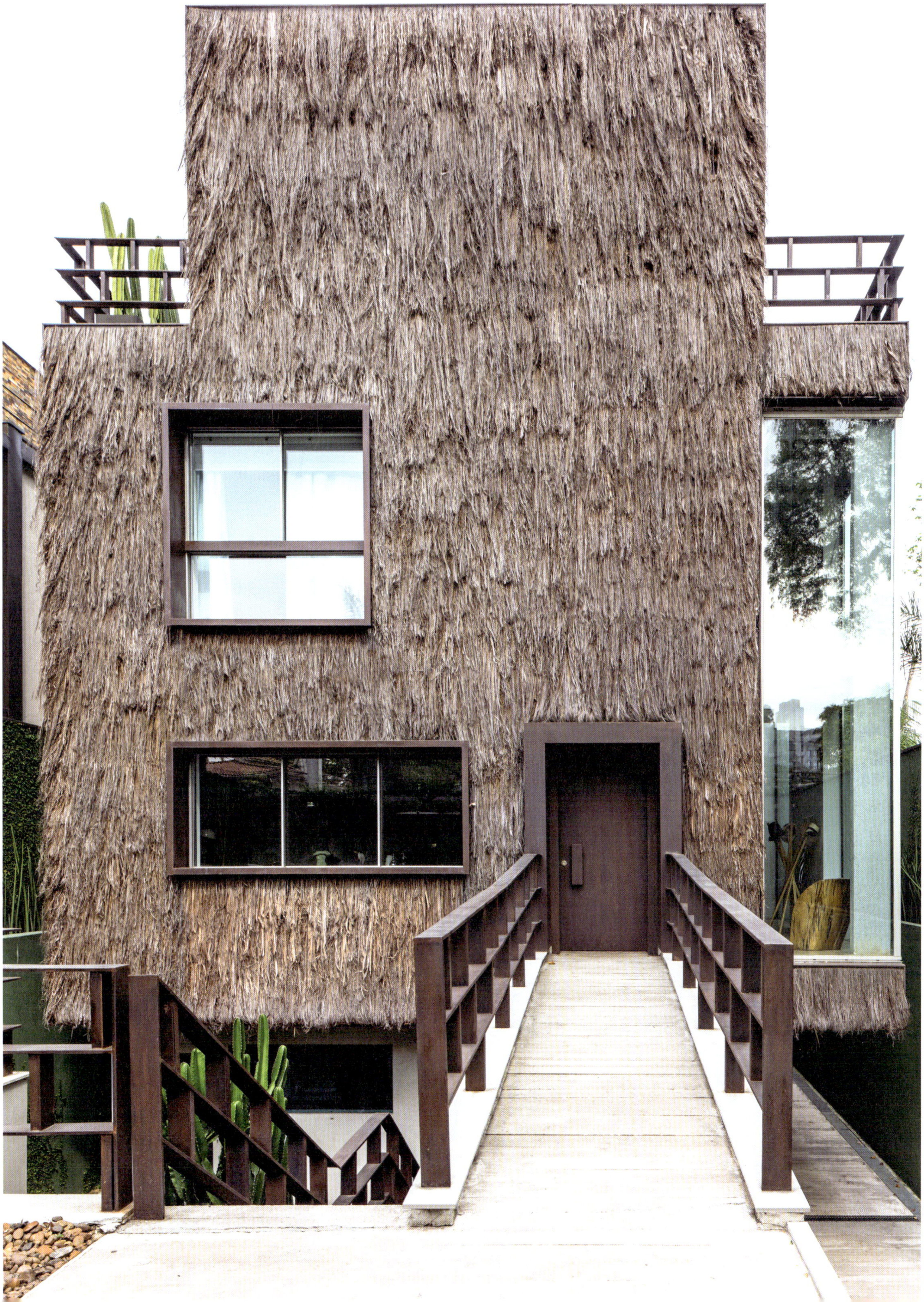

The Campana brothers describe the leather-clad bookcase as being like a vegetable that invades the house. In tandem with the brothers' commitment to the use of natural materials and traditional handicrafts in their practice is their passion for modernity. Functional rooms—the garage, kitchen, and bathrooms—are clean, hi-tech, and bold in their use of materials (marble, mosaic tiling, concrete) and color.

Zunino House

The home's open staircase is flanked by a voluminous leather-clad bookshelf that leads from the first floor to the top story and acts as the spine of the building.

Using the Sun as a Building Material

Every day during sunset, a cross is formed on an interior wall of Saint Bernard's Chapel in La Playosa in Cordoba, Argentina. Soon after, the vertical and horizontal arms of the cross begin to separate and disappear. The chapel was conceived by architect Nicolás Campodonico, who uses natural light as one of his primary materials.

"Architecture needs to be seen as transformative," he says. "Light, material, and space can change into new forms." It's a personal definition that guides the Rosario-based architect's work.

In Saint Bernard's Chapel, he transformed the 100-year-old brickwork of the original rural house into the building blocks of the intimate oratory. Located in the Pampa plains, there is no forest or stone in the area, and Campodonico wanted to use materials authentic to the location.

"What you have in abundance is soil, and brick is the combination of soil, water, and fire, so the brick is a natural material from this place," he says of the method he chose to construct and clad the building. The earthy tones of the box-like facade and its curvaceous interior walls thus reflect the environment as the sunlight transforms the brick. "Nature makes its own rules here," Campodonico says.

He used natural sunlight to full advantage in this sacred place of deep reflection, applying it in a very considered manner to deliver a reminder of Christ's crucifixion every day.

Vertical and horizontal poles, placed separately on an elevated exterior opening, project individual shadows onto the curved interior wall, changing position as the Sun moves. Their meeting in the formation of a cross mimics the cross on which Christ was crucified. Conceptualized around the hypothesis that Jesus carried the horizontal pole on his way to be crucified, the moment when the two poles meet thus marks the culmination of this journey.

Architect Nicolás Campodonico
Project Capilla San Bernardo
Location Cordoba / Argentina

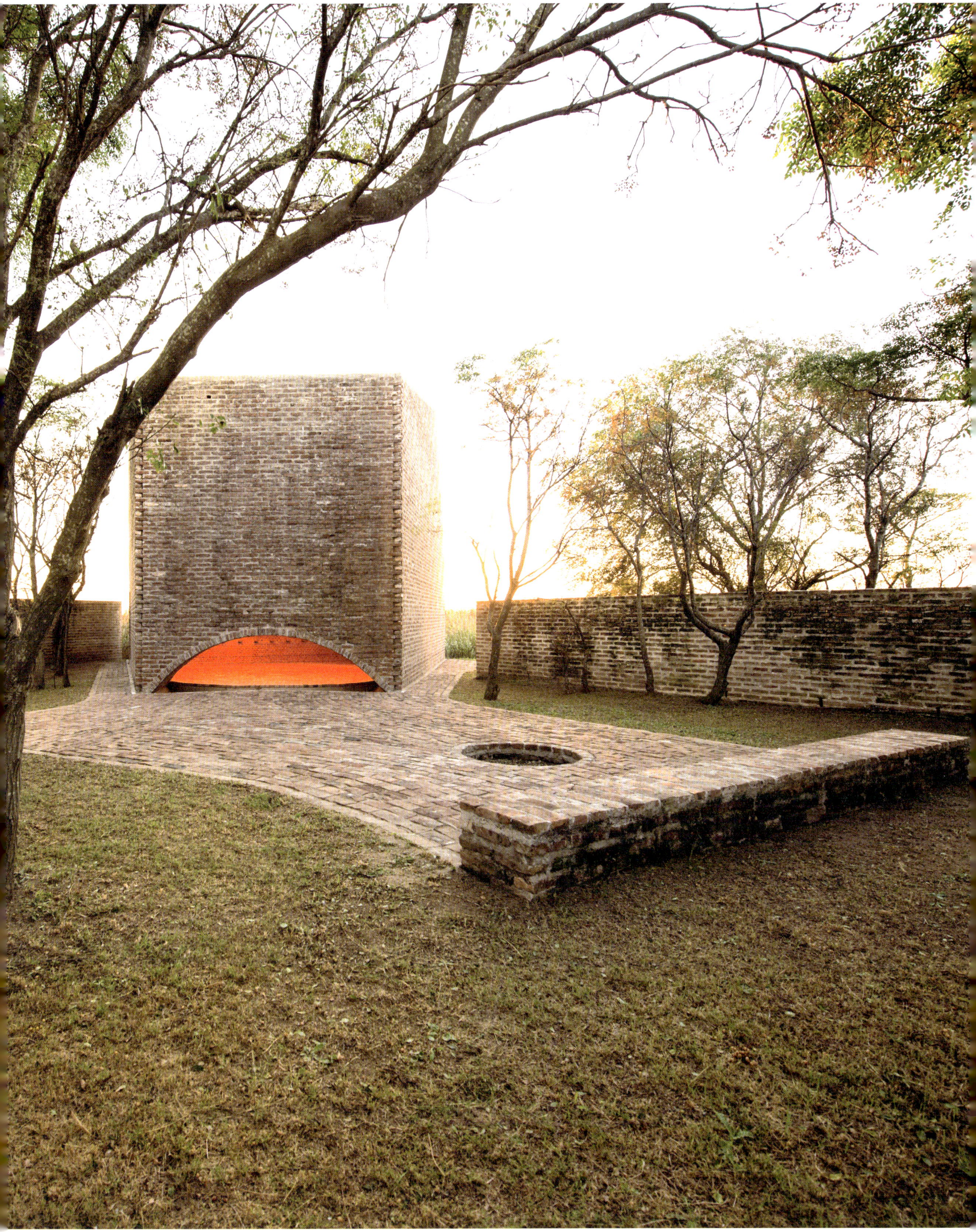

180   Capilla San Bernardo

The minimalist design of the exterior belies not only the sheer size of the space within, but also the complexity of the church's sculptural interior.

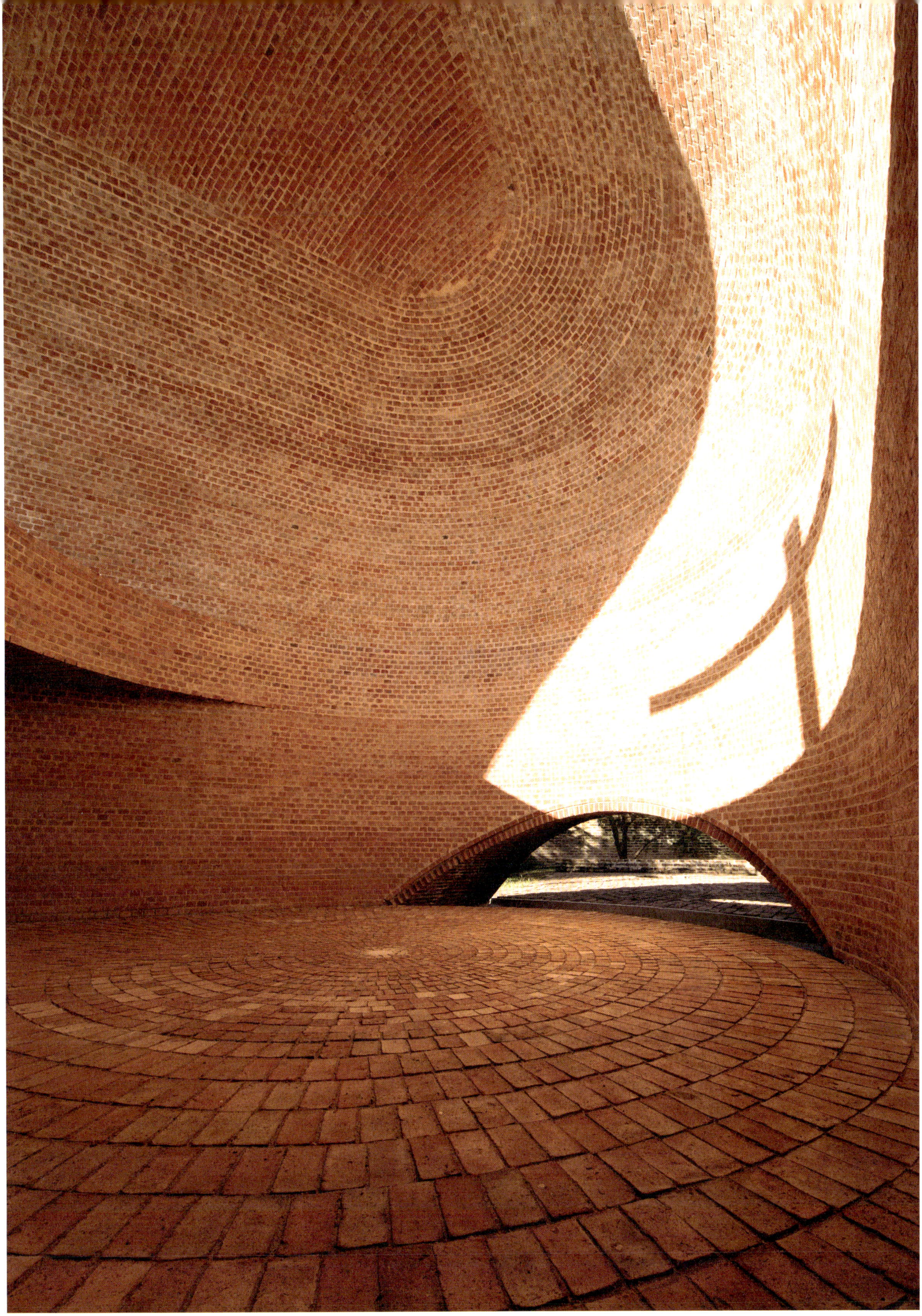

The earthy tones of the box-like facade and its curvaceous interior walls reflect the environment as the sunlight transforms the brick.

Capilla San Bernardo

The temporal existence of the crucifix's shadow as it moves across the bare-brick walls of the church lends gravitas to the spirituality of the space.

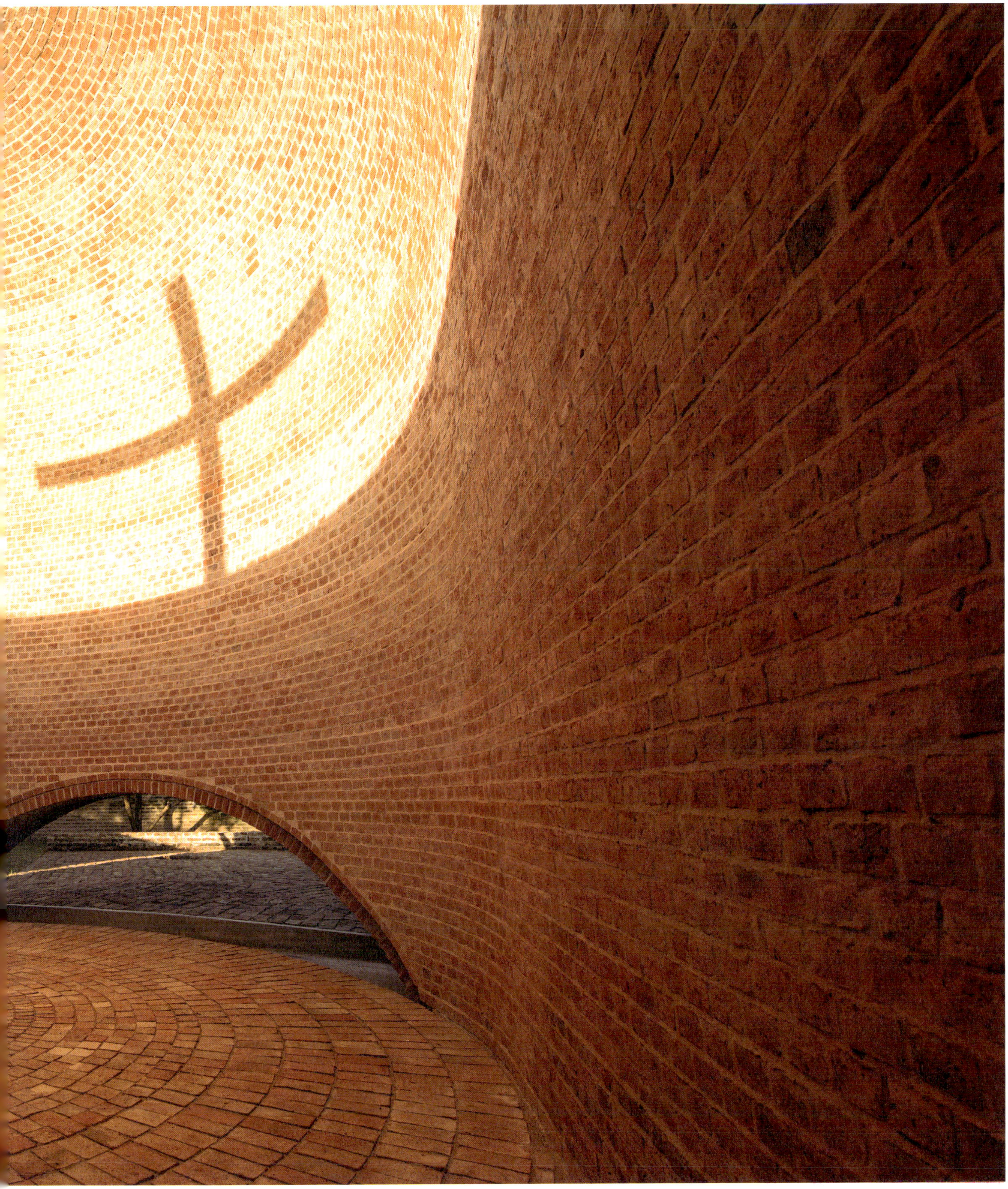

Opposites Balance an Island Home

Eugenio Ortúzar and Tania Gebauer make up Chilean architecture firm Ortúzar + Gebauer Arquitectos. Their studio is based on the island of Chiloé, where this expansive family home is also located. Eager to develop sustainable responses to living linked to the cultural and geographic environments of their projects, the studio designs buildings that have a strong relationship with their territory, culture, climate, and users. One way it achieves this is by using wood from the region, immediately connecting the architecture with its natural surroundings. This two-story house is no exception: the design employs reclaimed native wood for wall coverings, flooring, doors, and window frames. The main staircase comes from a long-gone traditional Chiloé house.

The structure is on a narrow plot of flat land on the island's hilly terrain, along the waterfront of an estuary. The concept capitalizes on the dramatic vantage points by compacting and angling the building's volumes to highlight particular aspects. The facade's floor-to-ceiling glass panels offer panoramic views of the serene aquatic landscape and allow it to blend into the hills behind, making it disappear from a distance.

From the rear, the home is equally unobtrusive, as it mimics the silhouettes of the region's traditional sheds and iconic wooden churches. Weathered, recycled zinc plates create the impression that the barn has always been there, and the solid facade provides the homeowners with complete privacy. The top level of the property overhangs the first floor, offering protection from the elements. The roof unifies the visually opposing elements of the house, giving no indication of the two extremes presented by the facades. It extends over a portion of the terrace, allowing daily life to flow easily outdoors, no matter the weather.

Architect Ortúzar + Gebauer Arquitectos
Project Pollo House
Location Quemchi / Chile

There is a deliberate attempt to make the house look rustic and timeworn, with its rusty corrugated paneling and chunky timber frame.

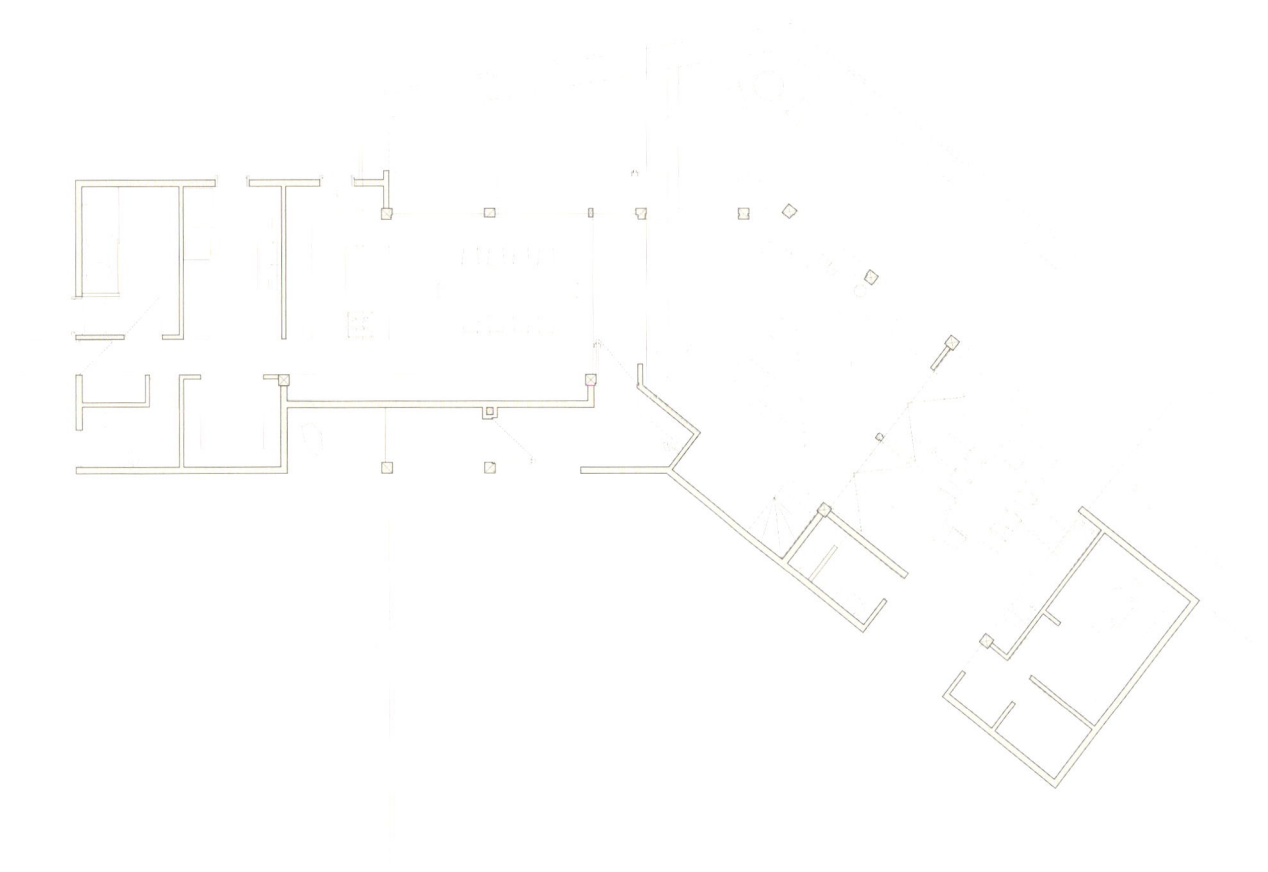

The floor plan of the house illustrates how the front elevation projects out from the rear elevation by several feet in each direction, the whole building following the lie of the land.

186 Pollo House

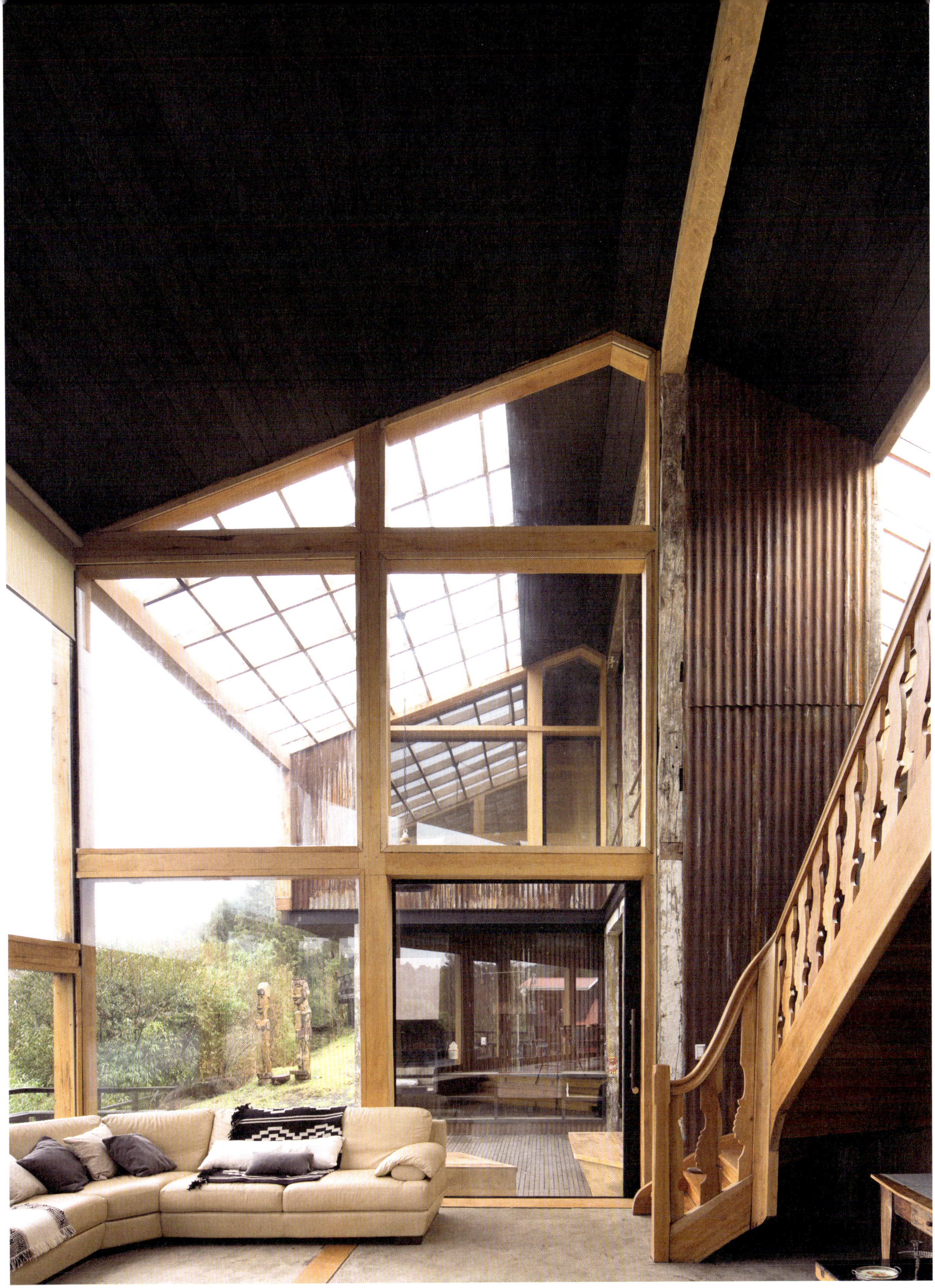

> The concept capitalizes on the dramatic vantage points by compacting and angling the building's volumes to highlight particular aspects.

While construction materials are in many ways traditional, the living quarters are resolutely contemporary. Fully glazed on the front, a vast double-height volume provides a communal gathering area that spills out onto open, partially covered decking.

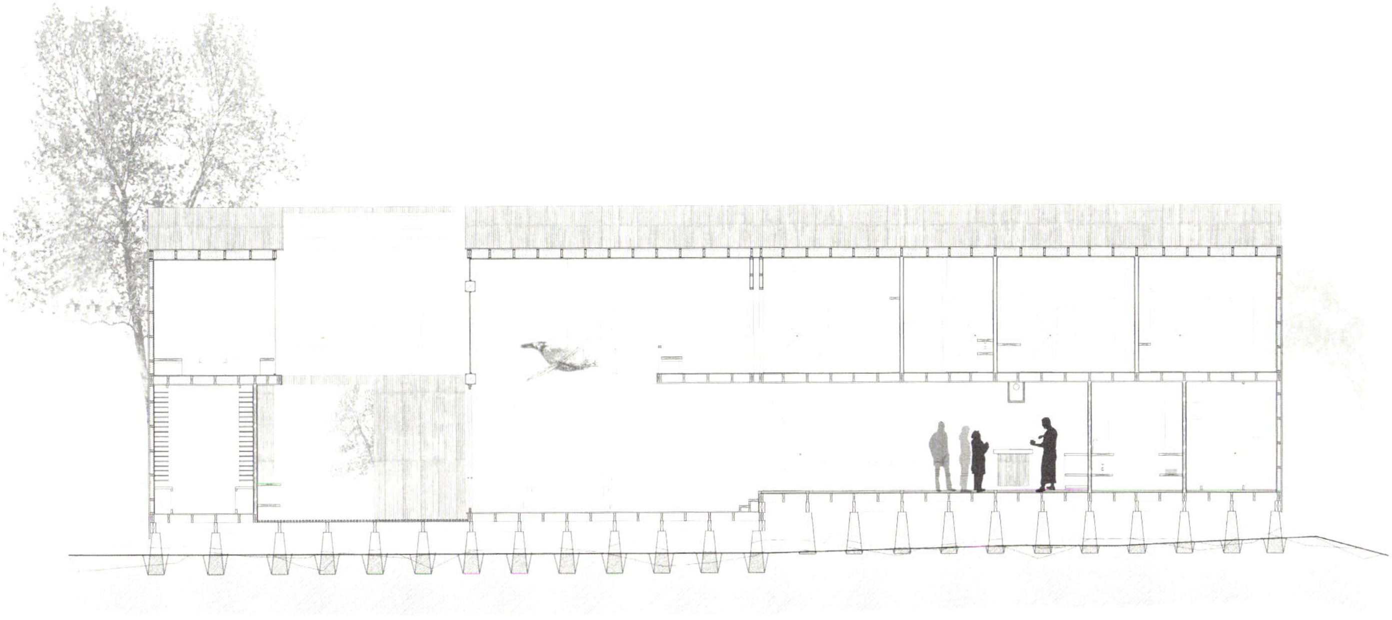

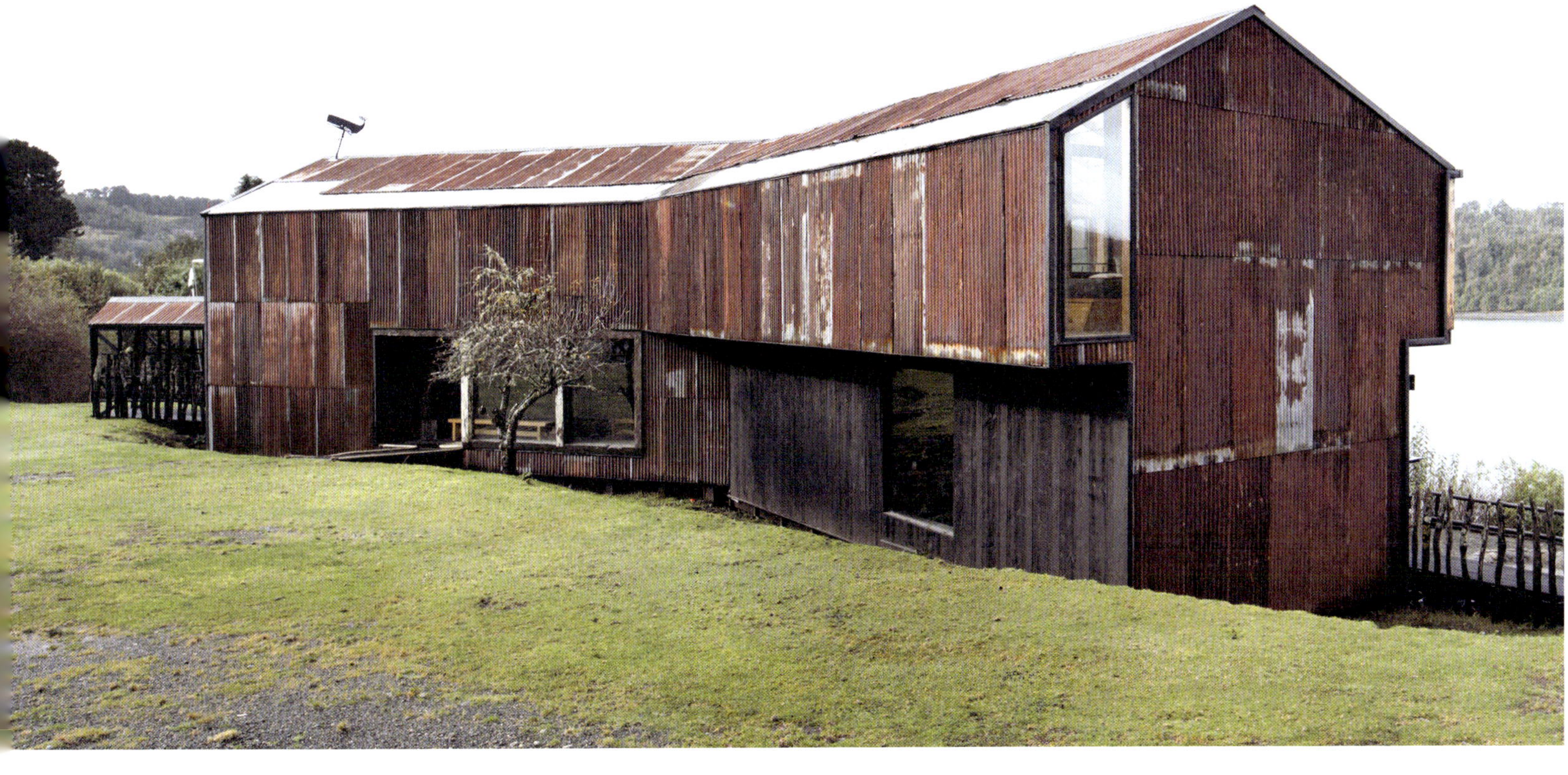

Cabins Camouflaged in Natural Reflections

Sacromonte Landscape Hotel is part of a boutique winery situated on the remote rolling hills of Maldonado, Uruguay. Thirteen contemporary hospitality "cabins" dot the undulating vineyards, reflecting the landscape and highlighting the serene isolation of the location.

MAPA, a creative studio that describes architecture as its "field of action," is recognized for creating novel materials while sensitively combining digital technology with natural realities. It made its mark on this project by designing structures that camouflage themselves from a distance but offer pleasant surprises close up.

"Sacromonte has a landscape of lush grassland, natural spring water reservoirs, and streams, surrounded by pristine vegetation, offering guests a wide range of scenarios," the architects explain.

The visual journey is literally and metaphorically reflective, with circular pools adding to the multisensory experience. Glimmering one-way mirrors cover the front of the cabins. By day, they reflect the landscape and weather conditions, while, at night, the interior lights blend in with the Milky Way, which is clearly visible.

In contrast, the facades at the rear are made from layered logs—a nod to the piles of wood typically found in such rural settings. The circular pattern of the logs is juxtaposed with the organic shapes of the local stones used for the low walls that serve as the foundation's base.

The steel carcasses of the cabins were prefabricated in less than 10 weeks in a factory in Montevideo, another example of MAPA's bent toward material efficiency and functional transformation. "When these modular metal structures leave the factory and the city, they cease to exist as such and become landscape shelters," say the architects. "They are no longer objects. Rather, they evolve into experiences."

Architect MAPA
Project Sacromonte Landscape Hotel
Location Maldonado / Uruguay

At dawn and dusk, especially, the cabins melt into the landscape, their mirrored facades reflecting the vast expanse of open sky.

Sacromonte Landscape Hotel

Seamless glazing provides those within the cabins with uninterrupted views across the rolling Uruguayan landscape.

The circular pattern of the logs is juxtaposed with the organic shapes of the local stones used for the low walls that serve as the foundation's base.

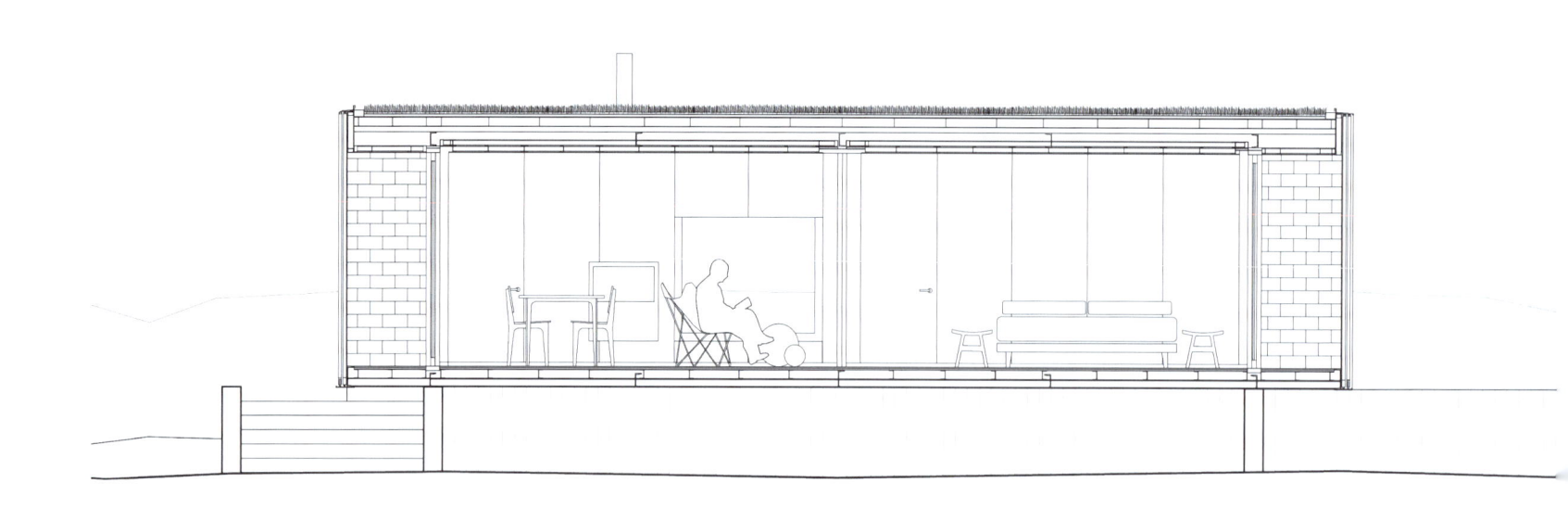

194 Sacromonte Landscape Hotel

Each cabin is, essentially, a rectangular volume split lengthways. To the front of the divide is one continual living space for sleeping, lounging, and dining. To the rear of the partition are the service spaces—kitchen, bathroom, and other utilities. Though the buildings themselves are nothing more than modular boxes, the low walls on which they stand and the shape of the decked areas follow the lie of the land so that the cabins nestle comfortably within the landscape.

Indigenous Group Gains Unique Language

The "New Andean Architecture" of Freddy Mamani has shaped the identity of El Alto in Bolivia, where the former bricklayer has fashioned over 60 buildings. Mamani's "cholets" (a name combining "chalet" with "cholo," a derogatory term for an indigenous person) are vibrantly colored edifices decorated in geometric acrylic paneling, glossy chrome, and reflective glass. They are an exuberant response to the social and economic power gained by the previously marginalized indigenous community in the region. A renaissance in native culture swept the country in 2005, when the first president from an indigenous population was elected.

In a city dominated by bland brick structures, the cholets are architectural emblems for the local Aymara people, the group to which Mamani belongs. "I did it as a cultural, economic, and social assertion through architecture," he explains, linking the paneled patterns inserted on the structures to the iconography found in the pre-Hispanic Tiwanaku ruins. "We're not afraid of showing our colors," he says of the Aymara people. He explains that his choice of bold shades—from fuchsia and sunset orange to cobalt and apple green—is inspired by the *aguayo* cloths used by Bolivian women to carry items on their backs.

The interiors are equally eclectic, with columns painted in an array of hues. Hand-sculpted and painted plaster-molded ceilings, neon LEDs, mirror paneling, and spectacular chandeliers add to the radical maximalism. These multi-use buildings often hold a retail space at street level, with a ballroom above for hosting events, and higher levels usually contain apartments.

The cholets have become symbols of cultural pride for a community once oppressed and persecuted. "This is a form of protest," explains Mamani, "because through architecture, we're showing who we are, what we want, what we like, and what we have." In addition to their unique dances, music, dress, and language, the Aymara now possess a distinct architectural style.

Architect Freddy Mamani
Project Neo-Andina
Location El Alto / Bolivia

Mamani's designs incorporate recognizable motifs and colors from historic and
archaeological sites, reviving them on a scale—and with a flair—never seen before.

Neo-Andina

While incorporating visual elements and colors from historic indigenous styles, Mamani's architecture also displays echoes of twentieth-century Asian architecture and Hollywood grandeur.

His choice of bold shades—from fuchsia and sunset orange to cobalt and apple green—is inspired by the *aguayo* cloths used by Bolivian women.

The exuberant facades and interiors present a very visual demonstration of the wealth and status of a new, indigenous, urban generation that is thriving on mining, industry, and international trade.

A Grid of Columns and a Roof: A Brief Overview of Architecture in Southeast Asia

Heat and the desire to escape it. These two factors have shaped much of the architecture in this region. While glass-enclosed air-conditioned volumes offer one way to do it, architects are increasingly opting to blur the lines between inside and out with lush greenery to keep cool.

01

Tropical Narratives and Urban Realities

Every society has a narrative or an indigenous structure that describes the origins of its architecture. In the Western world, it is Marc-Antoine Laugier's mythical primitive hut, where architectural elements are depicted as derivatives of nature—tree trunks as columns, branches as beams and roof.

02

Southeast Asia is a complex region. Although it comprises just 11 nation-states, it is culturally rich, with more than 100 ethnic groups spread over a territory encompassing 10,000 islands. Bearing in mind the diverse religious beliefs, complex colonial histories, and varied urban environments, is it possible or fruitful to establish an overarching perspective on the region's architecture?

Instead of taking a historical approach, I will look at two key factors that have influenced the way architecture is practiced and produced throughout the region. The first is the tropical narrative and its urban realities, and the second is the impact of global education and professional networks on architectural practice and experimentation.

01–02 The Hindu temple copmlex at Angkor Wat in Cambodia; this tradition was later merged with Modernist principals in what became known as "New Khmer Architecture".
03 Oasis Terraces by Serie Architects in Singapore.

In Southeast Asia, the origins of contemporary tropical architecture can be traced back to the indigenous Iban longhouse in Borneo. This traditional home consists of a row of rooms connected by a linear gallery, which acts as a communal space accommodating family gatherings, food preparation, festivities, and even funerals. Naturally ventilated and unglazed, the living area is elevated, and a large gable roof spans the entire building, sheltering inhabitants from tropical rain.

It is no coincidence that the roof is a primary element in Southeast Asian architecture. Apart from protecting inhabitants from the elements, the roof defines the internal living spaces, and the wide overhang creates an intermediary space between interior and exterior. However, tropical living conditions are not always compatible with, or desirable for, contemporary lifestyles. Large roof overhangs remain a common design feature in homes across the region, but interiors are typically enclosed with glass windows to allow inhabitants to enjoy air-conditioning.

Projects that resist hermetically sealed environments, such as Indonesian architect Andra Matin's houses and Durian Shed by Malaysia-based WHBC Architects, are an exception rather than the norm. One of the most innovative contemporary housing projects in Singapore is the Highland Road house by Linghao Architects. The two-story terraced house has been stripped to a bare minimum and boldly demonstrates harmonious tropical living. Communal living spaces are completely open to the elements, and the bedrooms are set back from the shared party wall to encourage ventilation throughout the building.

Beyond the physical structure of tropical buildings in the region, the use of plants as a design element has become increasingly popular. The single-family houses designed by Vo Trong Nghia (VTN) Architects in Vietnam and institutional structures by WOHA in Singapore exemplify this trend. While the "greening" of buildings has been decried by skeptics as greenwashing, VTN Architects uses plants in a manner that relates to a way of life, particularly within the dense urban fabric of Vietnamese cities. Aside from the obvious benefits of enhancing passive cooling and solar shading, the plants used in residential projects such as Stacking Green, House for Trees, and Binh House in Ho Chi Minh blur the boundaries between interior and exterior living spaces. These projects are conceived as climatically responsive prototypes that create microclimates and increase biodiversity, rather than merely "green" houses.

What differentiates a green Southeast Asian building from its global counterparts? To put it simply, the main difference between Stefano Boeri's Bosco Verticale in Milan and WOHA's Kampung Admiralty in Singapore lies in urban density and the pressures of urbanization in Southeast Asia. While Bosco Verticale is designed to produce energy, Kampung Admiralty is a public building with various communal, commercial, medical, and residential functions. It is the manifestation of a high-density tropical urban environment, and can be traced back to experiments with megastructures in the region during the late 1960s, when buildings were conceived as a series of "city rooms" that could be connected to other parts of the city.

Early experiments with megastructures became urban architectural models that have been furthered by various architects in Singapore over the years. From the communal voids of WOHA's Dawson public housing and School of the Arts to the large roof enclosures of Serie Architects' Punggol Oasis Terraces and NUS SDE4, they all aim to create breathable sociable tropical environments.

Inspired by global dialogues on megastructures and also by the Japanese Metabolist movement, a group of young architects—William Lim, Tay Kheng Soon, and Koh Seow Chuan—from Design Partnership designed the Golden Mile Complex and the People's Park Complex as models that address the needs of contemporary Asian city dwellers. While adhering to megastructure ideals, these buildings are also tropical in design. Unlike

04

megastructures such as Sewoon Sangga in South Korea or Nakagin Tower in Japan, they were intended to create social spaces and permeability, rather than focus on building technology.

Global Networks: From Nation-Building Experiments to Corporate Offices

While architects in Southeast Asia share a similar set of responses to the climatic and urban environment, is it possible to make connections in terms of networks and lineage? Can architects in the region be classified according to the teacher-apprentice lineage like the Japanese system, as observed by architecture professor Thomas Daniell, or to the political compass, as observed by architect Alejandro Zaera-Polo?

While certain lineage or collective positions do exist, they are generally fluid and less dogmatic than in other regions. Rather than indulging in theoretical investigations or seeking disciplinary autonomy, architecture in Southeast Asia tends to embrace the realities of the environment and industry. Using Le Corbusier's Maison Dom-Ino as an example, *pilotis* in Southeast Asia are simply a response to climate and social practices. Therefore, it is also not surprising when Japanese architect Fumihiko Maki commented, "We theorized, and you people are getting it built!" in response to the construction of the People's Park Complex.

Such a pragmatic approach can be tracked back to the efforts of a pioneering generation of architects in the region who established a new post-colonial national identity while addressing the pressures of urbanization and navigating the complexities of Cold War geopolitics. Although they were educated within specific colonial networks, their colonial influences were focused on educational pedagogy, technical capabilities, and systems thinking, rather than aesthetics.

Singaporean architect William Lim's humanist and urbanist approach, illustrated by his megastructure projects, can be traced back to his educational experiences with Alison and Peter Smithson at the Architectural Association and Jaqueline Tyrwhitt at Harvard.

Similarly, Cambodian architect Vann Molyvann's education in France and the influence of Le Corbusier can be seen in his use of cast concrete. Many of his buildings, particularly the National Sports Complex, also reveal his deep understanding of ancient Khmer waterways and the symbolic composition of the Hindu temple complex Angkor Wat. This merging of tradition with modernist principles gave rise to what is known as "New Khmer Architecture."

Indonesian architect Frederich Silaban's Dutch *bouwkunde* technical education was key to his pragmatic design for Istiqlal Mosque, Indonesia's national mosque. By carefully placing precast solar shading behind thin, repetitive columns, Silaban cleverly combined monumentality, nationalism, and a tropical sensibility in a single gesture, without traditional or colonial references.

Extensive material and typological experimentation during the early nation-building period contributed to the transformation of small architectural practices into large corporate firms, and small-scale itinerant groups of builders into professional construction companies across the region. The research and development of a modular construction system carried out by the Public Works Department in Malaysia, for example, led to the invention of the Standard Office Block, a generic office typology with large roof overhangs that could be readily replicated.

Experimentation with thin large-span roof structures for Subang Airport in Kuala Lumpur, Malaysia, by Booty Edwards and Partners, a private firm with British origins, led to further commissions for large-scale projects, prompting the formation of BEP Akitek. In Myanmar, the design of Rangoon University's Engineering

04 The Chaktomuk Conference Hall in Phnom Penh, Cambodia, designed by Vann Molyvann.
05 The ArtScience Museum at Marina Bay in Singapore, completed in 2011, it's architecture is inspired by a lotus flower.

College by British architect Raglan Squire led to experimentation with precast concrete ventilation panels. His practice subsequently developed into two successful large commercial practices—RSP Architects in Singapore and Squire and Partners in the UK.

Future Directions

Today, a new generation of architects is emerging. Unlike the pioneer generation, young practices today are not generally bound by ideological and political concerns. Globally connected through social media, architects are representing themselves online, and they are able to draw reference from their peers quickly and easily.

As more students are educated overseas, transnational networks are formed with affinities to global architectural discourse, rather than local culture and traditions. International education has also initiated a new crop of foreign practices in Southeast Asian countries. Vo Trong Nghia's decade-long education and work experience in Japan led to the establishment of VTN Architects with Japanese partners, who subsequently split from the company to form their own practices in Vietnam. The resulting firms, Takashi Niwa, NISHIZAWAARCHITECTS, and Sanuki Daisuke, are examples of Japanese architectural practices that are not geographically bound by traditional Japanese lineage.

In Indonesia, new architectural practices are forming as a by-product of an informal design cluster in Bintaro Jaya, a township in South Jakarta. Built during the 1980s and 90s, architecture and other design firms moved there to take advantage of low rent. A strong network between firms in the area led to the formation of the Bintaro Design District, an annual design festival celebrating creative output in the area.

While the region's architectural scene is gradually flourishing, it is crucial to address the challenges facing the built environment. Drawing inspiration from the "World Meetings" set up by Malaysian architect Lim Chong Keat and US architect and inventor Buckminster Fuller in the mid-1970s to bring architects from all over the world together to share common experiences and ideas, existing networks need to be further developed to rethink the role of architecture in addressing environmental, social, and political challenges facing the region. After all, the origin of Southeast Asian tropical architecture is premised on the typology of the Borneo longhouse, a radically simple enclosure that engenders social equality and protection against harsh natural elements.

Unlike the pioneer generation, young practices today are not generally bound by ideological and political concerns.

05

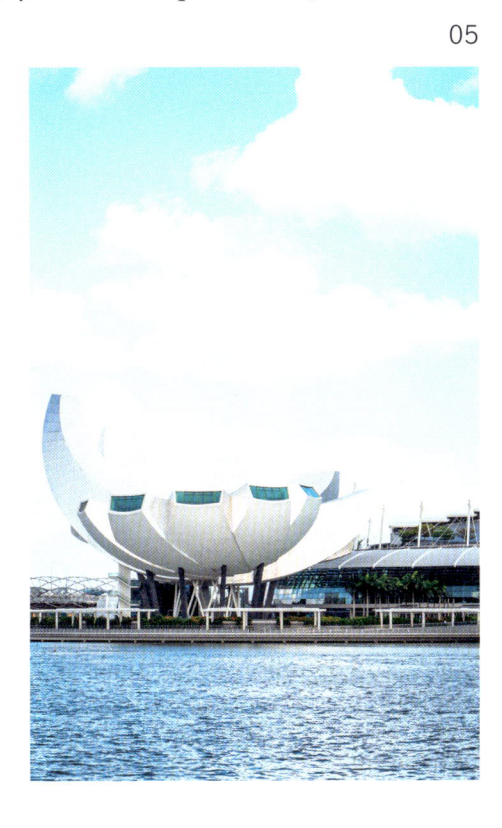

06

Calvin Chua is the founder of Spatial Anatomy, a Singapore-based firm that designs objects, spaces and strategies for cities. He also serves as an Adjunct Assistant Professor at the Singapore University of Technology and Design, leading studio research on peripheral territories in Asia.

Green Living in a Concrete Jungle

Architect WHBC Architects
Project Chempenai House
Location Kuala Lumpur/Malaysia

Taking inspiration from the tropical jungle around Kuala Lumpur, the design of this residential property incorporates the local ecosystem. The work of Malaysia's WHBC Architects, it is a concrete structure designed to capture dappled daylight while offering protection from direct sunlight and rainfall. The grid formation of the facade allows cooling breezes to travel through the interior spaces and invites the natural environment to penetrate living areas. "The perforated nature of the concrete structure allows the existing vegetation to grow into the volume of the house, thus softening the boundary between inside and outside," say architects Wen Hsia and BC Ang. These open rectangular frames sit at a depth of 3 feet (90 centimeters) to reduce the intensity of the sunlight entering the house. A series of concrete fins frame various openings to provide shade.

The sloping terrain of the plot allows most of the building to be raised from the ground, reducing dampness and humidity. This elevated position means that it sits among leafy canopies, offering an immersive experience for residents. The architects explain: "A seemingly heavy concrete box, it touches the ground lightly, places itself among the trees, and encourages the landscape to grow within it."

This environmental approach is particularly palpable in the swimming pool area and adjacent garden. Protected by the concrete volume and simultaneously cocooned by surrounding foliage, the extended horizontal position of these spaces maximizes the dense forest views. These vistas are equally captivating when approaching the house. A bridge, flanked by *Albizia* trees, leads to the entrance where a narrow walkway opens onto an internal courtyard and the main living space, the double-volume deck, and swimming pool. One level down is the garage and service area, while the top story houses the bedrooms with windows opening directly into the treetops.

The concrete grid creates a double facade on two sides of the house. The pool extends out beyond the living spaces so that the end is left open to offer panoramic views of the jungle outside.

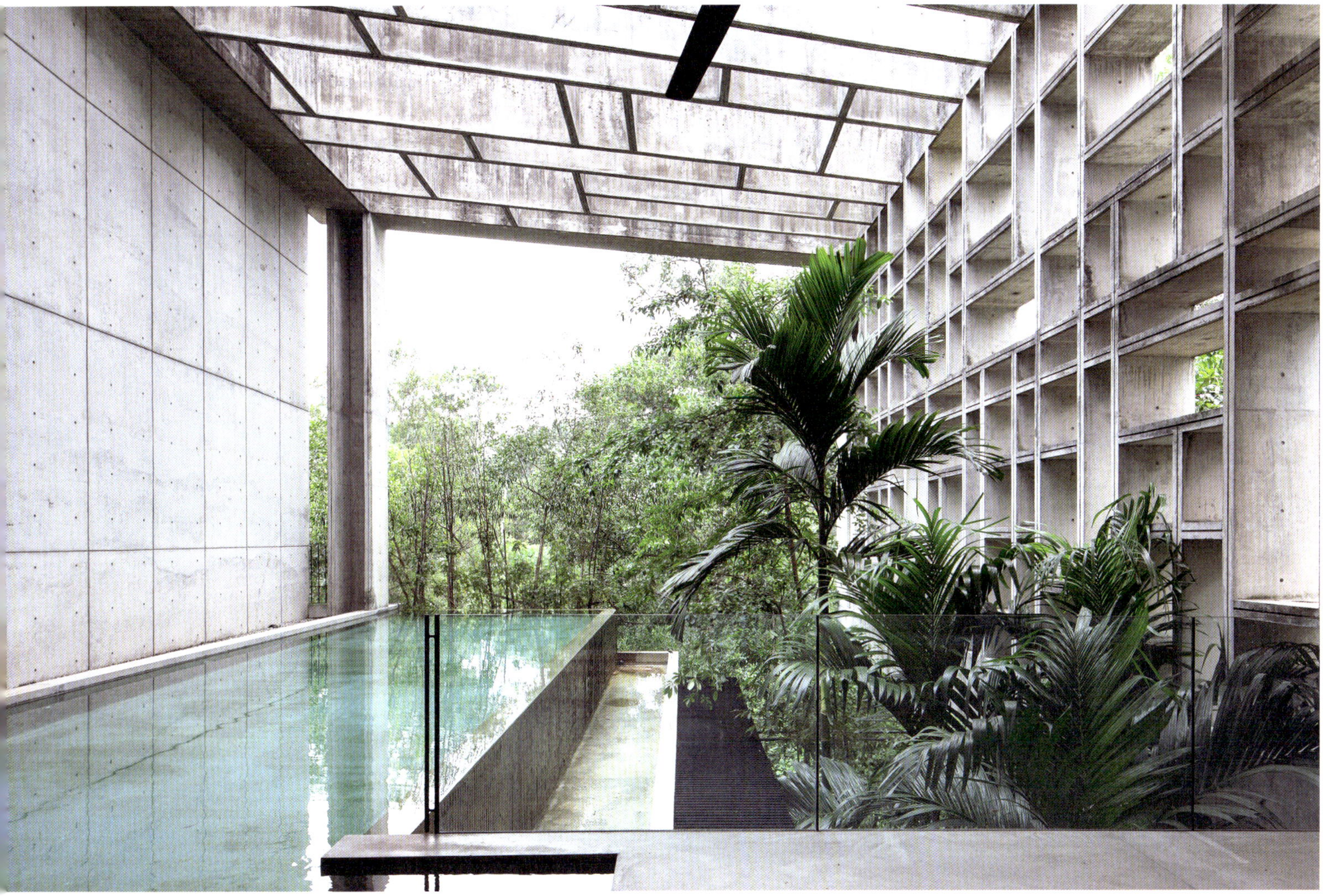

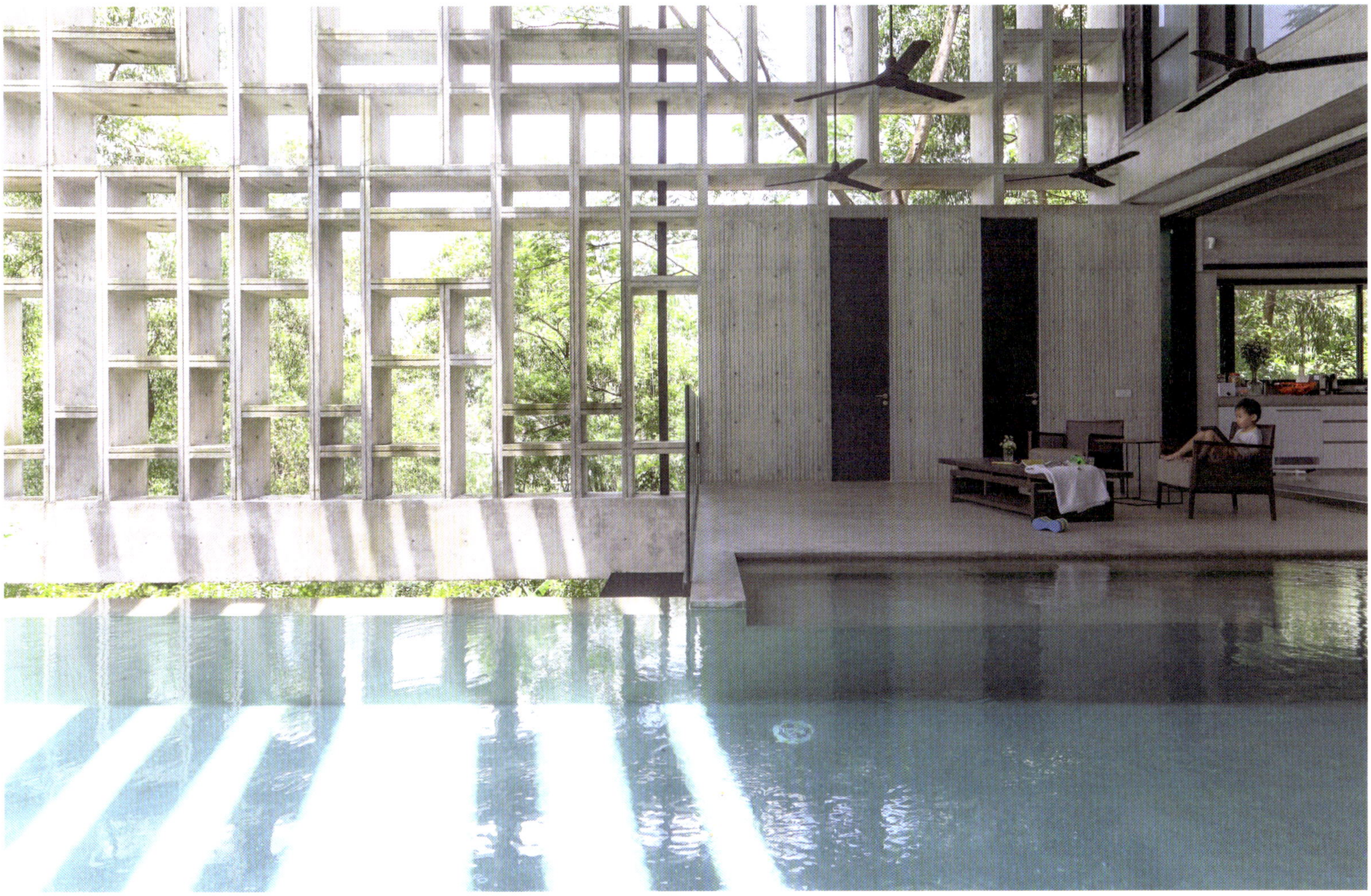

Protected by the concrete volume and simultaneously cocooned by surrounding foliage, the extended horizontal position of these spaces maximizes the dense forest views.

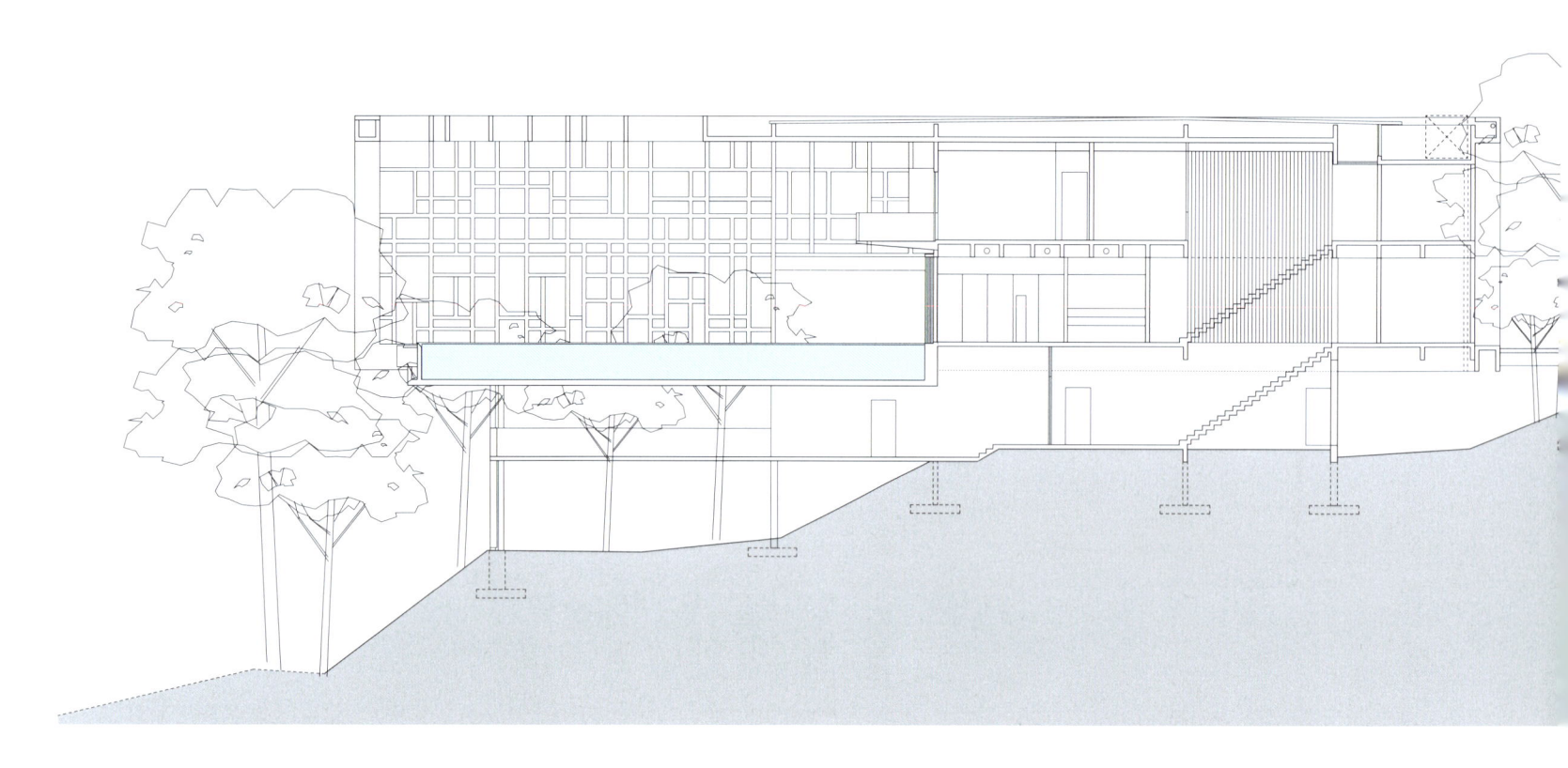

A side elevation of the house shows how it follows the natural lie of the land so that the entire communal space—living room, dining room, swimming pool—is raised off the ground on stilts. Concrete is the material of choice inside the house, as well as outside. The walls are left as raw concrete and complemented with highly polished stone floors and stairs in similar tones.

Chempenai House

211

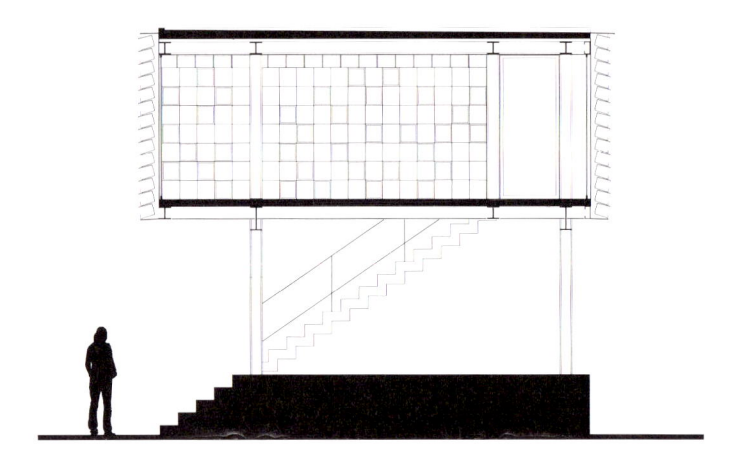

Meaning is Encoded in a Microlibrary

For multinational company SHAU, social and environmental responsibility are critical to every project it undertakes. So, it's apt that it produced a community "microlibrary" without disrupting the land on which it stands. Located in Taman Bima in Bandung, Indonesia, the library was constructed above an existing public-event stage. The city-owned site lies between middle-class housing and a less affluent village, meaning the library provides learning opportunities to a diverse community.

"Our intention was to add rather than take away," the architects explain. "We decided to enhance the open stage by covering it with the 'floating' library box, shading it, and protecting it from rain." The architects also relaid the stage and added steps that span its length.

I-beams and concrete slabs form the simple floor and roof structure, and over 2,000 white ice cream buckets make up the facade, placed between vertical steel ribs. This cost-efficient material shades the interior, and holes cut into certain buckets allow dappled daylight and air to pass through, naturally ventilating the interiors. Local artisans developed special tools to do the cutouts.

The buckets are tilted slightly downward to prevent rainwater from entering the building, and sliding doors inside the building can be closed during particularly harsh storms.

Equally well considered is the pattern in which the buckets have been placed, and the message they hold in their sequence. Cutout buckets represent "zeros," while closed buckets are "ones." Placed side by side, they form a binary code that embeds the phrase "buku adalah jendela dunia" (books are the windows to the world) onto the facade, repeating around the perimeter. This message is a metaphor for literacy, and the way symbols (or words in library books) become meaningful.

Architect SHAU
Project Microlibrary
Location Bandung/Indonesia

The buckets are arranged in such a way that the non-perforated vessels face in the opposite direction to those with holes. They represent "binary code" visually as well as symbolically.

This cost-efficient material shades the interior, and holes cut into certain buckets allow dappled daylight and air to pass through, naturally ventilating the interiors.

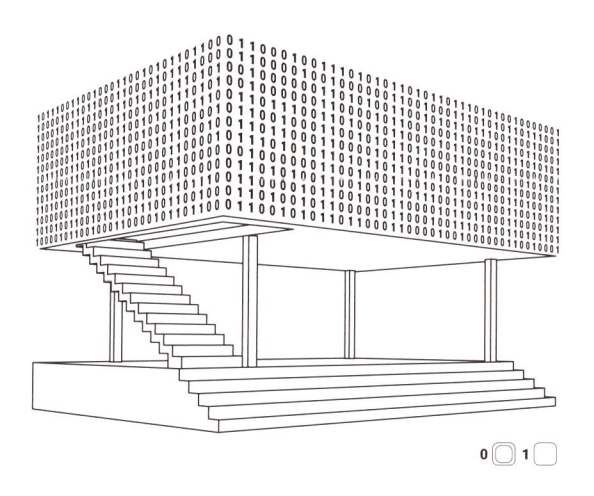

From a distance, the library's facade appears as if made from glass bricks. As you step into the room within, the effect is similar, with the bucket facade casting diffuse light that shifts as the sun moves across the sky. Lit from within at night, the facade sits like a lantern above the square, each of the buckets resembling a jewel-like light bulb on each "panel."

Microlibrary

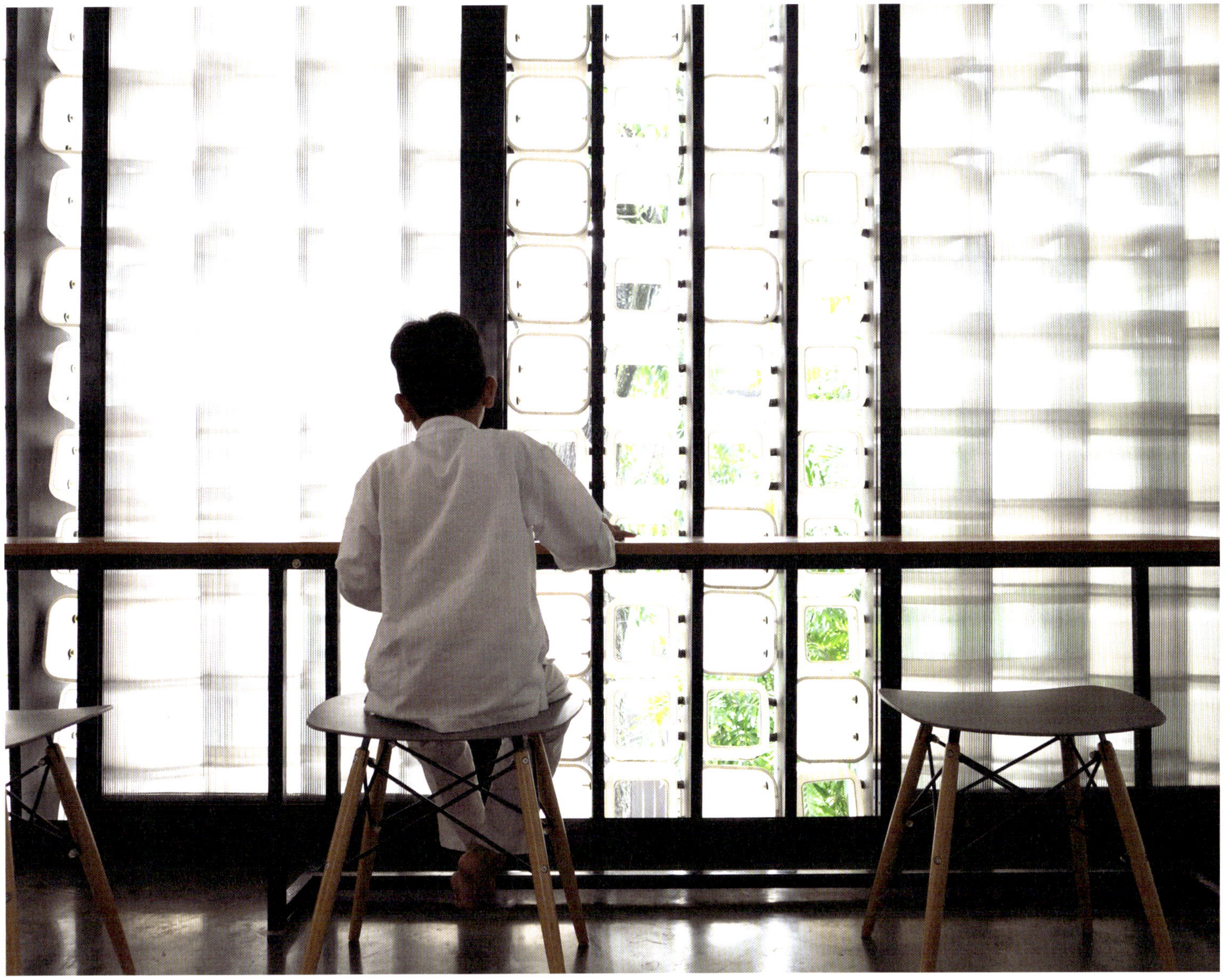

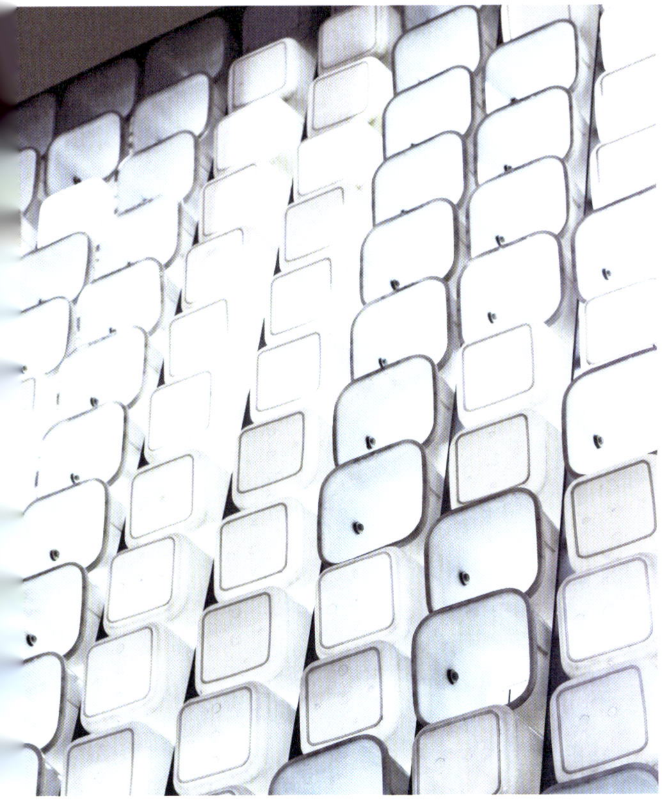

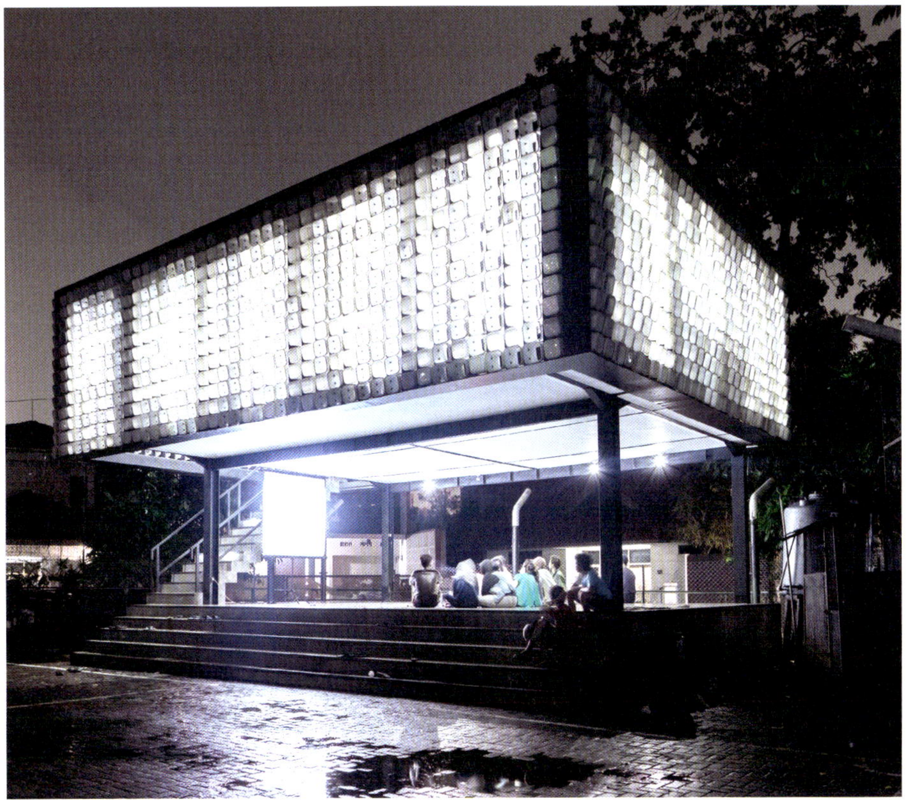

Plants Make Breathable, Healthy Walls

Architect   Formzero
Project   Planter Box House
Location   Kuala Lumpur / Malaysia

Malaysian architect Lee Cherng Yih founded architectural research studio Formzero intending to reintegrate urban architecture with tropical plants. He realized his passion in the home he designed for a retired couple in Kuala Lumpur, a structure covered with over 40 species of edible plants. Growing from concrete planters that form the building's facade, the plants make up an integral part of the couple's food supply.

"The house offers a sustainable, self-sufficient lifestyle," says Cherng Yih of the cross-ventilated low-energy abode that is at once a garden, house, and farm. The exterior features a split-bamboo texture, lending an organic feel while requiring minimal maintenance.

The planter boxes vary in size and layout, allowing plants to cascade over one another and forming green walls that can be appreciated from the open-plan interior with generous glazed windows and walls. Sunlight bounces through the leaves into the rooms, animating the walls.

The seemingly haphazard configuration of the interconnected planter boxes allows nutrients and water to pass from one to another, while also retaining stormwater and acting as irrigation reservoirs, meaning that the plants are nourished with minimal effort.

Outside, a box planted with a jasmine tree that originally stood on the land connects the property to the adjacent home. The recessed ground floor encourages public interaction, creating a thriving tropical landmark in the neighborhood.

The box planters create overhangs that cast shadows over the open terraces below—some of them deep enough for an entire room to be opened to the elements with little threat of penetration by direct sunlight or rain.

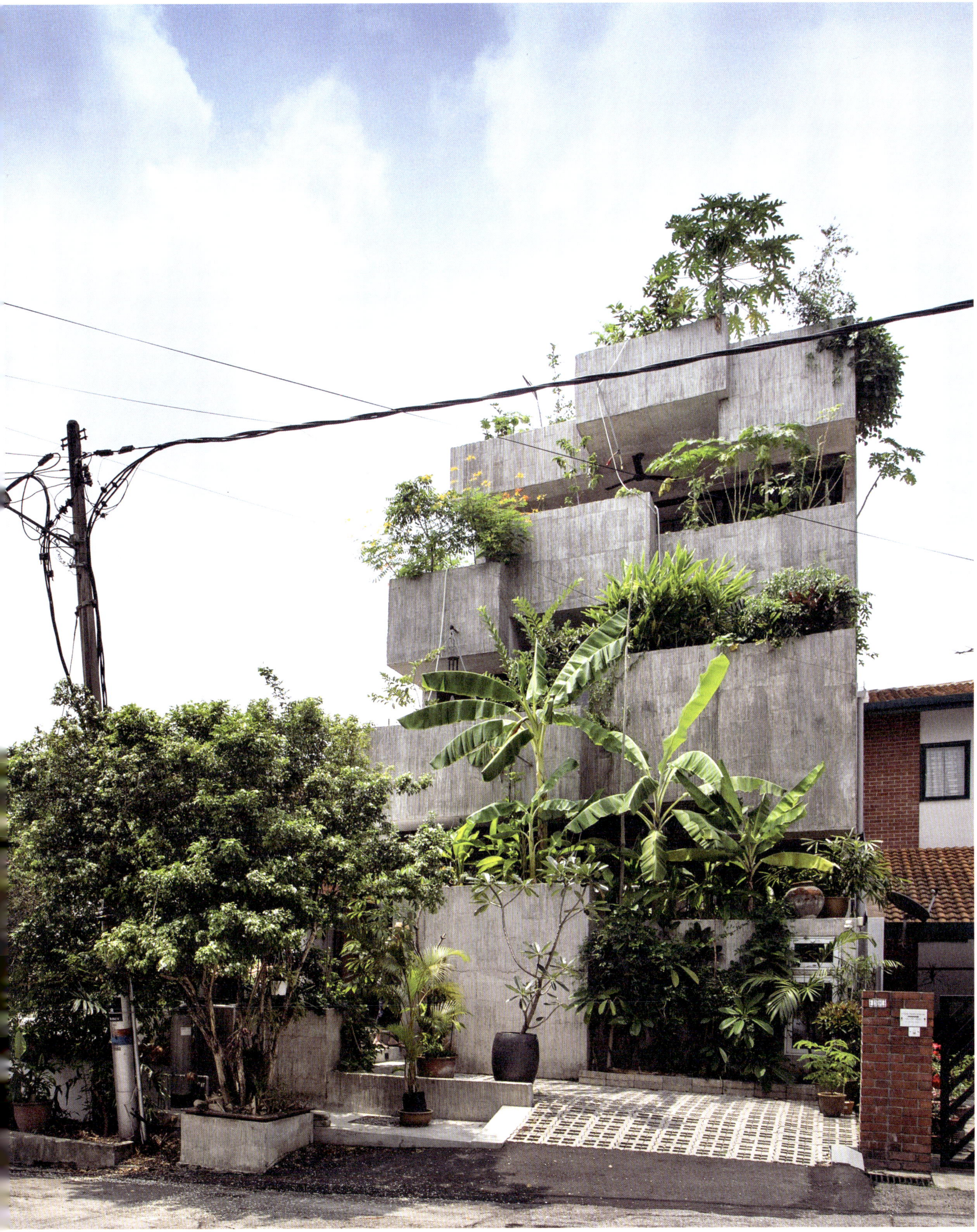

The recessed ground floor encourages public interaction, creating a thriving tropical landmark in the neighborhood.

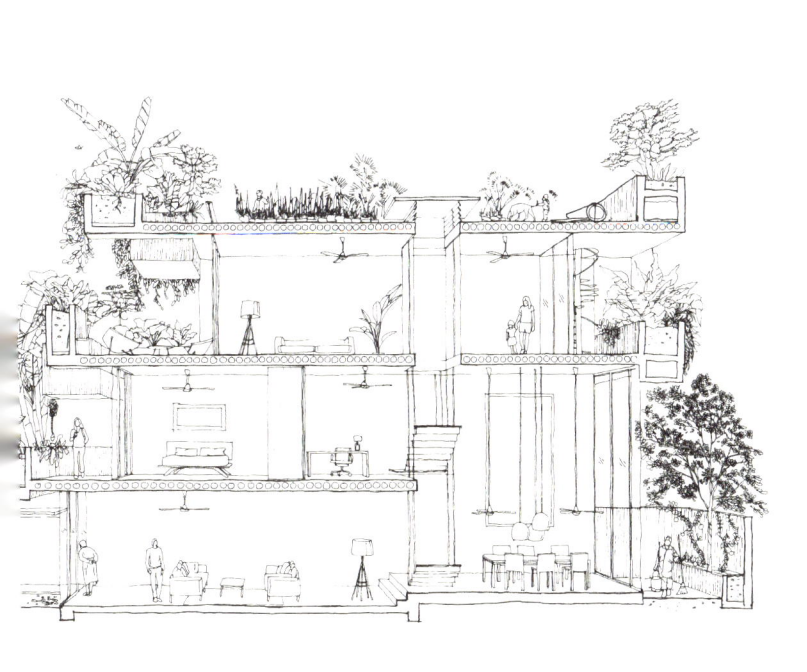

The voluminous interior combines double-height and single-height spaces, the different floors are accessed via a light and airy steel staircase that appears to float as it spans the width of the building. The mass of foliage sprouting from the box planters, as well as softening the rough-cast concrete of the facade, offers considerable privacy to the home's inhabitants.

Solutions for a Flood-Prone Landscape

Architect Palinda Kannangara Architects
Project Frame / Holiday Structure
Location Imaduwa / Sri Lanka

A Sri Lankan ethnomusician commissioned Rajagiriya-based Palinda Kannangara Architects to design a retreat for his family in Imaduwa in Galle, Sri Lanka, on ancestral land, which they had been forced to abandon due to constant flooding. He wished to reclaim it and renew his connection with the village where he had spent his childhood. The design needed to be cost-efficient, with a short construction period—before floods arrived—with little labor required. The building was completed in just two months.

"The structure attempts to negotiate a flood-prone landscape while making minimal impact on the environment," says architect Palinda Kannangara, whose practice focuses on experiential architecture that "hinges on simplicity and a connection with the natural environment." The transitory nature of the site necessitated the use of a steel exoskeleton, which makes the building resemble a viewing deck more than a home. It is easy to adapt, dismantle, and reassemble should the structure need to be moved to higher ground.

Three platforms—for living, dining, and a pantry—are connected to two separate bedroom wings with light bridges, angled toward views of the surrounding vegetation, creek, and distant mountains. There is reclaimed timber flooring inside and painted steel checker-plate flooring outside, along with a boardwalk constructed from reused scaffolding panels on galvanized iron tubes. "Very few walls exist, but where they are used in the bedroom, they are light-weight super-flex drywalls on timber frames," Kannangara explains. The only exception is the brick bathroom wall. Adjustable glass louvers surround the living area, allowing cross-ventilation and offering extensive views.

The home is integrated into the life and activities of the village, and connected to the surrounding farming community. Due to its elevated design, Kannangara says, "the everyday rhythm of the site has been retained," as villagers continue to use the land for their cattle, which graze under the structure, enjoying moments of respite in the shade.

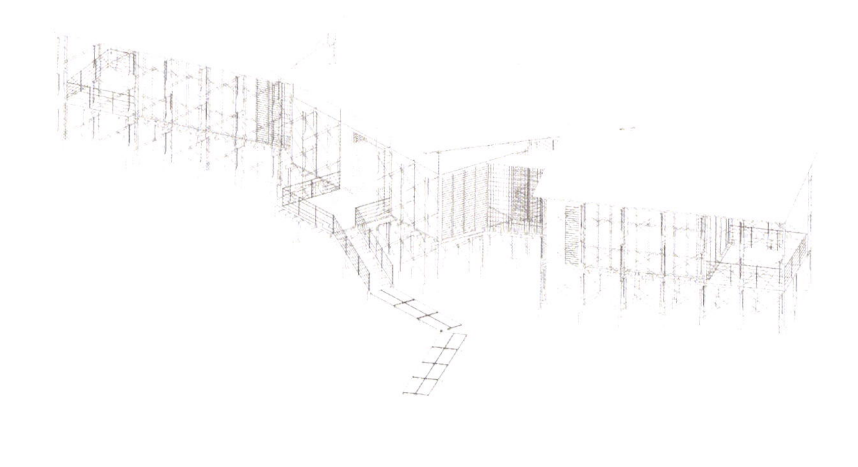

The dimensions of the house, and the rooms within it, are based on the modular length of the scaffold pole, which for this build was 5 feet (1.5 meters). This means that the floors of the living spaces are raised five feet above the ground.

221

The transitory nature of the site necessitated the use of a steel exoskeleton, which makes the building resemble a viewing deck more than a home.

Many materials were salvaged and repurposed during construction. For example, scaffolding platforms were reused for making paths and furniture, and leftover timber went toward the creation of kitchen counters.

Architect Farming Architects
Project VAC-Library
Location Hanoi/Vietnam

Lessons from a Mini Symbiotic City Farm

Homes in Hanoi often have small fishponds or aquariums alongside pots for growing vegetables (the latter due to contamination of plant life in the polluted Vietnamese capital). One of the city's innovative architecture studios, Farming Architects, has taken inspiration from this lifestyle trend to create VAC-Library, which includes these aspects.

The 592-square-foot (55-square-meter) public space in the residential hub of Duong Noi recreates a traditional rural scene in a vibrant city landscape. The production system blends horticulture, aquaculture, and animal husbandry to teach locals how to utilize plants and animals effectively.

Land, air, water, and solar energy are coupled with recycled by-products and waste to generate a self-sustaining ecosystem that is easy to replicate in a residential environment. The symbiotic process is based on aquaponics, which combines conventional aquaculture (raising aquatic animals) with hydroponics (cultivating plants in water). Fish excrement is broken down into nitrates, which are used to fertilize the plants, and the filtered water is circulated back to the fish.

"Children learn that koi fish are not just pets, and they can see how chickens are raised and that their excrement is also good for gardening," says Farming Architects founder An Viet Dung, who has a master's degree in environmental engineering.

The lessons gained from VAC-Library are meant to stimulate knowledge sharing among neighboring communities and encourage urban residents to explore similar options in their own living spaces. The architectural language of the structure, comprised of wooden beams, can be customized according to location and create an attractive feature, in keeping with the Vietnamese affinity for do-it-yourself.

The modular design of the structural elements means that the system can be customized to suit any location, by simply slotting in the light fittings, planters, and seating spaces where they work best.

225

The production system blends horticulture, aquaculture, and animal husbandry to teach locals how to utilize plants and animals effectively.

The design is particularly geared toward providing an open library space for children. Kids in the area and elsewhere can come here to play together, read books, and learn about this ecological model through their interaction with the structure.

227

The Light Touch of a Rural Watch Hut

Architect Narein Perera
Project Estate Bungalow
Location Matugama/Sri Lanka

In an estate in Matugama, Sri Lanka, at the point where a rubber plantation and jungle meet, lies a hillside bungalow that maximizes views of the undeveloped verdant landscape. Designed by Dr. Narein Perera, a senior lecturer at the University of Moratuwa in Sri Lanka, the dwelling is attuned with its surroundings.

Perera conceived a design inspired by the rural Sri Lankan watch hut, an elevated refuge used by farmers guarding their crops overnight. *Chena* agriculture is a traditional regional practice that involves cultivating a plot of land for a short time before moving on to another area, and the design and construction of farm buildings is led by this transitory approach.

The bungalow follows watch-hut principles. "It has a simple form that is elevated, protected yet connected, with maximum vantage, a single entry, and it is dismountable and reusable," explains the architect. "The most important factor, however, is that it touches the earth lightly."

By extending from the hill, secured by steel rods, the structure appears to float. "The materials are limited to steel, timber, and bamboo, with lines as thin as possible, imbuing it with a sense of flimsiness" says Perera.

Some of the bedroom walls (there is one en suite on each of the three levels) are clad in timber, forming a solid, protective layer. The eastern facade remains unclad, bringing the panoramic views inside.

Intended to be a temporary dwelling for the owner when he is overseeing the functioning of the estate, it is also a retreat for others. Therefore, rest and relaxation were paramount in the design, and only the necessities exist. Besides the bedrooms, there is a simple multifunctional room and a pantry. "Service and ancillary spaces are in existing buildings downhill, hidden by the tree canopy," says Perera. "This allows the occupier to disconnect from daily routines completely, and yet everything they need is provided."

The top-heavy nature of the building and the vast, multifunctional deck on the upper level give inhabitants the sensation of being suspended almost in mid-air as they take in the immense panorama beneath.

FIRST FLOOR PLAN
BEDROOM LEVEL 02

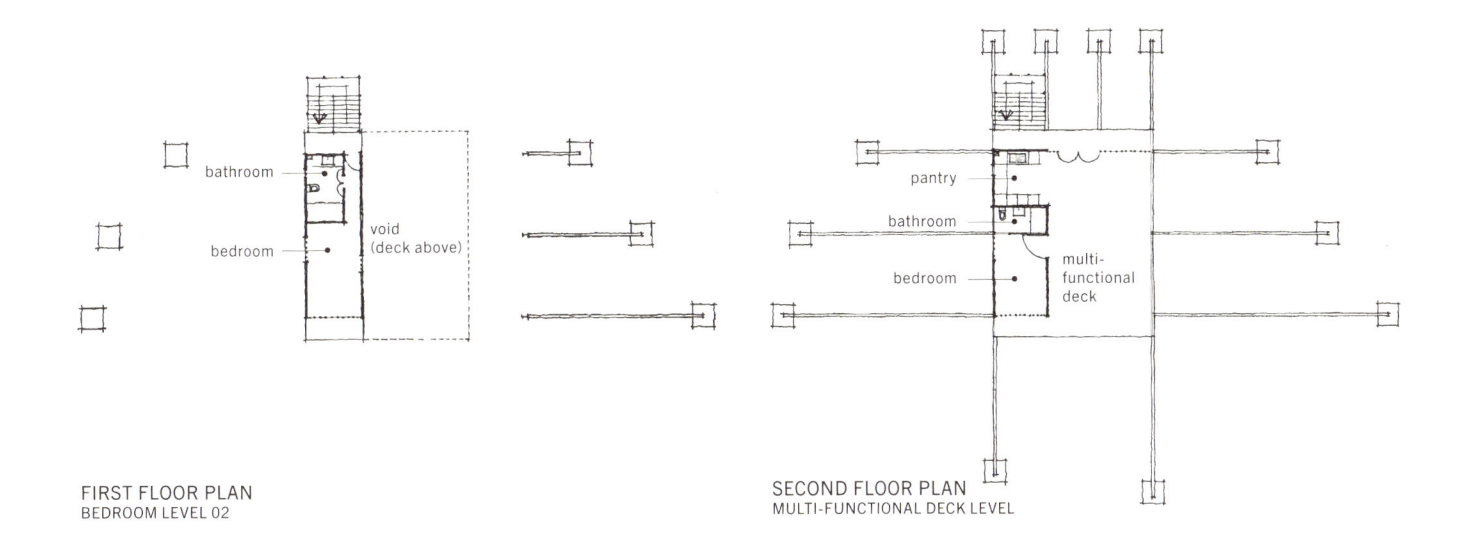

SECOND FLOOR PLAN
MULTI-FUNCTIONAL DECK LEVEL

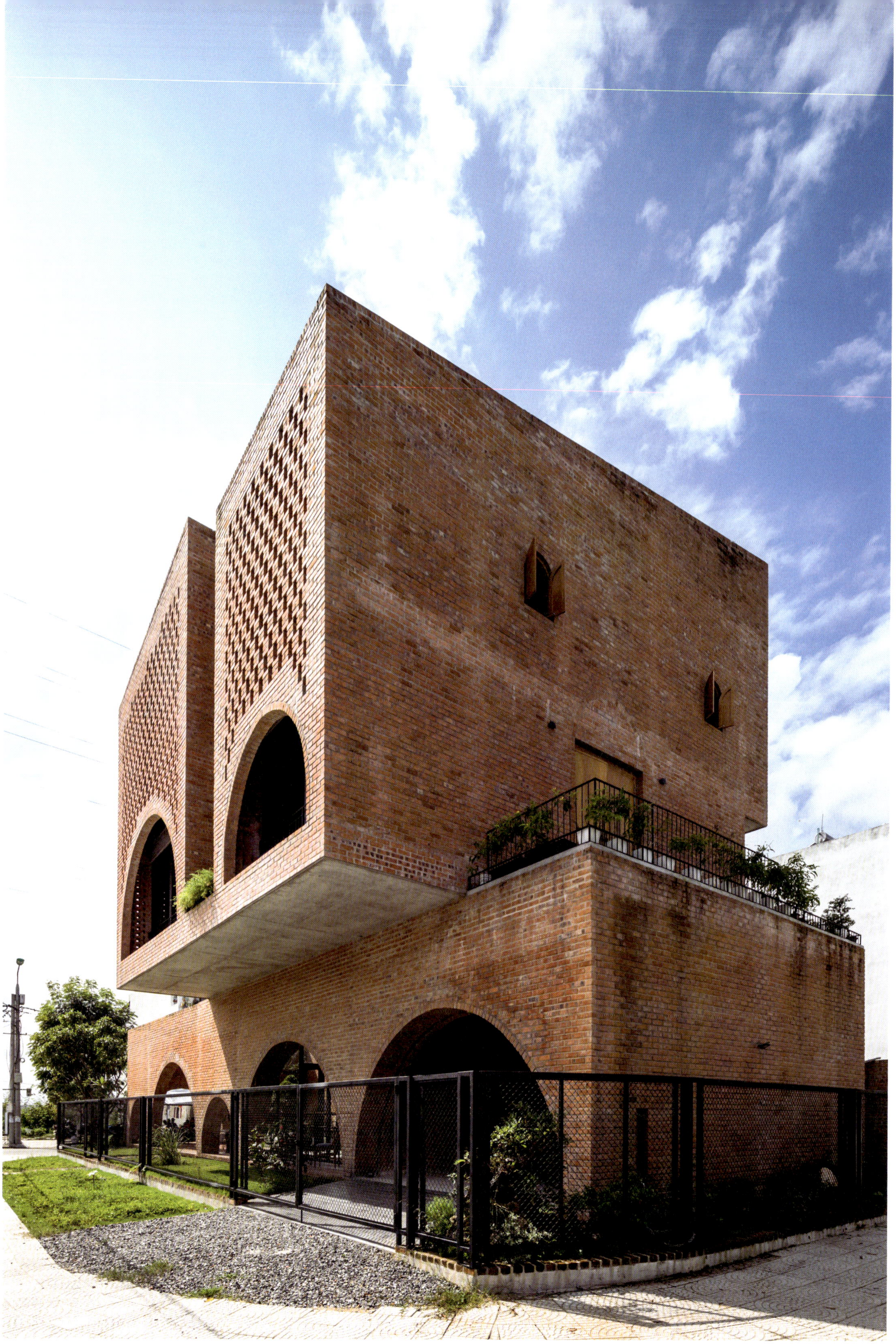

Ho Chi Minh City/Vietnam

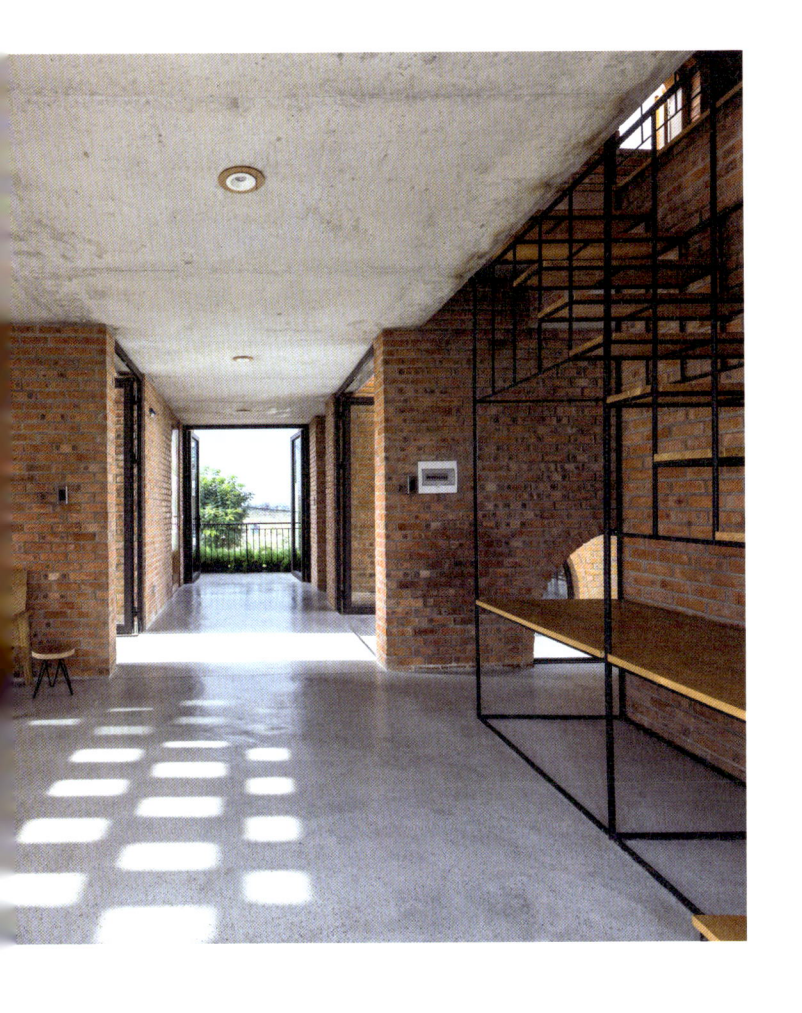

Tropical Space

This Ho Chi Minh City-based partnership creates what they call "emotive architecture." Amid rapid development, Tropical Space is actively reconnecting Vietnamese architecture with a sense of place.

Life and business partners Nguyen Hai Long and Tran Thi Ngu Ngon declare that the only common passion they share—besides a commitment to their family—is a deep love of architecture. The founders of Tropical Space, an architecture, interior, and landscape studio based in Ho Chi Minh City, are committed to environmentally friendly and sustainable building practices.

The couple met while studying at the University of Architecture Ho Chi Minh City when Nguyen was in his third year and Tran was a freshman. When they graduated, they settled in Ho Chi Minh City and worked at different architectural practices, before founding Tropical Space together in 2011.

"Confronted with the mess of Vietnamese architecture at that time," they explain, "we were motivated to review vernacular architectural values related to local materials and climates while focusing on the complex relationship between users, buildings, and environments." In the early 2010s, as Vietnam experienced significant urbanization and population growth—a phenomenon that continues to this day—the architects saw the architectural landscape become far removed from any traditional identity. "We wanted to use our designs to reopen the dialogue around optimizing the exchange of indoor and outdoor climates, and encourage communication between humans and nature."

This impetus led them to focus solely on projects in Vietnam, where they use design to help people live, work, and interact more comfortably in the tropical region, with a sensitivity toward their natural surroundings.

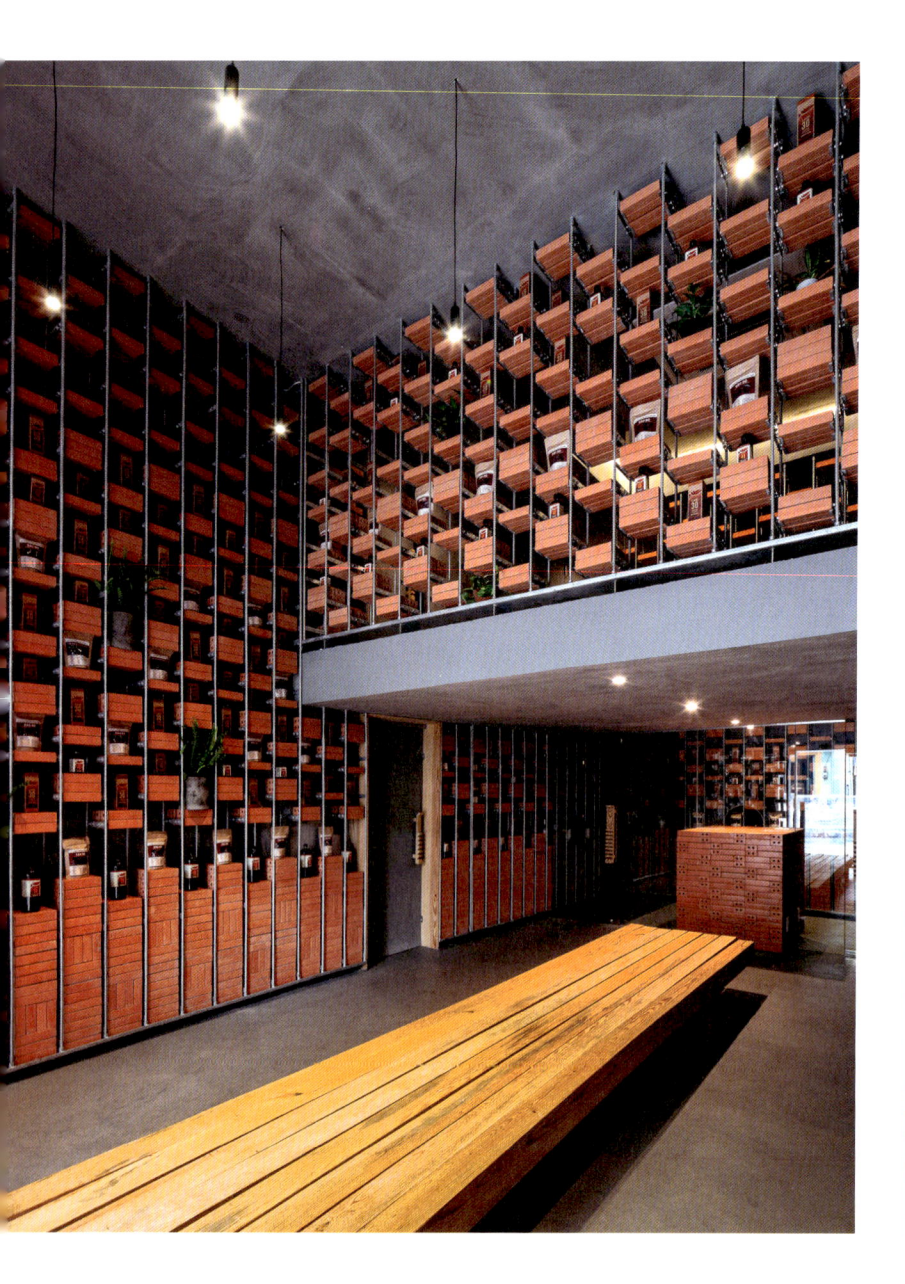

Pages 230–231: The Cuckoo House is a dwelling for a family of four living in Da Nang, Vietnam. Simple in its arrangement, the house sees three two-story volumes arranged on a ground-floor block that functions as a coffee shop. Essentially fully open plan, each volume serves as a separate functional space and is connected to the others via partially covered corridors.

Left and below: Commissioned to renovate inside and out for the Organicare Showroom, instead of adapting the existing facade of the building, Tropical Space simply attached a completely new framework to it. The stacks of tiles reduce in number the higher they go, creating an intriguing decorative design.

"Buildings are a means for architects to display human intelligence, sensations, and care for nature and society," Nguyen and Tran comment on their practice, which they call "emotive architecture." They tend to relate inside and outside environments to one another in a non-hierarchical way and see the intelligent use of light and materials as the most "emotive" components of their practice.

"We play with materials, sunlight, and shadows to arouse emotions and create beautiful experiences for users in the buildings we design," says Tran. This approach is apparent in Terra Cotta Studio, a workspace and sanctuary created by Tropical Studio for clay artist Le Duc Ha in Quang Nam Province. The square structure is constructed from a simple material palette of local clay bricks, bamboo, wood, and concrete. It features a perforated brick facade and transparent roof, meaning that the Sun transforms the interior as it moves, penetrating the brickwork and forming captivating checkered shadows. "In natural light, the surface, texture, and pattern of bricks are much more interesting," the architects state.

"Our work often starts with simple cubic volumes, which we develop in relation to natural light," explains Nguyen, whose fascination with brickwork stems from a family background in the traditional craft of ceramics. Learning about brick construction from his family, and living near the UNESCO World Heritage Site My Son Sanctuary with its historic fired-brick temples, informs the use of bricks in Tropical Studio's commissions.

In Ho Chi Minh City's Organicare Showroom, bricks are an adaptive tool in the flexible retail space that sells traditional Vietnamese fish sauce and organic products. As part of the renovation of an old commercial building, the architects formed a homogenous brick facade, with an interior steel-frame system. Bricks can be individually inserted into the interior walls as shelving, which can be adjusted according to product size and display needs. This ever-changing layout complements the perforated facade and creates a connection between

Below and right: A contemporary take on the traditional Vietnamese structure, this residential home in Long An Province comprises three separate open-plan spaces set on two floors beneath a deep sloping roof. The front yard is lined with hollow clay bricks.

the movement of the city outside and the interior, ensuring that the environmental context is not lost when stepping into the store. Dismantling brickwork is a concept that the architects are pursuing further. "It raises our interest in the construction and reuse of brick buildings so that the environmental impact is reduced and buildings become more sustainable," they state.

The environment is an ongoing concern, and Nguyen and Tran pay close attention to the natural world with design solutions that are adapted to the local climate and weather conditions. By observing the habitat of termites, they have come to question the adaptive processes of humans, and whether the way things have progressed has been counter-intuitive. Termites have continued to build the same type of home for thousands of years, despite dramatic climatic changes, seemingly adapting to embrace the environment. In contrast, humans have completely transformed their living spaces.

"In similar environments, with increasing pressures of global climate change, humans have changed and optimized the design, structure, materials, and technology of buildings to respond to climatic effects, for thermal comfort," Nguyen and Tran explain. "With human intelligence, we are constantly finding new techniques and ideas to construct buildings that protect us from environmental influences. However, it might be exactly these reactions and human activities in the built environment that have accelerated the impact on nature and resulted in environmental deterioration."

Influenced by how termites build their nests, their response has been to design buildings with expressive simplicity—in form, color, materials, and use of energy. "We want to encourage and inspire occupants to live a minimal lifestyle in tune with nature. By understanding the environment of each project, we can adapt buildings accordingly, reducing the energy required for mechanical cooling and lighting systems, while decreasing environmental impact and increasing health and well-being."

Above: The cube-shaped Terra Cotta Studio measures 23 × 23 × 23 feet (7 × 7 × 7 meters) and is organized on three floors within that space, with 24-square-inch (60-square-centimeter) modules that integrate shelves for displaying artworks. Surrounding the studio is a bamboo platform used for drying out terra-cotta products. This raised platform also separates the studio area from the workshop.

Opposite page: The company's design for a free-range rural chicken coop extends beyond the remit of a more conventional coop. The house is made from metal grills and Cemboard, which are combined in such a way as to provide light and shaded areas on a number of different levels, within a space that is also used for growing vegetables.

Tropical Space

"We play with materials, sunlight, and shadows to arouse emotions and create beautiful experiences for users in the buildings we design."

Tropical Space's design for a residential home in Long An Province illustrates this point. It is inspired by traditional Vietnamese structures that stretch fluidly from one end to the other in a deft application of spatial layering. "The continuous space between the functional areas inside and outside the house allows children to play and move freely," the architects explain. The kitchen and living areas at the northern end of the building take the cultural importance of Vietnamese cooking and entertaining into account, and provide space to accommodate many people.

The architects considered the prevailing wind direction through the seasons and maximized the flow of ventilation by dividing the sloping roof to form a courtyard with porous walls. Sunlight creates boundaries in the absence of structural divisions and generates transitional moments depending on its intensity and the varying shades of dark and light.

This home is a reflection of Tropical Space's impulse to create uncomplicated, harmonious, stimulating spaces, a practice not limited to humans. Its design for a countryside chicken coop turned a 215-square-foot (20-square-meter) garden into a playground for poultry. It includes shaded canopies (that also act as perches for children to rest on while enjoying the environment), designated spots for laying and hatching eggs, areas for chickens to scratch the ground, and ponds, with water drainage used to irrigate the surrounding vegetation.

Their one shared passion for architecture drives Nguyen and Tran to support nature while enhancing the quality of life for residents and users. Their work, however, reveals a plethora of congruous sentiments, indicating that their definition of architecture goes way beyond the norm.

Roof Tiles Become Cooling Agents on Walls

Architect Manoj Patel Design Studio
Project Residential Dwelling
Location Vadodara/India

The defining characteristic of this residential home in the Indian city of Vadodara is the tile-clad external walls. Conceived by Manoj Patel Design Studio, the building puts architect Manoj Patel's postgraduate studies in climate change and sustainable development into practice.

"Materials such as glass, aluminum, metal, and fiber sheets are often used to clad facades and create an eye-catching modern look," says Patel. "Those materials are costly and high in energy consumption," he explains, "and they are also unsuitable for Indian climates." Instead, he prefers to utilize salvaged and recyclable materials to create cool spaces in India's hot temperatures, provide local employment, and reduce construction costs. For instance, 40 percent of the red clay tiles decorating the southern and western walls of this house are reclaimed roof tiles.

The economical V-shaped tiles were each cut into five 1-inch-wide (2.5-centimeter) sections and laid in a diagonal zigzag formation. This pattern was chosen after extensive research to establish the composition that would best shelter the house from the Sun. The tiles have transformed the walls into functional, protective surfaces that maintain a comfortable temperature inside the building. Cleverly sited terraces on all three levels of the home serve a similar purpose—they invite air in and reduce temperatures through natural cross-ventilation. The tree canopy that hovers above them captures the breeze and shades the living areas.

The cutting and cladding of the tiles employed skilled local labor. As Patel notes, "By using simple, economical, and vernacular materials, craftsmanship is reinvented, merging tradition and modernity."

The architects' novel approach to cladding is not only more sustainable than many modern alternatives, but it has decorative benefits too. Entire walls of tiling intersect the modernist cuboid volumes with panels of earthy terra-cotta flair.

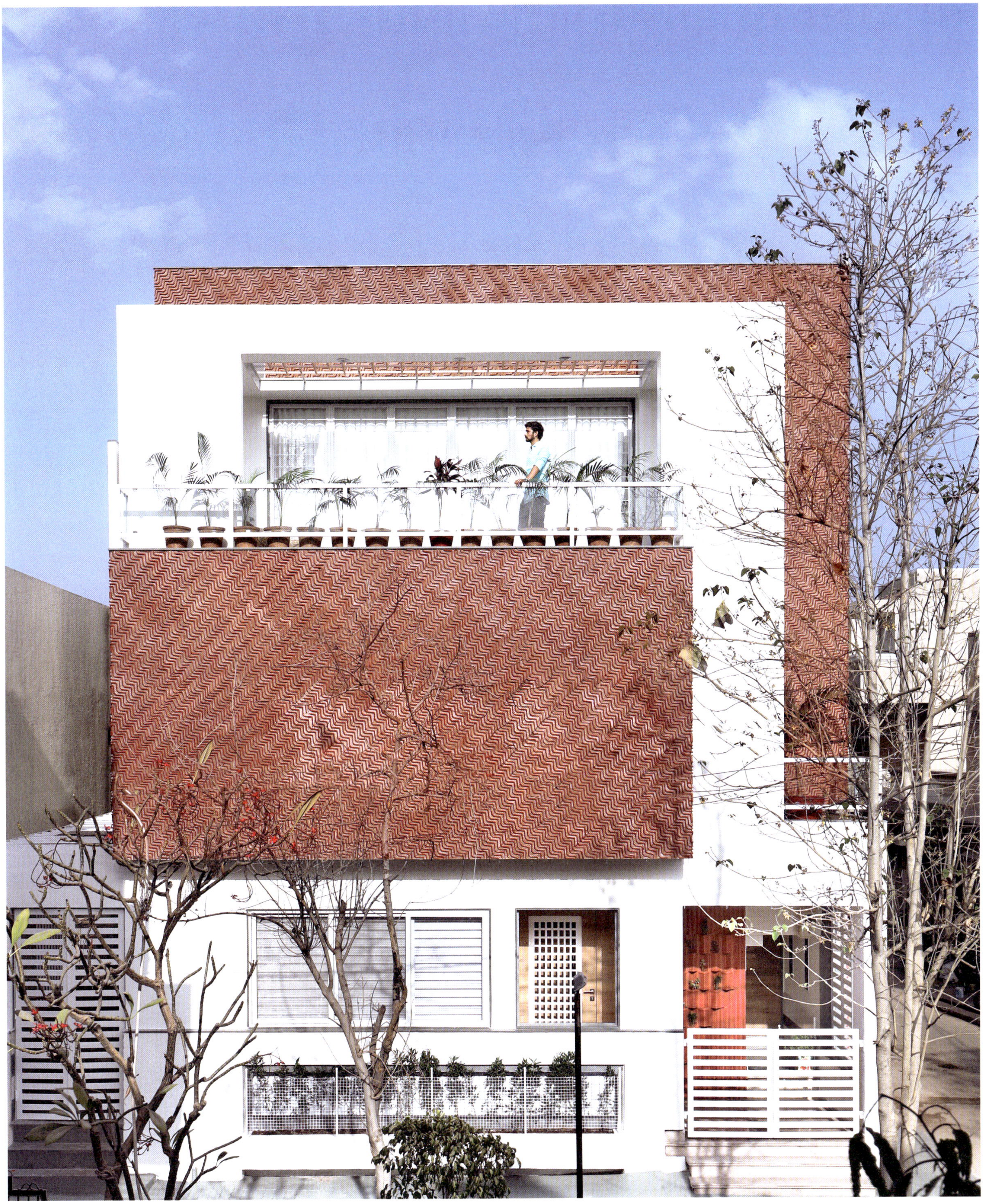

Natural Ventilation and Heat Protection

Architect Chaukor Studio
Project Minaret House
Location Noida/India

Chaukor Studio, in Delhi's satellite city of Noida, designs what it calls "regenerative architecture"—a user-centric, eco-friendly mode of building. In this home, the studio incorporated its philosophy by starkly contrasting the residence with the skyscrapers surrounding it. Adjacent to a golf course, the residence benefits from green, open vistas that allow the minaret and multilayered facade to serve as examples of such architectural regeneration.

"This is part of a greater exploration to restore, renew, and revitalize the lost wisdom of formal expressions of the art of buildings," the architects explain. Studies on climatic principles, social circulation patterns, and local materials culminated in a home that embodies a distinct identity rooted in Indian heritage.

The central minaret functions as a wind tower, drawing fresh air in from outside and allowing hot air to escape, eliminating the need for air-conditioning and thus reducing energy consumption. The layered facade of the building and small, deep openings on the southwest wall provide shade and further cooling.

Social interaction is equally well considered: public and private zones are segregated, and spatial volumes are adapted to accommodate specific purposes. Intimate rooms with low ceilings, narrow entrances, and small windows lead off from larger gathering areas, allowing both private comfort and harmonious coexistence. Movement is encouraged by large terraces that connect double-volume living areas in the way that ancient city streets would have joined one place to another.

Inspired by the colors that exemplified and unified the ancient cities of India, Chaukor Studio covered the facade, boundary walls, parapet, and porch with a yellowish plaster. Made from Rajasthan's Jaisalmer dust, white cement, and stone aggregate, the uneven, rough texture adds to the perceptual depth of this arresting home.

The minaret offers a common recognizable motif from vernacular architecture. Building up toward it, the stepped facade creates a series of terraces that connect the family areas to one another while using outdoor spaces as communal extensions of private rooms.

The central minaret functions as a wind tower, drawing fresh air in from outside and allowing hot air to escape, eliminating the need for air-conditioning and thus reducing energy consumption.

Weather Protection and Material Reverence

"This house is not about how it looks, but what it overlooks," say architects Gauri Satam and Tejesh Patil of Mumbai-based studio unTAG Architecture & Interiors. They are referring to a 1,000-square-foot (93-square-meter) retirement farmstead they designed in the Sindhudurg district of western India. The architects' quest for simplicity led them to explore unique design solutions sensitive to their context. The home's placement in the heart of a mango-and-chikoo grove, nurtured by the homeowners for 15 years, was integral to achieving the seamless connection between house and orchard. Located on the slopes of a hillock, it overlooks another through jackfruit, cashew, and palm trees.

The abode descends with the topography in a series of 12-foot-wide (3.5-meter) interlinked spaces that contain the bathroom, bedroom, living area, veranda, and deck.

The entrance connects the living areas with the kitchen and service court, where a rural hearth is enclosed by a stone *jali* that transforms the space with shaded patterns throughout the day.

Sourcing materials conducive to the native climate is a critical component of unTAG's architectural practice. In this instance, the cost-effective chira stone (laterite) from a quarry just two miles (three kilometers) down the road was an obvious choice for the load-bearing structural elements of the home. Its porous properties mean that it behaves like earthenware. It is suitable for the area's monsoons and it also reduces interior temperatures naturally. The local terracotta roof tiles on the overhanging pitched roof minimize the penetration of direct sunlight, while the dark gray Indian Kotah stone of the interior walls and floors provides heat insulation. The teak and jackfruit window and door frames, crafted from the rafters of a dismantled Hindu temple in a nearby village, display the architects' affinity for reusing noble materials.

Architect unTAG
Project Vrindavan
Location Sindhudurg/India

Seen from across the mango grove, the home has a low profile. The chira-stone walls and deep pitch roof complement the rustic, rural ambience of the farmstead.

The design of this dwelling has a modernist twist, particulalry in the geometric patterning of the *jali,* whitewashed walls, the cantilevered staircase, and the large expanses of plate glass.

Sourcing materials conducive to the native climate is a critical component of unTAG's architectural practice.

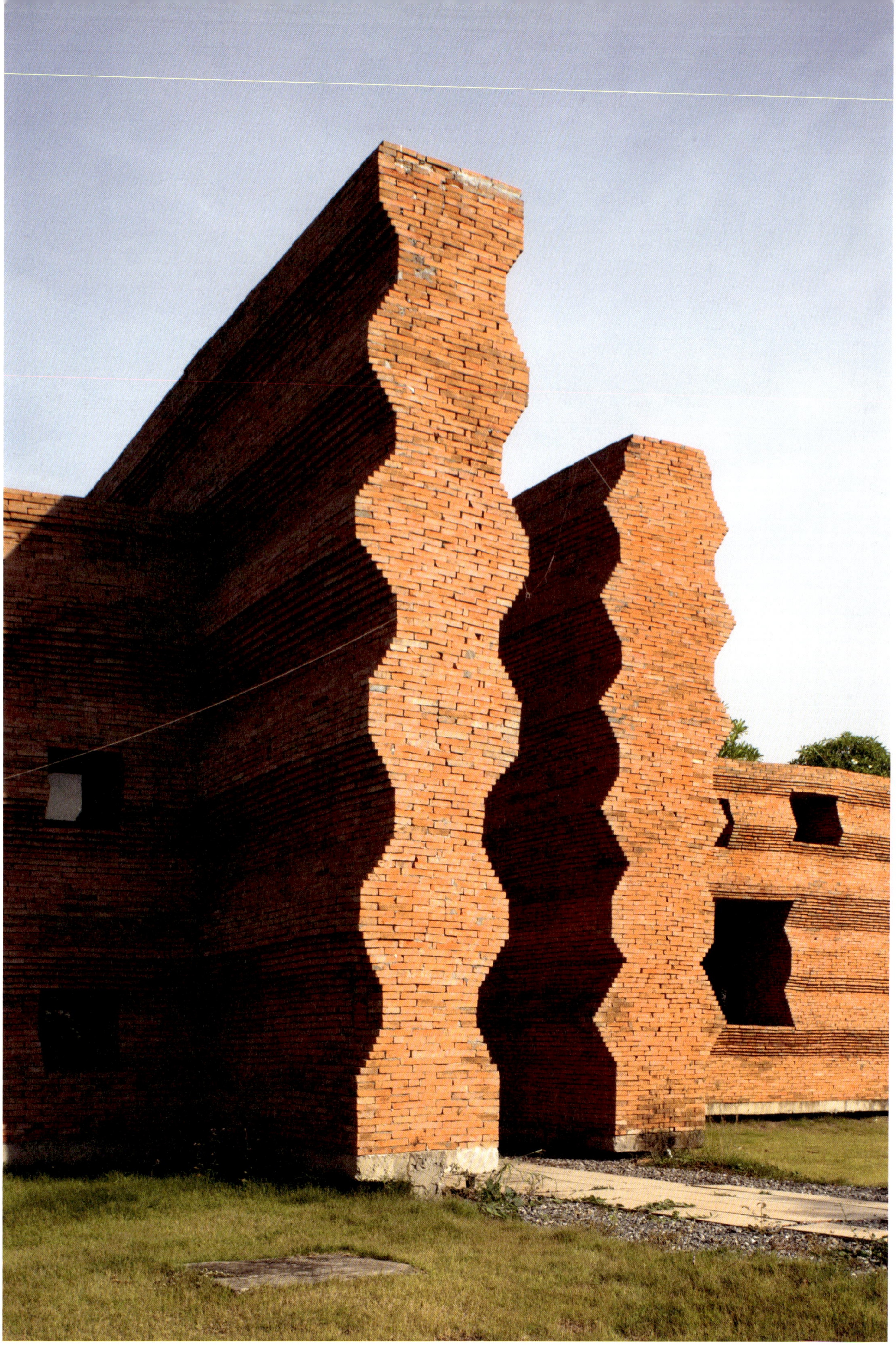

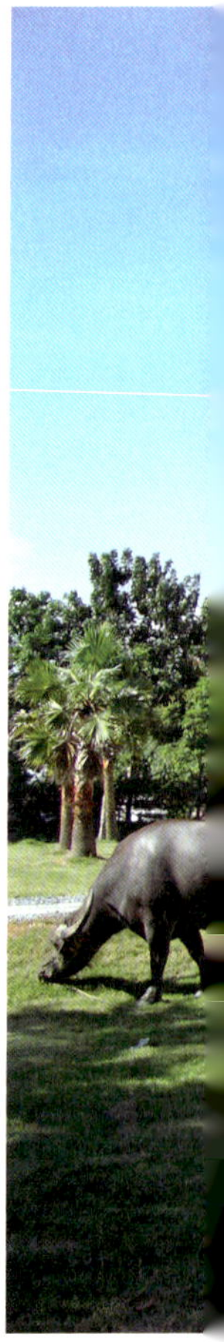

Bangkok/Thailand

Bangkok Project Studio

Bangkok-based Boonserm Premthada draws from a material palette of humble and overlooked items, which he hopes to elevate through the power of design.

Thai architect Boonserm Premthada understands the value of patience. He founded Bangkok Project Studio in 2003, a year after graduating with a master's degree in architecture from Chulalongkorn University, but his first architectural projects were not completed until 2011. Since then, however, he has achieved worldwide recognition. He was one of the winners of the 2018 Global Award for Sustainable Architecture, under the patronage of UNESCO, and, in 2019, he received the Royal Academy Dorfman Award for his sensitivity to local contexts.

Although based in Bangkok, Premthada is not interested in working within the congested city sprawl. He focuses on Thailand's countryside. "The rural area needs architects to create opportunities and an economy so that people do not have to relocate and struggle in cities," he explains of his opinion that there is no need for additional city structures. "I prefer to work in less-developed places because I know that my architecture is meaningful to people there." Commissioning artisans from the small towns in which he works, he instills every project with traditional local knowledge.

In this way, he attempts to unlearn what he was taught during his studies. "What I learned at university are rules and formulas, but I have found that they do not work everywhere. What I have learned from villagers is necessity and priority. I have learned about humanness, human instincts, and that we should aim for natural learning—the simple way."

Premthada uses endemic materials and traditional crafts in an effort to respect his country's innate wisdom. He founded Bangkok Project Studio to "prove

"My motivation is to help owners see things from a different perspective, to resolve misunderstandings, and counter the lack of self-identity."

a point that there should and must be other ways of designing for different cultures, geographies, and climates." He sees many property owners swayed by trends they see in the "Western" world. "But they are living in Thailand, and they are limited by budget, time, and the availability of skilled labor," he says of the reality. "My motivation is, therefore, to help owners see things from a different perspective, to resolve misunderstandings, and counter the lack of self-identity."

The Kantana Film and Animation Institute in Nakhon Pathom Province embodies this idea of celebrating a unique Thai identity. By using 600,000 handmade bricks on the school's 26-foot-high (8-meter) walls, the project prevented a local brick company from going out of business and it highlighted the potential of a simple, locally available material.

"I specifically select ordinary overlooked materials because I want to enhance their value with design," Premthada explains. Inspired by local houses made of wood, he used a cheap plywood reinforced with steel for the structure of the Wine Ayutthaya, a wine bar and eatery on the banks of a river in what was formerly the capital of the Kingdom of Siam. It has four multi-level platforms and five spiral staircases that create visual intrigue amid the towering trees on-site.

At Elephant World in Surin Province, where humans and elephants live together in harmony, glass blocks usually used to decorate bathrooms are the primary material for certain buildings. "I pick up the nearest and easiest things in each area," Premthada says of his chosen building blocks. "My definition of materials extends to water, wind, sunlight, trees, and even old

Bangkok Project Studio

Pages 244–246 and above: The towering brick walls of the Kantana Institute have a distinctive wave-pattern in cross-section. They are also staggeringly thick. The masonry is punctuated at regular intervals with apertures, which serve to ventilate the spaces between the inner and outer skins of the edifice while providing quiet enclaves for sitting and relaxing.

Bangkok Project Studio

"My definition of materials extends to water, wind, sunlight, trees, and even old buildings. Space is about things you can see, but place is something you remember."

buildings." All of Premthada's projects align with his ideas around space versus place. "Space is about things you can see, but place is something you remember," he states. A sense of place is powerfully envisioned at Elephant World, where a brick observation tower is integrated with the highland landscape. It allows visitors to climb to the top and look down at the elephants, watch them roam freely, and gain a new perspective on the animals that usually tower over them on land. Premthada's design makes it difficult to forget such a place.

Sensory experiences are a high priority in these projects, and the choice of material and the way they are used stimulates unexpected perceptions.

Premthada finds ways to develop what he calls the "poetics in architecture" by making abstract ideas concrete. At the Wine Ayutthaya, the smells of plywood and wine, and one's movement up the winding staircases to gain different views, are part of the ingrained memory of a visit.

Blurring the lines between the built and natural environment is a signature approach for Bangkok Project Studio.

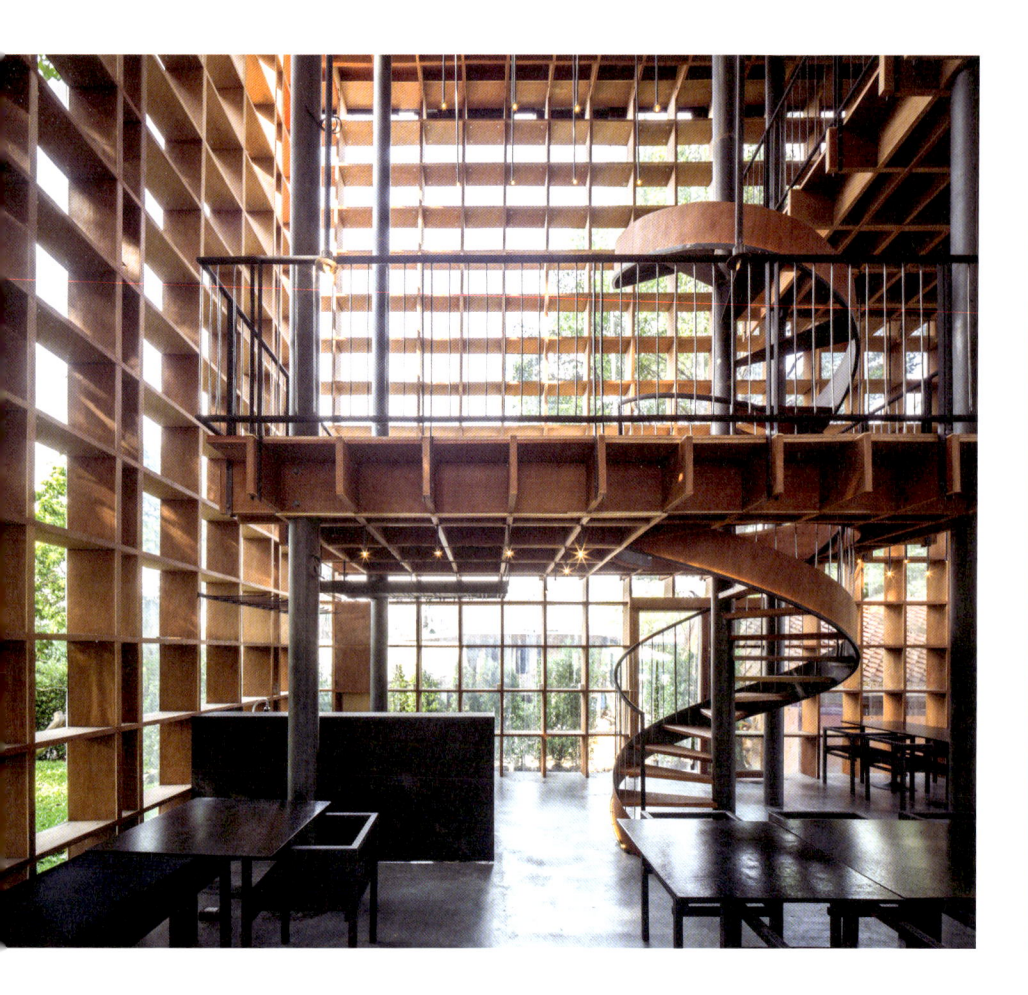

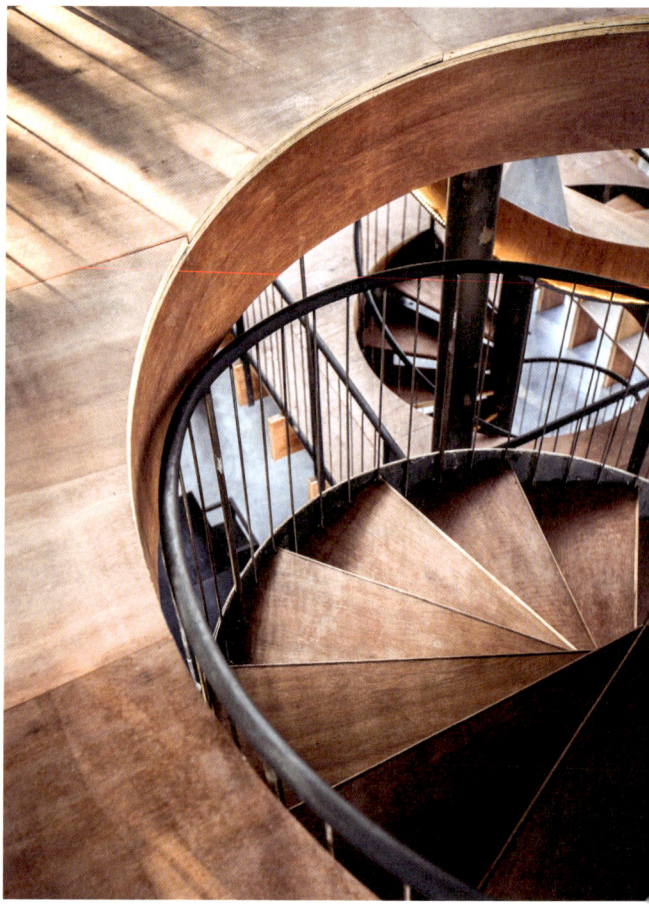

Sound (or the lack thereof) has become another mechanism Premthada employs—a focus he draws from being born with just 30 percent auditory ability in one ear. "Humans principally rely on one sense of perception: sight. But when you close your eyes, you wake up other senses," he explains of atmospheric architecture, which heightens the awareness of one's surroundings.

The courtyards at the Kantana school encourage interaction, humanizing the educational institute. The sensory experience in this environment is purposefully considered; tall brick walls limit visual stimuli, thus amplifying the sound, smell, and temperature.

"It is different from the walls of the elephant museum, which ensure that when elephants enter the museum, they are not disturbed by sound from outside." Blurring the lines between the built and natural environment is a signature approach for Bangkok Project Studio; Premthada describes his designs as "borderlessness." He avoids lines between urban landscape, architecture, and interior, preferring a blended integration of the total environment. This approach is particularly evident in a project currently underway in Samut Prakan. The Mangrove Learning Centre for the Thai Red Cross Society is a rehabilitation center for the elderly with a light footprint, among the trees of a mangrove forest.

Having set out to create meaningful architecture, it appears that the patience with which Premthada embarked on his career is paying off. A portfolio of memorable places, constructed with local materials, traditional skills, and innovative adaptations, is serving a multitude of different purposes—for humans, nature, and animals.

Opposite page and above: At the Wine Ayutthaya, the use of plywood for construction transforms the perception of a material that is typically used in furniture making. The single-volume space measures 1,296 square feet (121 square meters) and is an impressive 29.5 feet (9 meters) in height. In a fun twist, the spiral staircases are reminiscent of corkscrews.

Locating Chinese Architecture

It's a telling detail that a Chinese word for "architecture" didn't emerge until the 20th century: Instead, the people behind traditional structures were seen as artisans. As many such buildings are razed to make way for high-rise developments, a renewed interest in vernacular is emerging.

What is Chinese architecture? This question, which can be asked of the building traditions of any culture, is deceptively simple. One answer could simply be any architecture within China's borders. Or, perhaps Chinese architecture is that which is designed and constructed by Chinese architects. Neither of these answers, however, seems entirely satisfactory—geopolitical borders expand and contract, and people move across them. One could also provide a temporal clarification to the question: is there a moment at which defining Chinese architecture became necessary? Rather than attempting to give a neat answer to the question of what Chinese architecture is, or, even less productively, to deconstruct it, I would like to trace the contours of the concept of "Chinese architecture" to locate some of the key historical tensions that animated it in the twentieth century.

The Question of Origin

The Chinese word for "architecture"—*jianzhu*—first came into usage in the early twentieth century. Before its emergence and the institution of architecture as the profession we know today, the skills needed to design and engineer structures like temples, pagodas, pavilions, and archways were possessed by artisans—*jiangren*. The names of these individuals, noted for their skills in timber frame construction, are often obscured by the fact that they worked collectively in guilds, challenging the modern concept of authorship and individual genius that pervades contemporary architectural practice. One of the few exceptions to this historical condition is the Lei family, seven generations of carpenters and artisans who served the Qing court (1636–1912) for more than two-and-a-half centuries. They created the standards and codes that dictated the specific form and style of buildings for Qing nobility, and

01 The Forbidden City palace complex in Beijing.
02 A classical garden and bungalow in Hangzhou, eastern China.
03 Waterside buildings in Fenghuang Ancient Town in Hunan Province, South China.

documented their work through a vast number of architectural models of not just single structures, but entire garden and palace complexes. The Leis were not only instrumental in shaping the landscape of imperial China; the maps and models they created of its architecture, including the Forbidden Palace and Temple of Heaven, form an archive that has been studied by historians of Chinese architecture.

The Qing dynasty collapsed in 1912. In the decades leading to its demise, foreign empires took advantage of its weakened state and deployed both historians and troops to either study or loot the territory. It was also during this time that the preservation and study of Chinese architectural heritage became both a scholarly and imperial project. Objects ranging from sculptures to stele were being wrested from their original context, only to reemerge in museum vitrines and on mantelpieces around the world. Japan, Great Britain, France, the US, and Germany produced prolific historians and collectors of East Asian material culture. The photographs, maps, drawings, and textual descriptions of religious and imperial architecture made by individuals like Itō Chūta, Ernst Boerschmann, and Heinrich Hildebrand are valuable accounts of Chinese architectural history. They are inflected by both deep scholarly interest and thinly veiled imperial ambition.

This outsourcing of Chinese architectural heritage and history was followed by the establishment of the Society for Research in Chinese Architecture in Beijing in 1930. The organization comprised historians of both Chinese and foreign backgrounds. This occurred at a time when the so-called "First Generation" of Chinese architects, who studied in Japan and the West in the 1920s, returned home. One of these architects and key figures in Chinese architectural history is Liang Sicheng, who, like several other members of his cohort, trained in the Beaux-Arts tradition at the University of Pennsylvania. Liang was born in Japan to exiled Chinese parents. He married fellow student Lin Huiyin, who was denied entry into the architecture school because of her gender. Liang became the student of noted Beaux-Arts architect and designer Paul Cret. Unlike other students who became practicing architects, both Liang and Lin became architectural researchers, steeping themselves in ancient Chinese building manuals and architectural treatises. Amid the Second Sino-Japanese War (1937–45) and the Chinese Civil War (1927–45), the couple traveled throughout the country's hinterlands to locate, document, and analyze traditional architecture that had rarely been visited by any historian, foreign or domestic.

Liang and his colleagues used a variety of research methods to define the singularity of Chinese architectural form. They each had their own analytic frameworks. Boerschmann, the German architect and historian who traveled extensively throughout China in the early decades of the twentieth century, was interested in spatial arrangement and the connection between architecture and religious practice. Liang, on the other hand, was preoccupied with questions of construction and anatomy. These projects and expeditions occurred during a time of war and political turmoil in China. The task of locating, documenting, and preserving these sites was, therefore, not only an attempt to safeguard but also to articulate a national identity, albeit tinged with anxiety over the loss of tradition in the face of rapid modernization.

The Question of the Other

Chinese architectural history written during the early twentieth century was embedded within larger geopolitical entanglements: the Qing dynasty fell, Japan rose as an imperial power, and the Chinese Nationalists and Communists battled for control. On the one hand, these histories were an attempt to construct a lineage of cultural heritage on the eve of the birth of the modern Chinese nation. On the other hand, they were imperial projects of categorization and knowledge production. However, within these histories written by both Chinese and foreign historians, two aspects of the built environment are frequently overlooked. The first is the vernacular and hyper-local. The other is the foreign and colonial. To grapple with the question of what Chinese architecture is, we need to focus on the latter, while understanding that these two conditions are rarely experienced in isolation.

04

The influence of cultures east, west, and south of the borders of the Chinese empires emerges in differing degrees of legibility. Boerschmann, for example, made no mention of the Western-style architecture and urban planning in major cities like Guangzhou. His interest lay in the pagodas, temples, ancestral halls, mosques, and prayer towers—sites of religious and spiritual significance. Regarding the architecture of Islam, he attempted to make connections between these "West-Asian" typologies and the architecture of Taoism, Confucianism, and Buddhism. This overarching theme of spirituality and religious practice reflects a broader argument: Chinese architecture, for Boerschmann, was an antidote to Western industrialization and secularization. Even though his research countered the West's prevailing attitude that Chinese architecture lacked progress and evolution, his analysis propagated an interpretation of Chinese culture as counter to a Western idea of modernity and progress.

However, within stone's throw of the temples and pagodas that Boerschmann so methodically recorded in Guangzhou was the architecture of Western imperialism. In 1842, the Treaty of Nanjing opened up Chinese cities to foreign trade. The number of foreign settlements multiplied in subsequent years, proliferating mainly along China's coastline and waterways. Each of these sites had its own approach to governance and was subject to the rule of not just a single empire, but often multiple overlapping empires. Tianjin, a city on the northeast coast of China, is a prime example. In 1900, it contained no less than nine foreign concessions in addition to a Chinese walled city, leading historian Ruth Rogaski to describe it as not just a colony, but a "hyper-colony." Each concession built structures that evoked their respective metropoles, ranging from Paris to Saint Petersburg. Other cities were more stylistically cohesive, but no less foreign. Harbin, a city in the far reaches of northeast China, was occupied by Russians and built in a style that could be mistaken for the handiwork of Victor Horta, the Belgian architect and designer of art nouveau. The northeastern city of Qingdao was leased to the German Empire and is now known for Wilhelmine-era architecture with a hint of oriental flair. The residents of these dissonant imperial spaces encountered the "foreign" not only through the transplant of architectural style but also through the introduction of modern urban planning and technological infrastructure.

The Uses of Chinese Architecture

At the turn of the twentieth century, Chinese architectural history was written in the twin shadows of nation and empire. The projects undertaken by individuals like Liang Sicheng and Ernst Boerschmann attempted to locate and narrativize tradition. Their work was prophetic: many of the sites documented in these histories were destroyed or irrevocably damaged during the Chinese Cultural Revolution (1966–76). The concept of Chinese architecture took on additional urgency after the establishment of the People's Republic of China in 1949. In the early years of the republic, Chinese architects were tasked with creating buildings and sites that would be legible as both "Chinese" and "modern." In other words, they were responsible for creating the image of "New China."

The results often took the form of postmodern pastiche. Take, for example, Chang'an Avenue, a wide thoroughfare between Tiananmen Square and the Forbidden City in Beijing. The so-called Ten Great Buildings that run along the avenue were designed by Zhang Bo, a former student of Liang Sicheng and Lin Huiyin, and include the Great Hall of the People, Minority Culture Palace, and the Beijing Railway Station. These buildings place recognizable motifs of Chinese architecture—pavilions, curved hip-and-gable roofs, archways, and ornamented columns—atop concrete, glass, and steel structures that reference Soviet neoclassicism and American Beaux-Arts. In this sense, Chang'an Avenue became modern not by way of rupture, but continuity. The selective import of Western modernity and architectural tradition was grafted onto fragments of Chinese architecture to form an image of New China that was legible to both domestic and international audiences.

Today, Chinese architecture operates on the global stage. Like the First Generation of Chinese architects at the turn of the century, many of the architects highlighted in this volume trained in the top architectural education institutions in Europe and the US. They worked for the studios of OMA and Steven Holl, and then established their own firms in China. Rather than pastiche, there is renewed interest in vernacular architectural practices that widen our understanding of the ecological, as well as a sensitivity to typologies that define traditional Chinese architecture. For example, the *hutong* (timber frame construction) and *feng shui* patterns continue to emerge as sophisticated, if not subtle, motifs. A critical question for contemporary Chinese architectural practice, however, is how to negotiate the parameters of "Chinese architecture" within the forces of nationalism and neo-imperialism, both of which are taking hold within Chinese domestic and international policy. The historiography of Chinese architecture in the twentieth century has shown that the concept is not without its own politics and intimacies to an ever-present West. As architectural firms led by Chinese architects begin to gain the attention of Western media, their work deserves to be analyzed in a way that is both celebratory and critical.

Rather than pastiche, there is renewed interest in vernacular architectural practices that widen our understanding of the ecological.

04 Portrait of Mao Tse Tung on the wall of the Forbidden City in Beijing.
05 The terminal building of Daxing New International Airport, Beijing, designed by British-based firm, Zaha Hadid Architects.
06 Nathan Road in Hong Kong.

Mimi Cheng is a doctoral candidate whose research focuses on global histories of modern architecture, with emphasis on postcolonial theory and cross-cultural studies.

Talking in Circles with Mountain Forms

Treewow Villa O is a tiny 860-square-foot (80-square-meter) hotel in the quiet Chinese village of Zhongcun, at the foot of Siming Mountain in Yuyao, Zhejiang Province. Rotterdam- and Shanghai-based creative architecture atelier MONOARCHI, under lead architects Xiaochao Song and Keming Wang, wanted to create a comfortable retreat between an ancient bamboo forest and stream. The structure is 26 feet high (8 meters)—the height of an adult bamboo plant. Built on steel columns, it makes as little impact on the site as possible.

MONOARCHI adapted its interest in public projects and urban design for this hospitable dwelling; the two levels, accessed by a spiral staircase, direct inhabitants' flow through their cylindrical formation. "When the guest enters the terrace on the first floor, they will start to experience the circular sequence of spaces—from the eave along the terrace to the connected interior," explain the architects.

The wooden retreat was constructed by hand using a traditional method, giving the non-linear eave an "extremely high error-tolerant rate," which, the architects say, is the way rural construction respects the laws of nature. Song and Wang worked closely with local artisans, utilizing their construction skills to advance the design.

Three non-concentric circles stand above one another—the terrace, interior encasement, and undulating roof, which unwraps to offer another terrace with a view of the mountains and an old tea factory across the water. Fifty-seven trusses support the walls and roof, and they are positioned in such a way that the eave curves up and down—revealing different views and concealing specific windows for privacy, without restricting the flow of natural ventilation. The curve of the roof mimics the contour of the mountains, placing Treewow Villa O in direct communication with its undulating landscape.

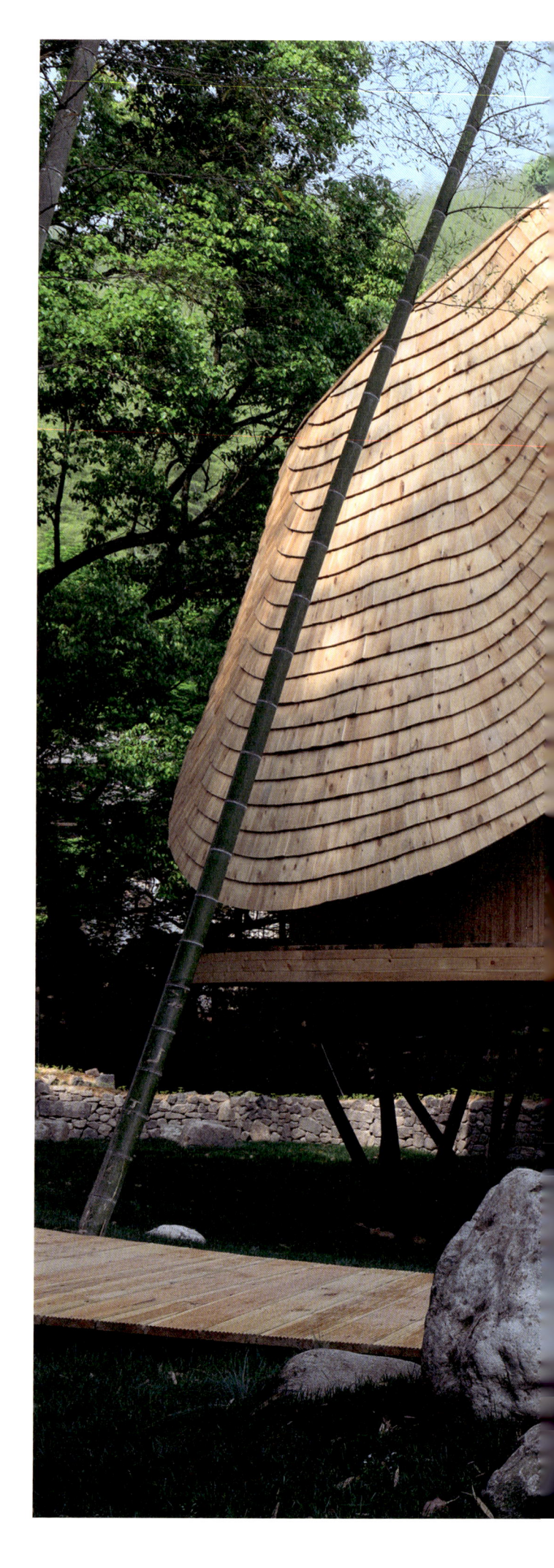

Architect MONOARCHI Architects
Project Treewow Villa O
Location Yuyao/China

Aerial and side views of the villa demonstrate the complexity of the roof design, and how its organic, undulating curves emanate from three non-concentric circles.

Treewow Villa O

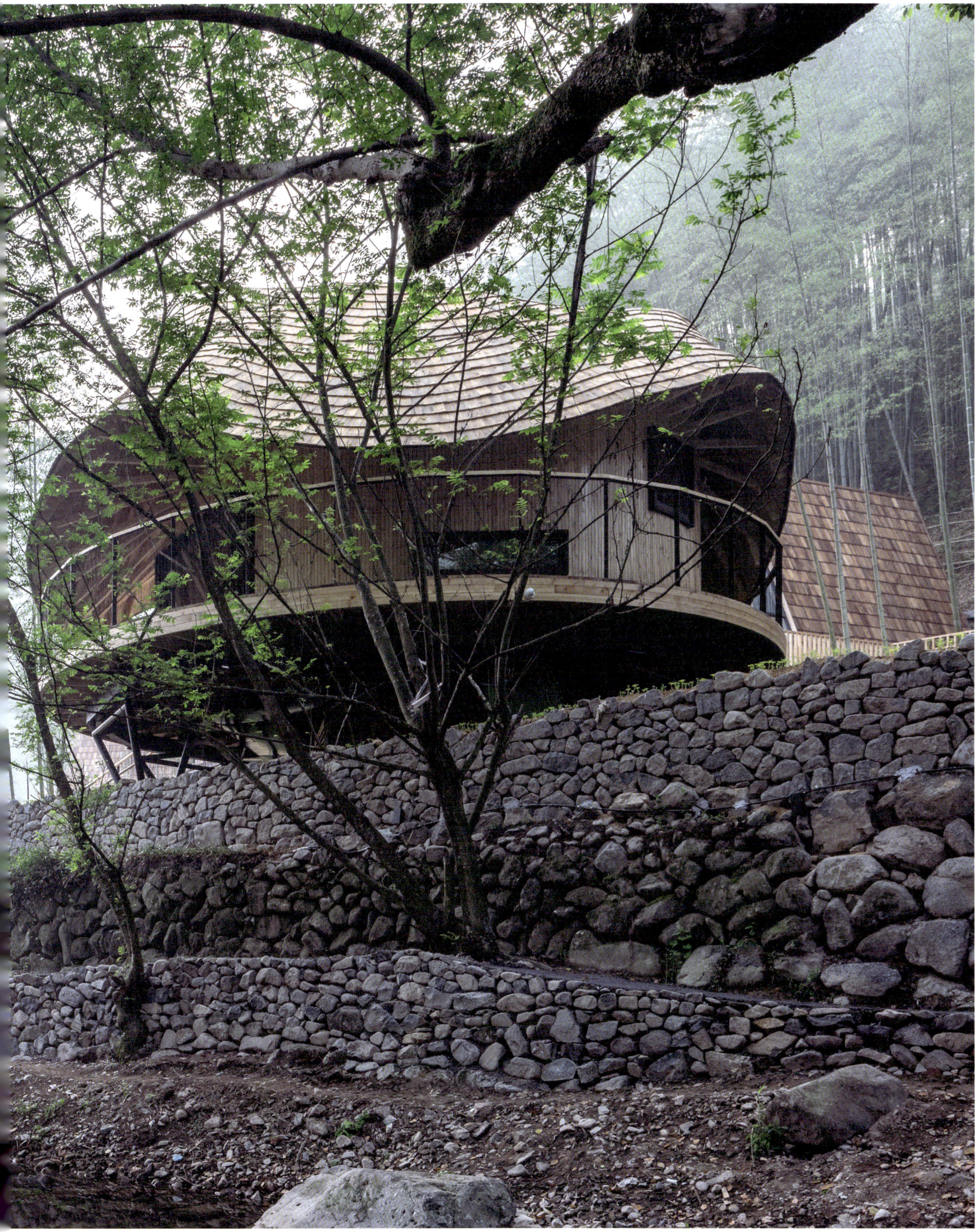

"When the guest enters the terrace on the first floor, they will start to experience the circular sequence of spaces—from the eave along the terrace to the connected interior."

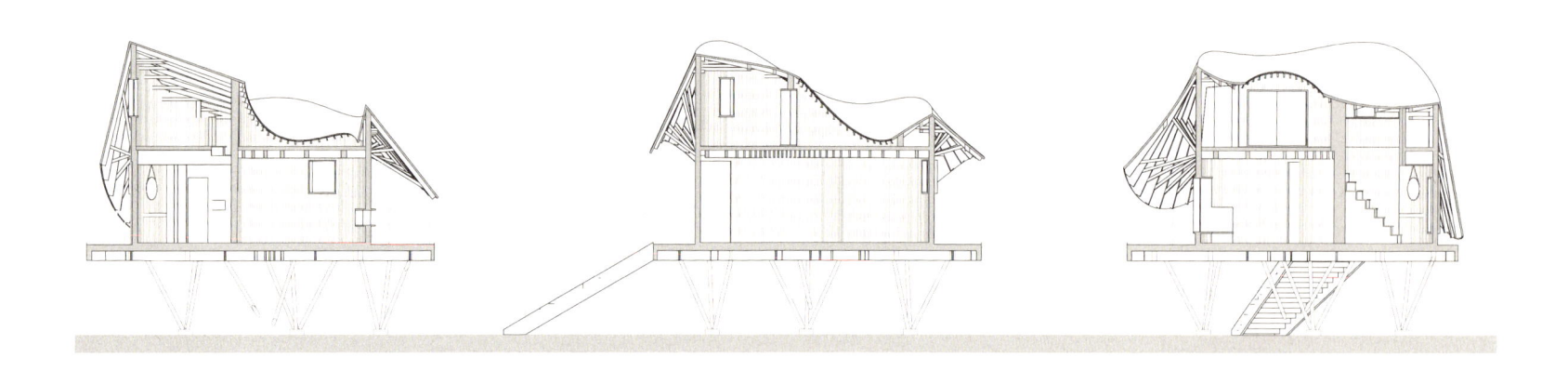

Cross-sections of the villa from three different angles offer views into the sculpted interior spaces that can only be imagined from the outside, so deep are the eaves of the roof. In time, the wooden tiling on the external surfaces of the villa will weather and take on a patina that blends in even more with the natural surroundings.

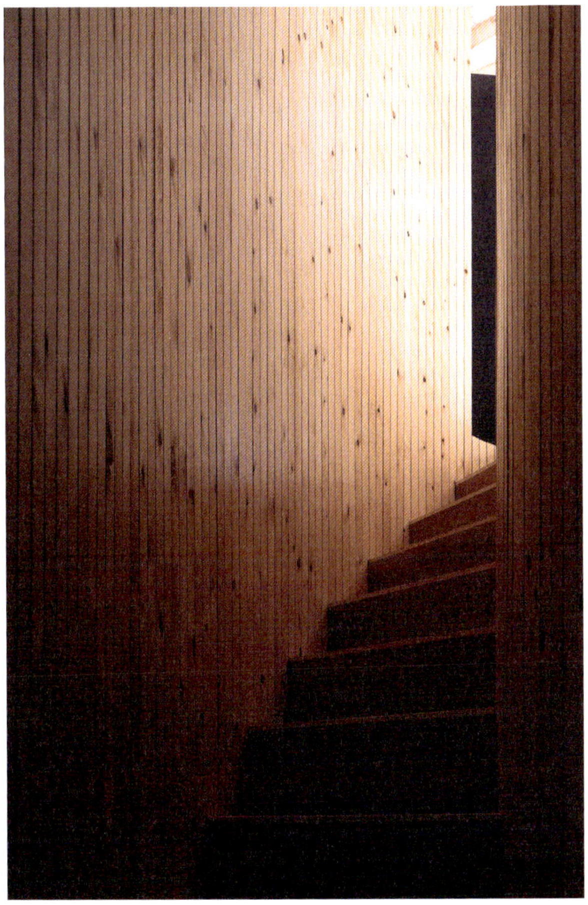
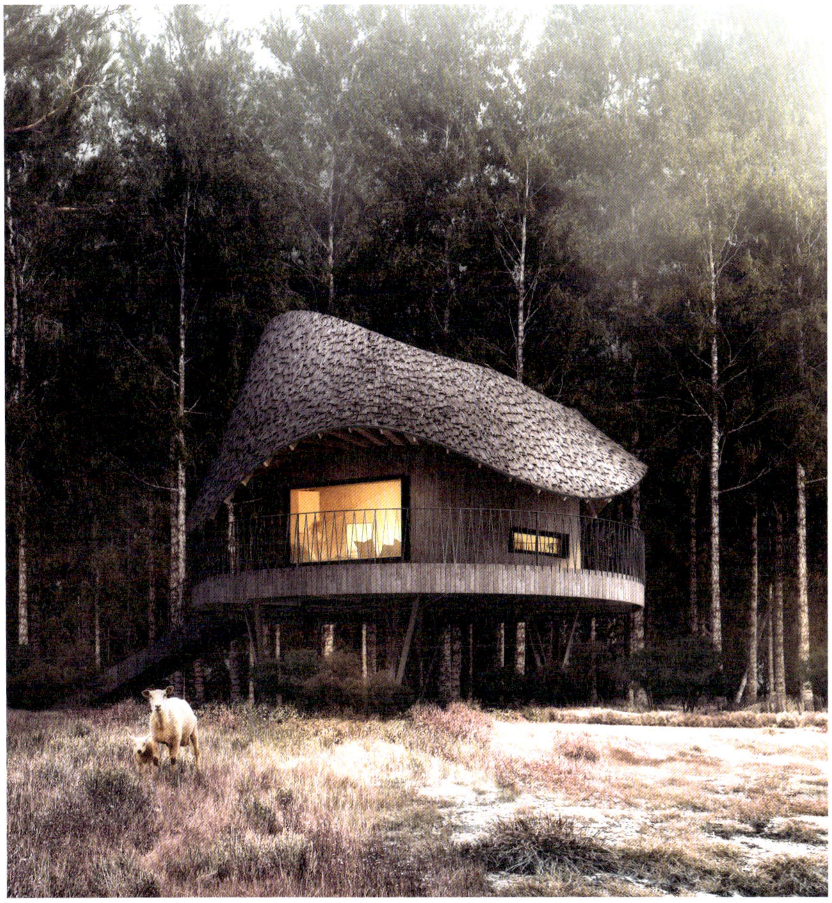
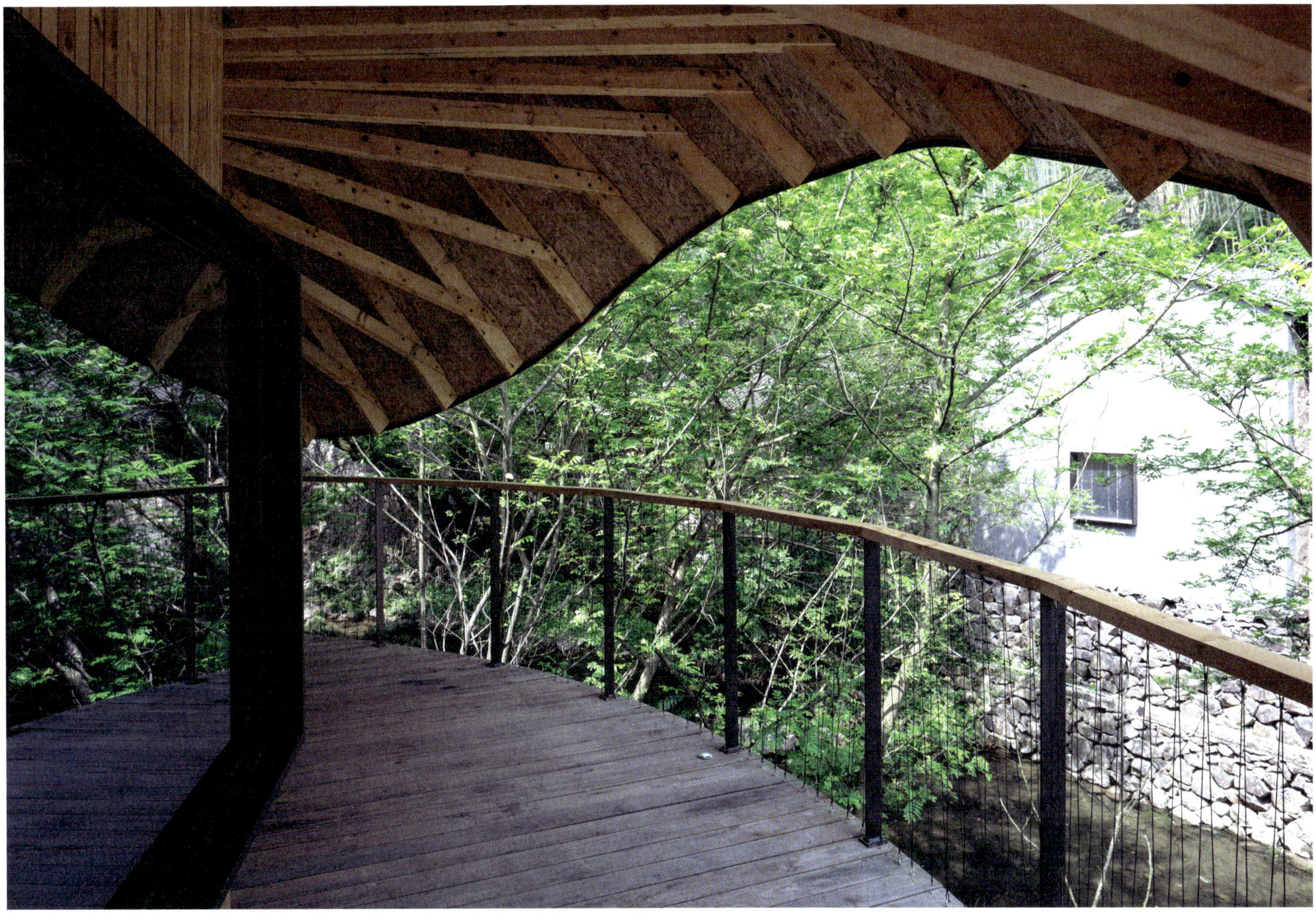

Keeping Village Traditions Thriving

Architect WEI Architects
Project Xiaoxi Jia (Springstream Guesthouse)
Location Chixi / China

Xiaoxi Jia (Springstream Guesthouse), in the Chinese village of Chixi in Fuding County, is a "protective development." WEI Architects, a company that aspires to create "cultural, humanistic architecture," was invited to renovate a dilapidated house in the village, typical of many disused properties in the area. It demonstrated that a project like this could help revitalize forgotten villages by building a guest house that generates much-needed income for the community.

Under the direction of architect Na Wei, materials were locally sourced, with over 80 percent recycled from the area or reclaimed from the original building, including the Chinese fir timber and stone bases of the old house. Local villagers with building skills were employed to keep traditional construction methods alive, exemplified by the mortise-and-tenon structure and specially made window and door frames.

The curving clay-tile roof covering the veranda replicates the wooden eaves of the original house. The rounded peaks of the mountains that tower above the site informed the shape of the roof. "The moment I set foot in the village, I was touched by the environment, and this feeling drove the entire design process of this project," says Wei.

"We wanted our construction to respect this harmony," she says. "Like planting a tree, we intend for Xiaoxi Jia to spring from its local environment and grow into the surroundings, naturally." The height of the main house and floor plan match those of the original building, partly due to the preservation of one of the gabled masonry walls. Inside, the layout is based on the local tradition of arranging rooms around a central hearth.

The subtropical monsoon climate, with annual typhoons, necessitated a study of seasonal wind directions, leading to unique window designs (including roof lights) that promote ventilation and convection, dehumidify, and achieve passive cooling.

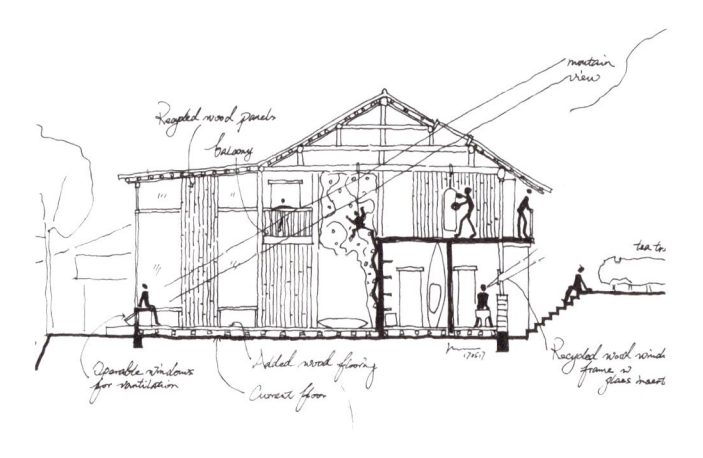

A section drawing demonstrates the orientation of the house in relation to the mountains. Many aspects of the building's design were informed by the surrounding landscape—in particular, the curved shapes of the tile-covered roofs.

263

Springstream Guesthouse

Inside the dwelling, the architects have made a conscious effort to preserve the walls and finishes of the original building.

Materials were locally sourced, with over 80 percent recycled from the area or reclaimed from the original building.

Springstream Guesthouse

A series of copper seams incorporated into the poured-concrete floor direct guests from the entrance of the home toward doors leading to the tearoom and a terrace facing the stream.

Springstream Guesthouse

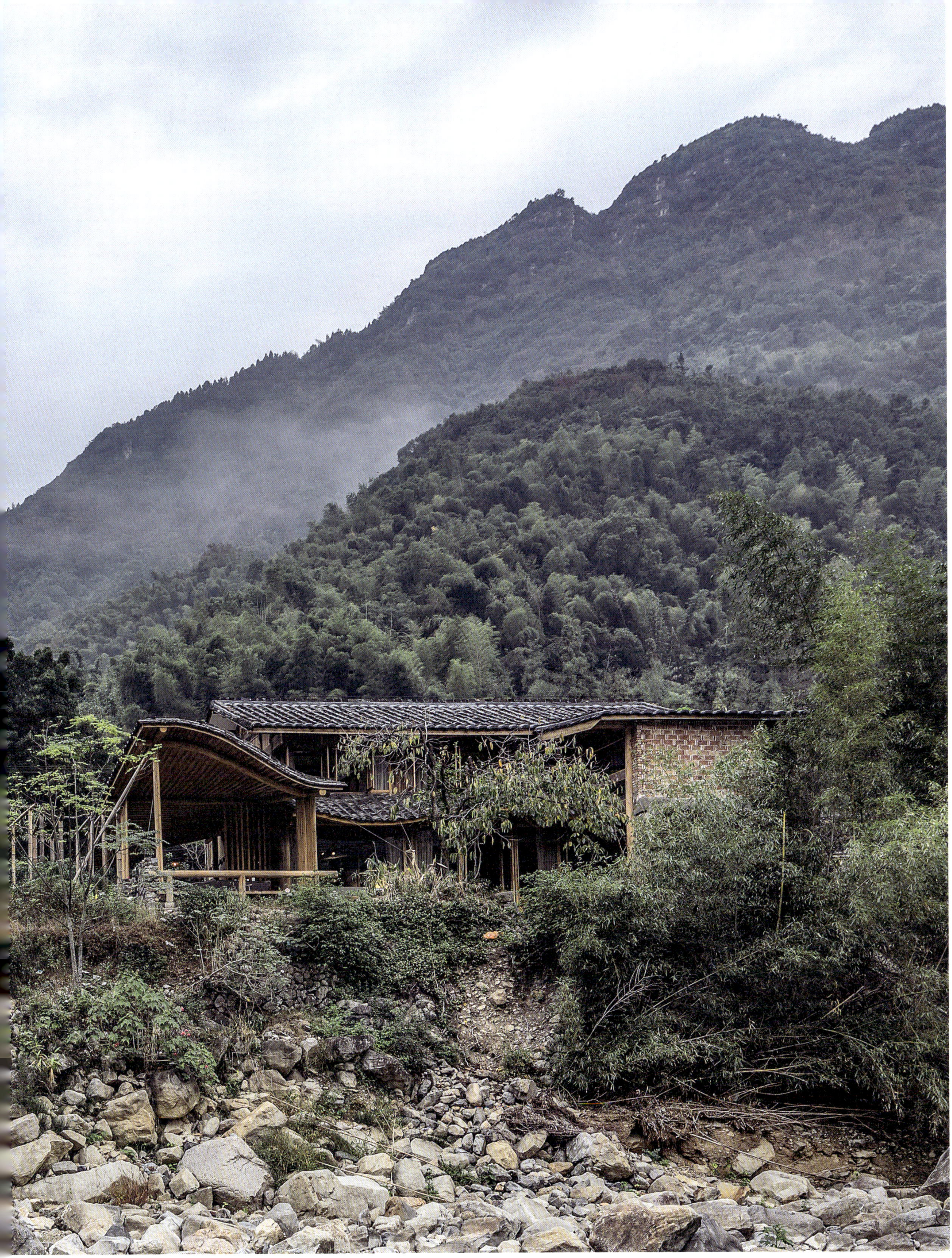

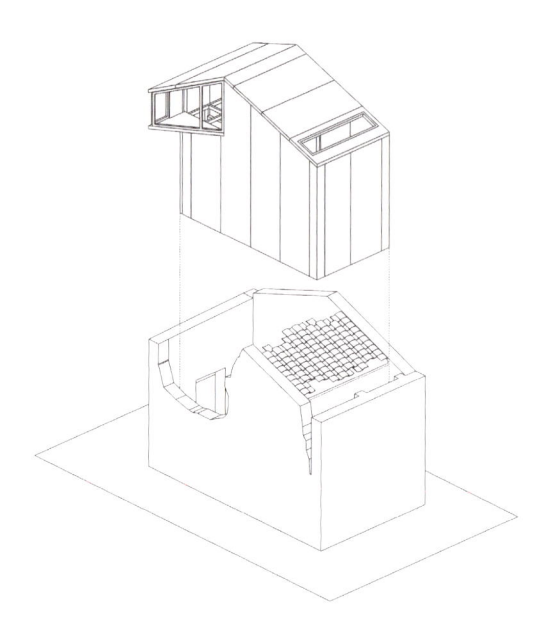

Building New Homes within Old Abodes

In the deprived area of Shangwei, which is surrounded by the modern urban hub of Shenzhen, the local government is legally obligated to renovate uninhabitable properties. However, the fragile state of the dilapidated and abandoned brick buildings means that any construction work affects the adjacent structures.

People's Architecture Office, a multidisciplinary studio dedicated to social improvement through housing and urban regeneration, developed the Shangwei Village Plugin House as a way of preserving the original structures and building new dwellings inside them, allowing the old homes to be inhabited again. This house-inside-house approach provides a quick and affordable alternative to razing buildings and rebuilding from scratch, or relocating communities, encouraging development that is sensitive to the existing urban fabric. It uses a low-cost modular building system of prefabricated panels that increase energy efficiency.

Structural connections are integrated into each section, meaning that homes can be built in less than a day with unskilled labor using just one tool, reducing disruption. At the Huang family home, Plugin House acts as structural reinforcement, as the roof had partially collapsed. Additional space was added by placing the bedroom on a mezzanine level, and a corner window offers a panoramic view of village rooftops. A skylight replaces the section of the roof that had collapsed, drawing more natural light into the home.

The Fang family's Plugin fits exactly within the original home's walls. The original roof had completely fallen in, so there was an opportunity to insert a clerestory window, inviting sunlight into the bedroom.

In both structures, separate units are used for heating and cooling, and composting toilets compensate for the lack of sewerage systems in the area.

Architect   People's Architecture Office
Project   Shangwei Village Plugin House
Location   Shenzhen / China

Each Plugin House is different to the next, as its form and dimensions are dictated not only by the site for which it is designed, but also the extent to which the existing building is damaged.

Structural connections are integrated into each section, meaning that homes can be built in less than a day with unskilled labor using just one tool.

The Plugin House will frequently sit within the walls of existing buildings, so its design needs to incorporate creative solutions for bringing natural light to the rooms within.

Shangwei Village Plugin House

273

274 Shangwei Village Plugin House

While nestled within original buildings that are sometimes hundreds of years old, the Plugin House does not attempt to conform architecturally. Out of necessity, largely owing to financial constraints, it remains true to its materials and is unadorned basic both inside and out.

275

Architect   RSAA
Project   Tongling Recluse
Location   Anhui Province / China

Crumbling Walls Serve a Spatial Purpose

The international architecture and urban design studio RSAA was founded with a mission to build a bridge between Western and Eastern styles of architecture. The firm was commissioned with Büro Ziyu Zhuang to redevelop Tongling Recluse, a small home in a remote village in China's Anhui Province. The ruins of the abandoned dwelling built into the side of a mountain provided a rich source of inspiration for the project.

A combination of the local Huizhou and Yanjiang styles, the traditional structure was transformed using the original bricks through an ecologically considered design. "Local craftsmen used old materials and tiles salvaged from other buildings to rebuild it with traditional techniques," say the architects. "In this way, we responded to the native culture with a vernacular, sustainable concept."

To make the most of the home's vantage point overlooking the village, increase circulation, and enhance user experience, they extended the house toward the mountain, and another volume enlarges the living room on the north-south side. The addition of a second story further increases living space, and a striking copper-plated staircase connects the two levels. Curved walls separate the new rooms from the original building, creating intriguing sinuous interior spaces. The new walls are integrated with the old structure, but they are clearly visible and play an integral role in partitioning the rooms. The terrace, living room, dining room, kitchen, and courtyard are arranged in a westward line, according to the level of privacy required in each room.

The streamlined design includes a traditional folding roof, and extended eaves create a wide veranda. When viewed from above, the black-tiled roof complements and contrasts with its lush mountaintop surroundings.

The dwelling comprises two double-height volumes connected via a glazed two-story passageway.

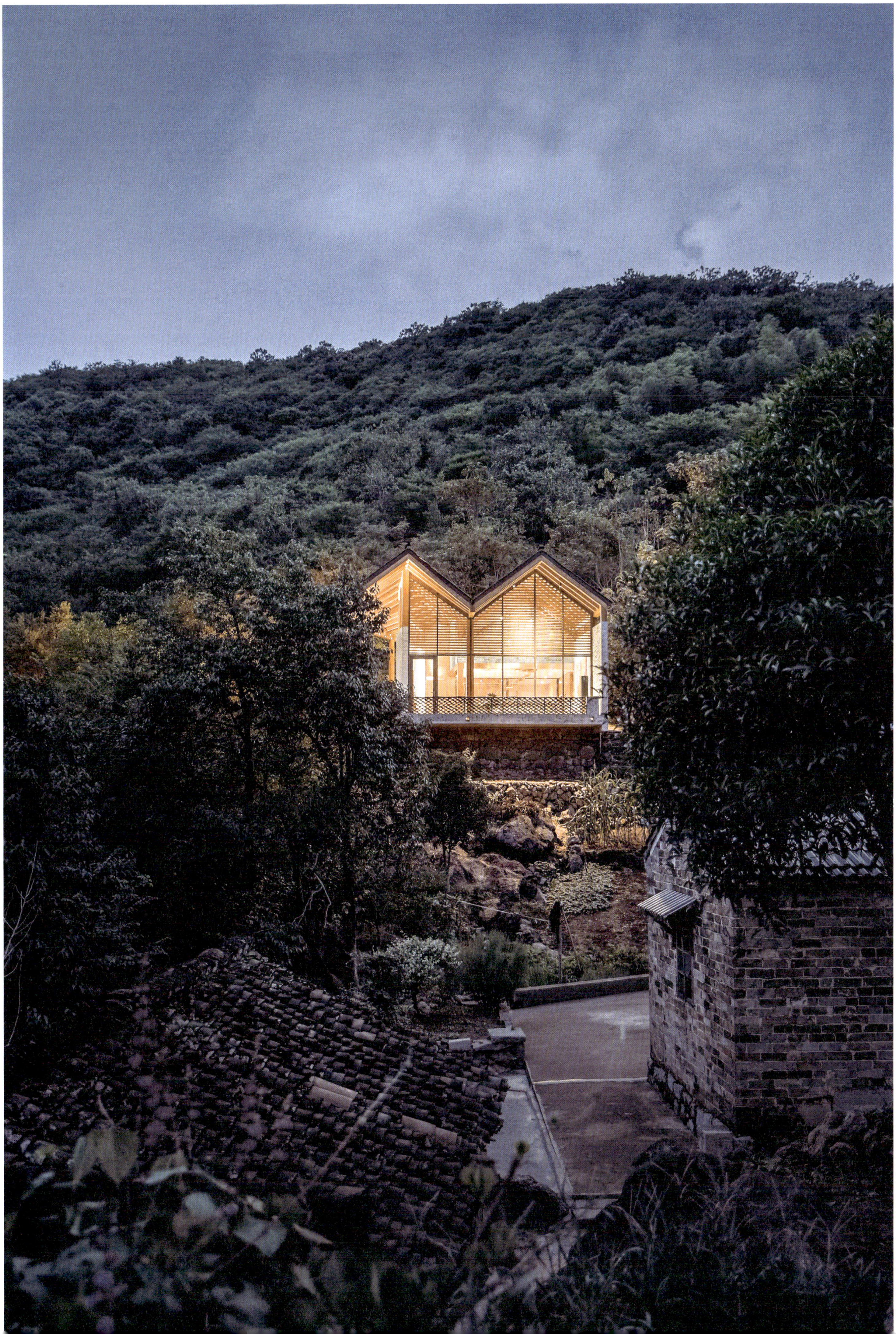

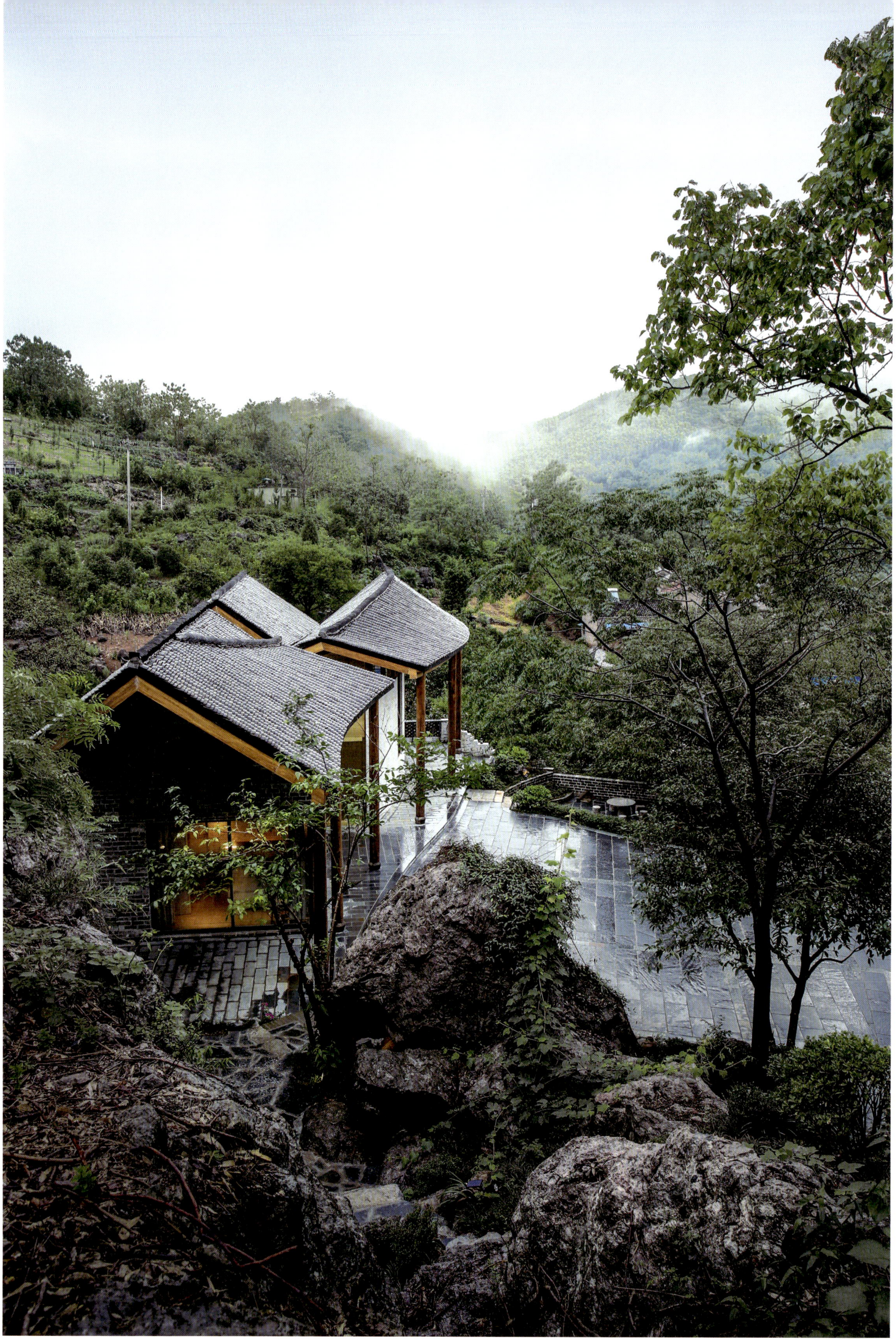

Exterior details—in particular, the two narrow pitched roofs that span the living room and the use of black slate for patio and roof tiles—mimic the local environment's undulating hills.

Tongling Recluse

The streamlined design includes a traditional folding roof, and extended eaves create a wide veranda.

The architects made no attempt to mask or conceal the walls of the original building, but used stone of a different color deliberately to mark the line at which old becomes new. The copper staircase appears to float at the center of the living room. Its position allows for the seamless transition from the double-height space to two separate floors.

282

Shanghai/China

Neri &Hu

Renowned the world-over, the defining characteristic that unites this interdisciplinary practice's body of work is an ethos that can be summed up in a single word: "meaning."

The architectural practice Neri&Hu calls itself a "Design Research Office," a moniker referring to its approach. The company, based in Shanghai, with an office in the UK, also extends to interior, product, and graphic design, ensuring coherence across their projects.

"Interdisciplinary research is part of our process, intrinsically intertwined with every project from the start," say studio founders and husband and wife Lyndon Neri and Rossana Hu. "Architecture is the foundation of everything we do, but we see design as a holistic discipline."

Both from Chinese families—Hu was born in Taiwan, and Neri grew up in the Philippines—the couple met in the US, where they completed their studies. They pursued undergraduate architectural studies at the University of California, Berkeley. (Neri is three years older and jokes that when Hu was deciding which profession to practice, he wooed her toward architecture with his beautiful drawings.) Neri went on to complete a master's degree at Harvard, while Hu graduated with a master's degree from Princeton. After many years in the US, where they spent a large part of their careers working for Michael Graves Architecture & Design, they launched their own office in 2004, in Shanghai, returning to their families' homeland.

The accolades they have accumulated since then attest to their success. Their awards include a World Architecture Festival Award in 2014, Wallpaper* Designers of the Year 2014, Maison&Objet Asia Designers of the Year 2015, and ICONIC AWARDS Interior Designer of the Year 2017, among a multitude of others. Recognized internationally, having worked

Pages 282–283: In Qinhuangdao, the Aranya Art Center sees a series of galleries surrounding a deep circular void that functions as a communal space for the city's residents. The opening has seating arranged around its edges so that it can function as an amphitheater, and is filled with water to create a pond between shows.

Above and opposite page: Rethinking the Split House saw the architects transform a dilapidated 1930s lane house—originally occupied by a single family—into three separate state-of-the-art apartments. New insertions and skylights allowed the architects to do so while preserving the split-level formation, a defining characteristic of lane house typology.

> "Our role is to represent the culture 'as it is,' in an authentic way, not to pretend to be someone else, or from another time, trying to be something we are not."

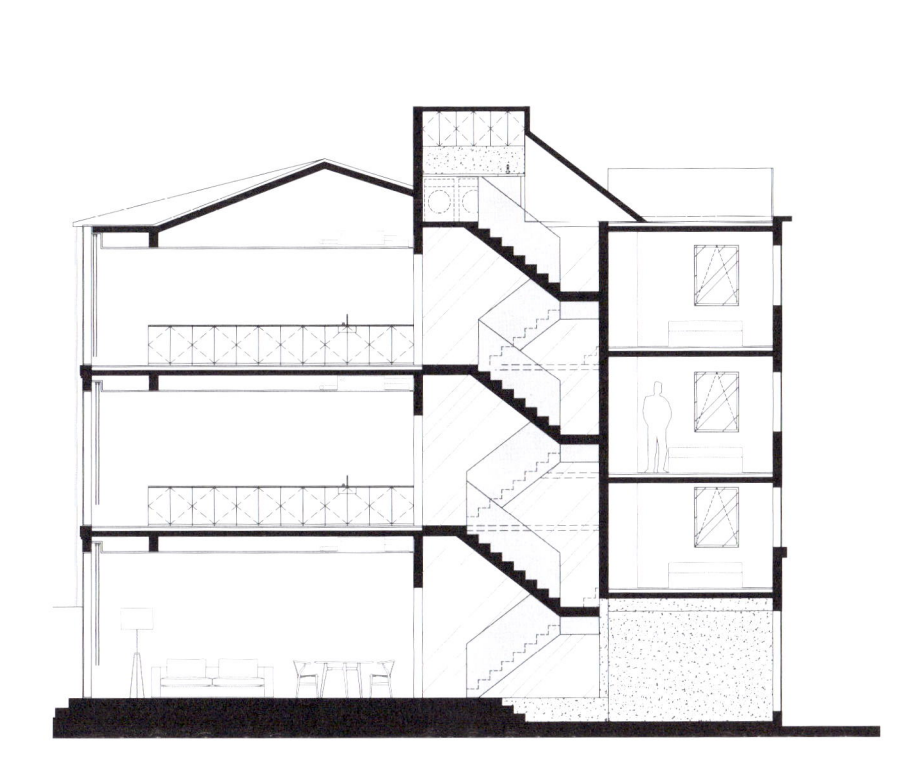

with brands such as Artemide, Poltrona Frau, Selfridges, and hotelier Ian Schrager, it's the work they are doing in China that stands out.

"We have a desire to tell the world that China does more than just 'copy,'" the architects say, referencing the country's infamous reputation for replica designs. "Our role is to represent the culture 'as it is,' in an authentic way, not to pretend to be someone else, or from another time, trying to be something we are not."

They do this through an investigative process that places people at the heart of their projects, interlacing them with meaning. "We feel an obligation in everything we design," Hu and Neri explain, "to be conscious of our social responsibilities." It is this ideology that has shaped Neri&Hu's approach to restaurants, retail stores, hotels, theaters, offices, homes, and chapels. "Meaning" is the ethos that unites them all.

Such meaning is equally relevant when the office transforms existing structures. In three seminal renovation projects in Shanghai (The Waterhouse at South

Bund, Rethinking the Split House, and Design Republic Design Commune), it conducted thorough research into the significance of the original buildings, preserving what it could while sensitively restoring the architecture and maintaining its character. Instead of hiding the original structure, the architects prefer to expose the layered patina like a scar, celebrating the history of a building.

"If not taken seriously and rigorously researched, a project that deals with old and new can easily become a fashion statement. It can be just about proportion and texture without much depth," explain the architects about the philosophies around adaptive reuse, heritage, memory, identity, and urban regeneration that guide their practice.

The Tsingpu Yangzhou Retreat, a 20-room boutique hotel in Yangzhou, demonstrates the office's sensitivity to time, place, space, and culture. Several of the old buildings on the site needed to be adapted, and new structures were necessary to accommodate the hotel's capacity requirements. Echoing the traditional courtyard vernacular of Chinese architecture, the architects unified the old and new volumes with a grid of walls and pathways, creating various courtyard enclosures.

The grid formation creates public spaces that flow toward more private rooms, typifying Neri&Hu's precise considerations for where public and private should meet and separate. The corridors that lead the way and divide these spaces are clad with detailed brickwork, reflecting light in different patterns to entice guests to venture through passageways and explore the building.

"While it is a very functional material, we like to give the brick a more poetic reading when using it as a building material," Hu and Neri explain. For this reason, the studio often purposefully exposes the brickwork in its projects.

In Suzhou Chapel, the brick walls feature arresting textures, "interweaving with one another to create a choreographed journey leading into the building," the architects explain.

"If not taken seriously and rigorously researched, a project that deals with old and new can easily become a fashion statement. It can be just about proportion and texture without much depth."

Opposite page: Much inspiration for the redesign of the New Shanghai Theater came from the concept of "theater" itself. The carved spaces of both the interior and exterior atriums create scenes of varying spatial and lighting configurations as the visitor moves through the areas, intensifying as they progress deeper into the building.

Left and above: On the historic Yuyuan Road in Shanghai, a low-slung brick wall becomes the unifying element in a project that aims to bring a sense of cohesion and communal character to a group of 10 disparate old and new buildings. The architects drew inspiration from vernacular Chinese urban typologies, such as the *nongtang* alleyways of Shanghai.

Above: Elevator manufacturer Schindler's headquarters in the Jiading District of Shanghai focus on two different material palettes. At ground level, a gray-brick podium represents the material heritage of the project's locale, since this is a common building material in China. Above the podium, minimalist glass boxes offer a subtle reference to the company's Swiss background.

Opposite page: Designed as part of a hotel resort, Suzhou Chapel combines dark brick walls with a white cube that appears to float above them. The design is an inversion of the local vernacular of white rendered walls and black roofs. Within the chapel, a mezzanine level is lined with wooden battens that reach upward to form a vaulted ceiling.

This architectural poetry reflects the deep personal interests Neri and Hu have in other forms of cultural expression—from literature and theater to music, art, and food. They bring these passions into their projects, adding to the creative cultural dialogue in which they exist.

"We believe in architecture and design as powerful cultural forces," they state. "The functional aspects are less interesting for us, although as professionals, they are a prerequisite—your design must work on a very practical level. But we believe in the subtext over the obvious and the poetic over the utilitarian."

Intensive research into the historical context of a site and its surrounding cultural and physical environment ensures that their projects are meaningful for the people and places they serve.

Recently, they have focused on projects outside China's major cities, in smaller towns where there has been a progressive governmental shift toward local materials, typologies, and cultures. "It helps to provide viability for disappearing villages, and maintains some cultural memory for a nation that is moving too fast, too soon," the architects say.

That does not mean they are ignoring their base of Shanghai, where they see the urban sprawl as holding a unique identity—its own "natural" landscape of sorts—which they find inspiring. "In a sense, the urban fabric is 'natural' for humanity," they state. "Cities are built by humans as ants build ant farms. The integrity of a place lies not in how 'natural' it is, but how authentically human it is. At this point, we are not looking to return to living in caves or tree houses, but to live with other people in harmony."

In Shanghai, this means navigating between a forever-changing inner-city landscape and the traditional neighborhoods that seem stuck in a past era. It provides an opportunity for projects such as the New Shanghai Theatre. Built during the 1930s, with many iterations since then, Neri&Hu sought to rediscover its original grandeur while designing a building relevant for the present day with the potential to become a lasting and significant landmark in the future.

At ground level, under its imposing stone structure, fluted bronze walls resembling shimmering stage curtains convey a sense of weightlessness as they guide visitors inside. The entrance, set back from the pedestrian walkway, offers a sheltered plaza that invites public circulation and blurs spatial boundaries. Passersby can glimpse through the "curtains" and see the theatricality of the interior.

"Architects need to think deeply about the questions posed by a building," Hu and Neri insist. "It's never about style. It's never about a look. It should always be about meaning."

Opposite page and above: The site proposed for the Tsingpu Yangzhou Retreat was already dotted with small lakes and existing structures. Taking inspiration from Chinese vernacular architecture, the architects developed a design in which courtyard areas give hierarchy to the spaces, framing views of the sky and blurring the lines between interior and exterior.

A Museum Saves a Sand Dune from Ruin

Architect OPEN Architecture
Project UCCA Dune Art Museum
Location Qinhuangdao / China

Beijing-based OPEN Architecture decided to build the UCCA Dune Art Museum in the heart of a sand dune as a way of saving the seaside environment of China's Bohai Bay in Qinhuangdao from imminent destruction. "We wanted to protect the vulnerable dune ecosystem, formed by natural forces over thousands of years," say the architects. "Because of the museum, these sand dunes will be preserved instead of being leveled to make space for ocean-view real-estate developments, which has happened to many other dunes along the shore."

Applying the notion of art as it first materialized on cave walls, the museum is a series of cave-like cells carved into the sand. Ten interlinked galleries and a café, all organically shaped, represent primal, timeless forms.

The architects maintain a belief in "the innovative power of architecture to transform people and the way they live while striking a new balance between man-made and nature." The museum design manifests this vision with rectangular skylights, windows, and entryways that provide natural light and invite the sky, sea, and sand to be part of the cavernous interior experience.

A spiral staircase allows visitors to emerge from the concealed structure onto a cylindrical lookout point, enhancing appreciation of the beach setting, where the museum's sandy rooftops undulate congruently with the landscape. These sand-covered roofs insulate the building from the heat, while a low-energy, zero-emission heat pump replaces traditional air-conditioning.

Covering the complex geometry of the concrete shells is formwork made from small strips of wood and—in areas with tighter curvature—more elasticized materials. Applied by hand by local builders (some whom were former shipbuilders), these wall finishes were intentionally left irregular and imperfect. They call for the appreciation of manual labor in a museum where human creativity and nature are equally cherished.

There is a deliberate asymmetry throughout the design of the museum—both in its layout and in its construction. The building's concrete curves mirror the windswept arcs of the sand dunes.

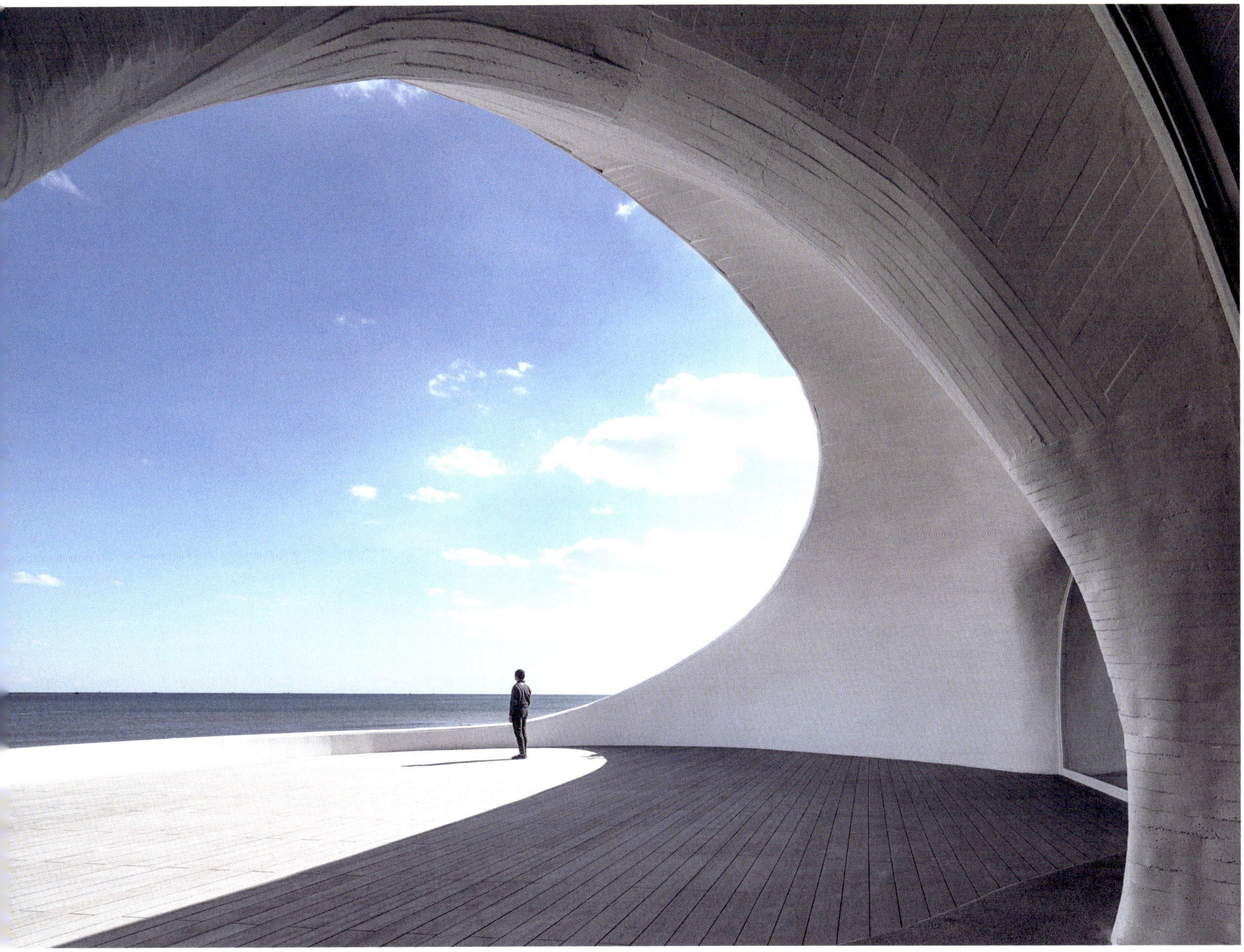

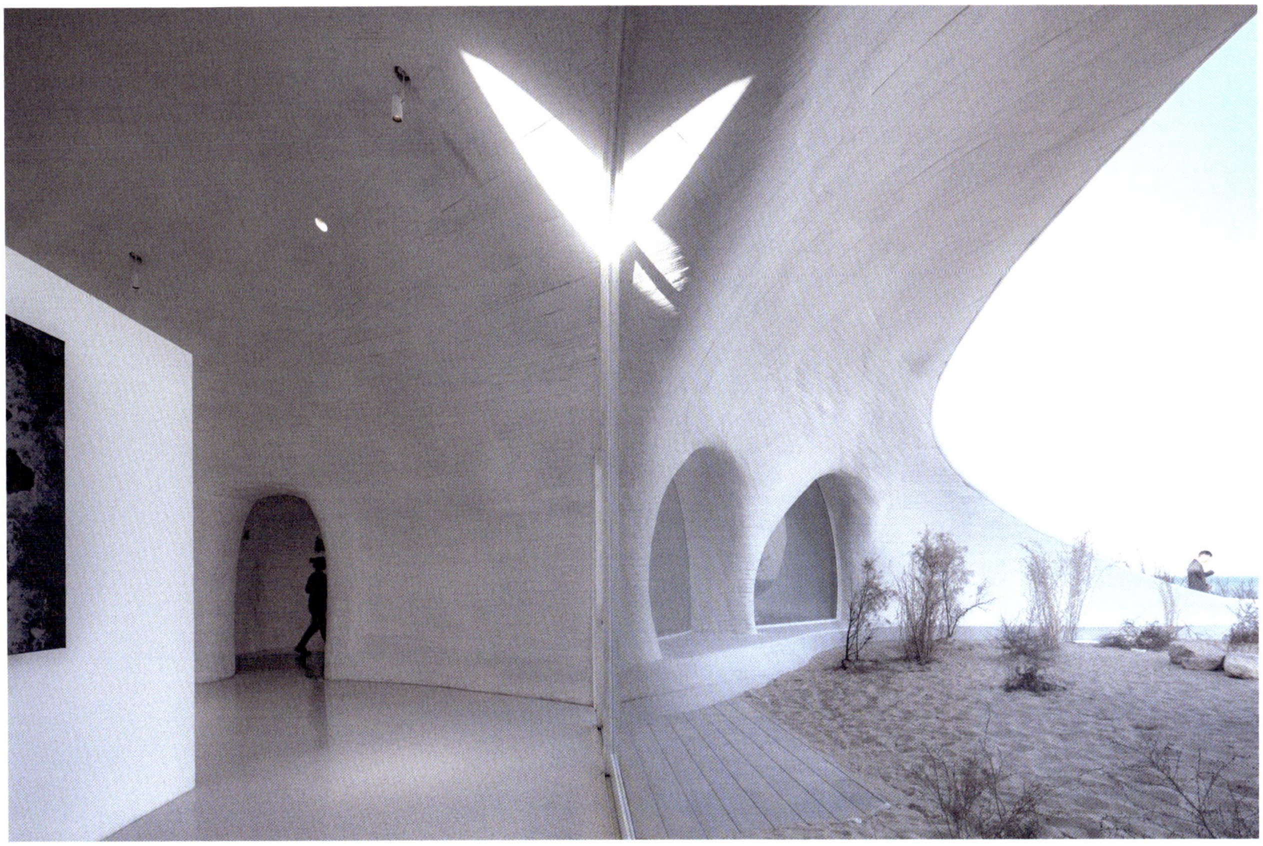

UCCA Dune Art Museum

At times, one can forget that one is several feet underground, so bright and expansive are some of the museum's spaces.

Openings throughout the building frame different views of the sea and sky. Shadows cast on the gallery walls shift as the natural light changes through the day.

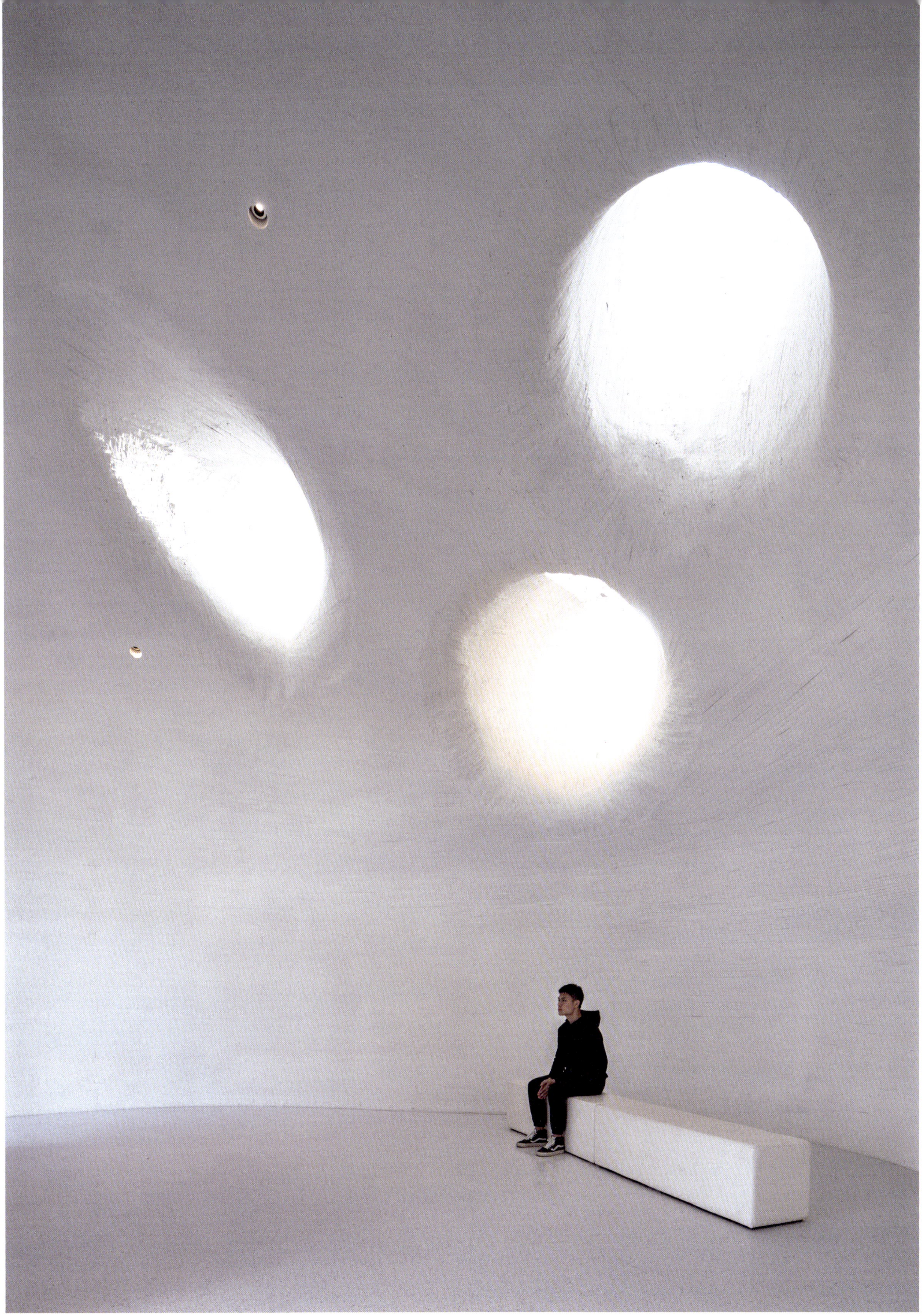

Sand-covered roofs insulate the building from the heat, while a low-energy, zero-emission heat pump replaces traditional air-conditioning.

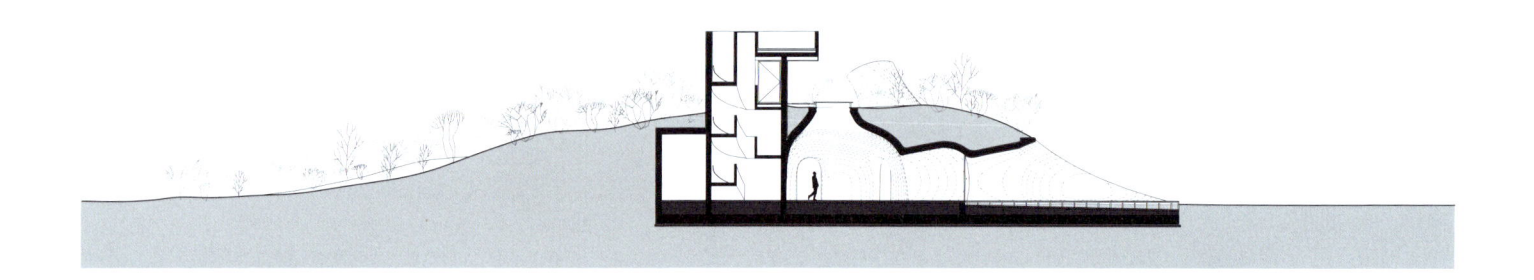

298   UCCA Dune Art Museum

A side elevation shows the extent to which the sand dune has been excavated to allow the museum to lie almost completely concealed beneath the surface, while an aerial view shows the footprint of the museum as it breaks out into the open from beneath. With new plant growth in spring and summer, the structures become further concealed by vegetation.

299

Index

Arquitetos Associados
  Brazil
  arquitetosassociados.arq.br
  Claudia Andujar Gallery
  Photography
  Leonardo Finotti
  168–173

Atelier Masomi
  Niger
  ateliermasomi.com
  Regional Market /
  Hikma /
  Niamey 2000 /
  Artisans Valley
  Photography
  Maurice Ascani (66),
  James Wang (67–69),
  Torsten Seidel (70–71),
  Atelier Masomi (72–73)
  66–73

Bangkok Project Studio
  Thailand
  bangkokprojectstudio.com
  Kantana Institute /
  The Wine Ayutthaya
  Photography
  Spaceshift Studio
  (244, 246–251),
  Bangkok Project Studio
  (245)
  244–251

CAAT Studio
  Iran
  caatstudio.com
  Mahallat Residential
  Building No. 3
  Photography
  Parham Taghioff
  38–40

Campana Brothers:
Fernando + Humberto Campana
  Brazil
  campanas.com.br
  Zunino House
  Photography
  Leonardo Finotti
  174–177

Chaukor Studio
  India
  chaukorstudio.com
  Minaret House
  Photography
  Mohd Javed
  238–239

Comunal
  Mexico
  comunaltaller.com
  Social Housing
  Production
  Photography
  Onnis Luque
  144–147

Dar Arafa Architecture
  Egypt
  dararafa.com
  Al Abu Stait Mosque
  Photography
  Tariq Al-Murri (42 top),
  Essam Arafa (43–49)
  42–49

Driss Kettani Architecte
  Morocco
  drisskettani.com
  Laâyoune Technology
  School
  Photography
  Driss Kettani
  54–59

Farming Architects
  Vietnam
  farmingarchitects.com
  VAC-Library
  Photography
  An Viet Dung
  224–227

Fernanda Canales
  Mexico
  fernandacanales.com
  Casa Bruma
  Photography
  Rafael Gamo
  Architectural Project
  Fernanda Canales and
  Claudia Rodríguez
  Landscape Project
  Claudia Rodríguez
  Team
  Hugo Vargas, Aarón Jassiel
  and Alejandra Téllez
  Construction
  CM2 (Luis Cayuela)
  Structural Engineering
  Grupo SAI (Gerson Huerta)
  126–131

Formzero
  Malaysia
  formzero.net
  Planter Box House
  Photography
  Ameen Deen
  216–219

Freddy Mamani
  Bolivia
  Neo-Andina
  Photography
  Tatewaki Nio
  196–201

Frida Escobedo
  Mexico
  fridaescobedo.net
  La Tallera /
  Hotel Boca Chica /
  Laboratorio de
  Vivienda Infonavit /
  Mar Tirreno /
  Serpentine Pavilion
  Photography
  Rafael Gamo (154–155, 158–161),
  Courtesy GRUPO HABITA
  @undinepröhl (156–157)
  154–161

Kéré Architecture
  Germany
  kere-architecture.com
  Doctors' Housing /
  Gando Primary School Extension /
  Centre de Santé et de
  Promotion Sociale /

National Park of Mali /
Lycée Schorge /
Dano Secondary School /
Gando Teachers' Housing /
Gando School Library /
Songtaaba Women's Center
Photography
*Courtesy of Kéré Architecture
(92–93, 100, 101 bottom),
Erik-Jan Ouwerkerk (94–95),
Iwan Baan (96, 97 top right,
97 bottom),
Andrea Maretto (97 top left),
Daniel Schwartz (101 top)*
92–101

Kunle Adeyami / NLÉ
Nigeria and
The Netherlands
nleworks.com
Floating School
Photography
*Courtesy of NLE /
Kunlé Adeyemi*
74–77

Local Studio
South Africa
localstudio.co.za
Hillbrow Counselling
Centre
Photography
Dave Southwood
14–15

Localworks
Uganda
localworks.ug
Mannya Multipurpose
Hall
Photography
Will Boase Photography
102–105

Malan Vorster Architecture Interior Design
South Africa
malanvorster.co.za
Tree House Constantia
Photography
Adam Letch
22–27

Manoj Patel Design Studio
India
manojpateldesignstudio.com
Residential Dwelling
Photography
Tejas Shah
236–237

MAPA
Uruguay and Brazil
mapaarq.com
Sacromonte
Landscape Hotel
Photography
Leonardo Finotti
190–195

MONOARCHI Architects
China
monoarchi.com
Treewow Villa O
Photography
*Chen Hao (256–259,
261 top left, bottom),
Monoarchi (260 bottom,
261 top right)*
256–261

Narein Perera
Sri Lanka
Estate Bungalow
Photography
*Lakmal Galagoda (228),
Malaka Weligodapola (229)*
228–229

Neri & Hu
China
neriandhu.com
Aranya Art Center /
Rethinking the Split House /
New Shanghai Theatre /
Yuyuan Road Redevelopment
Project / Schindler City /
Suzhou Chapel /
The Brick Wall
Photography
*Pedro Pegenaute
(282–287, 289–291),
Dirk Weiblen (288)*
282–291

Nicolás Campodonico
Argentina
nicolascampodonico.com
Capilla San Bernardo
Photography
Nicolás Campodonico
178–183

OPEN Architecture
China
openarch.com
UCCA Dune Art Museum
Photography
*Zaiye Studio and
WU Qingshan*
292–295

Orkidstudio
Kenya
orkidstudio.org
Swawou Girls' School
Photography
Peter Dibdin
86–91

Ortúzar + Gebauer
Arquitectos
Chile
ortuzargebauer.com
Pollo House
Photography
Federico Cairoli
184–189

OUALALOU + CHOI
France and Morocco
oplusc.com
Fez Medina Renovation
Photography
Lilia Sellami
50–53

Palinda Kannangara Architects
Sri Lanka
palindakannangara.com
Frame / Holiday Structure
Photography
Luka Alagiyawanna
220–223

Index

People's Architecture Office
China
peoples-architecture.com
Shangwei Village
Plugin House
Photography
*People's Architecture
(270–271,
273 bottom,
275 Bottom),
Zhan Changheng
(272, 273 top,
274, 275 top)*
270–275

Porky Hefer—Vernacular
Architecture and Design
South Africa
animal-farm.co.za
The Nest @Sossus
Photography
Katinka Bester
16–21

PRODUCTORA
Mexico
productora-df.com.mx
Centro Cultural
Comunitario
Teotitlán del Valle
Photography
Luis Gallardo
112–117

Ramos Castellano
Arquitectos
Cape Verde
ramoscastellano.com
Terra Lodge
Photography
Sergio Pirrone
78–85

Roth Architecture
Mexico
sferik.art
SFER IK Museion
Tulum
Photography
Fernando Artigas
138–143

RSAA
China
rs-aa.com
Tongling Recluse
Photography
Shengliang Su
276–281

Saota
South Africa
saota.com
Kloof 119A
Photography
Adam Letch
28–33

SHAU
Indonesia
shau.nl
Microlibrary
Photography
Sanrok Studio
212–215

TACO (Taller de
Arquitectura Contextual)
Mexico
arquitecturacontextual.com
Pórtico Palmeto
Photography
Leo Espinosa
132–137

Taller Hector Barroso
Mexico
tallerhectorbarroso.com
Entre Pinos
Photography
Rory Gardiner
118–125

TAX (Taller de
Arquitectura X)
Mexico
kalach.com
Torre 41
Photography
Yos hi Koitani
148–153

Tropical Space
Vietnam
khonggiannhietdoi.com
Cuckoo House /
Organicare Showroom /
Long An House /
Terracotta Studio /
Chicken's House
Photography
*Oki Hiroyuki (230–231,
233–234),
Quang Dam (232, 235)*
230–235

unTAG
India
Vrindavan
Photography
Courtesy of unTAG
240–243

WEI Architects
China
weiarchitects.com
Springstream
Guesthouse
Photography
Jin Weiqi
262–269

WHBC Architects
Malaysia
whbca.com
Chempenai House
Photography
*Ben Hosking
(206, 207 top, 209),
Kent Soh (207 bottom,
208 bottom, 210–211)*
206–211

Feature Picture Credits

The Search for South African Archicture
Chris Howes/Wild Places Photography/ Alamy Stock Foto (8); Images of Africa Photobank/Alamy Stock Foto (9 top); meanderingemu/Alamy Stock Foto (9 bottom); Greg Balfour Evans/ Alamy Stock Foto (10); frederic REGLAIN/ Alamy Stock Foto (11); ilyas Ayub/ Alamy Stock Foto (12 top); Katinka Bester (12 bottom); Eric Nathan/ Alamy Stock Foto (13)

Beit Beirut: Architecture Shaped by War, Collective Memory, and Democracy
Frans Sellies/getty images (34); Iain Masterton/Alamy Stock Photo (35 left); Michele Burgess/Alamy Stock Photo (35 right); agefotostock/Alamy Stock Photo (36); Lensleb/Alamy Stock Photo (37)

West African Architecture: Yesterday, Today, and Tomorrow
Eitan Simanor/Alamy Stock Foto (60); adam eastland/Alamy Stock Foto (61 left); Anthony Pappone/getty images (61 right); Rob Fenenga/Alamy Stock Foto (62); Tope Adenola (63); Courtesy of NLE/ Kunlé Adeyemi (64); MOISE GOMIS/ getty images (65)

The Architecture of Mexico's Evolving Identity
Konstantin Kalishko/Alamy Stock Photo (106 left); Rik Hamilton/Alamy Stock Photo (106 right); Michael Dwyer/Alamy Stock Photo (107 left); Witold Skrypczak/Alamy Stock Photo (107 right); Lucas Vallecillos/Alamy Stock Photo (108); Witold Skrypczak/ Alamy Stock Photo (109 top); John Mitchell/ Alamy Stock Photo (109 bottom); Rafael Gamo (110); agefotostock/Alamy Stock Photo (111 top); Universal Images Group North America LLC/DeAgostini/ Alamy Stock Photo (111 bottom)

Brazil: Uncertainties and Stabilities
Fred Pinheiro/Alamy Stock Photo (162); Dmitri Kessel/getty images (163 left); Dircinha Welter/getty images (163 right); Nelson Kon Fotografias (164); ITPhoto/ Alamy Stock Photo (165); Foto Arena LTDA/ Alamy Stock Photo (166); David Wall/ Alamy Stock Photo (167)

A Grid of Columns and a Roof: A Brief Overview of Architecture in Southeast Asia
Zoonar GmbH/Alamy Stock Photo (202 left); Mike Fuchslocher/ Alamy Stock Photo (202 right); Hufton + Crow (203); Igor Prahin/ Alamy Stock Photo (204); Thomas Dutour/ Alamy Stock Photo (205 left); Riccardo Bianchini/Alamy Stock Photo (205 right)

Locating Chinese Architecture
Yin Wenjie/getty images (252); zhangshuang/getty images (253 left); Peerawat Kamklay/getty images (253 right); Grant Faint/getty images (254); Xiaodong Qiu (255 left); DuKai photographer/getty images (255 right).

BEYOND THE WEST

New Global Architecture

This book was conceived, edited, and designed by gestalten.

Edited by Robert Klanten and Andrea Servert

Project and profile texts by Tracy Lynn Chemaly

Preface by Tracy Lynn Chemaly and Faye Robson

Captions by Anna Southgate

Regional essays by Graham Wood (8–13),
Doreen Toutikian (34–37),
Mathias Agbo Jr. (60–65),
Natalia Torija Nieto (106–111),
Pedro Vada and Marina Pedreira de Lacerda (162–167),
Calvin Chua (202–206),
and Mimi Cheng (252–256)

Editorial management by Adam Jackman

Design, layout, and cover by Johanna Posiege

Photo Editor: Mario Udzenija

Typefaces: Garamond Premier by Claude Garamond and Robert Slimbach;
Trade Gothic by Jackson Burke;
and Trade Gothic Next by Jackson Burke, Akira Kobayashi, and Tom Grace

Cover photography by Dirk Weiblen

Backcover photography by Spaceshift Studio (top and bottom), Sergio Pirrone (center left), and Ben Hosking (center right)

Printed by die Keure, Bruges

Made in Europe

Published by gestalten, Berlin 2020

ISBN 978-3-89955-879-1

© Die Gestalten Verlag GmbH & Co. KG, Berlin 2020

All rights reserved. No part of this publication may be reproduced or transmitted in any form or by any means, electronic or mechanical, including photocopy or any storage and retrieval system, without permission in writing from the publisher.

Respect copyrights, encourage creativity!

For more information, and to order books, please visit www.gestalten.com

Bibliographic information published by the Deutsche Nationalbibliothek. The Deutsche Nationalbibliothek lists this publication in the Deutsche Nationalbibliografie; detailed bibliographic data is available online at www.dnb.de.

None of the content in this book was published in exchange for payment by commercial parties or designers; gestalten selected all included work based solely on its artistic merit.

This book was printed on paper certified according to the standards of the FSC®.

MIX
Paper from responsible sources
FSC® C009115